The Mystery of Christian Marriage through the Ages

The Mystery of Christian Marriage through the Ages

The Scriptures and the First Thousand Years

ANNA M. SILVAS

CASCADE *Books* • Eugene, Oregon

THE MYSTERY OF CHRISTIAN MARRIAGE THROUGH THE AGES
The Scriptures and the First Thousand Years

Copyright © 2020 Anna M. Silvas. All rights reserved. Except for brief quotations in critical publications or reviews, no part of this book may be reproduced in any manner without prior written permission from the publisher. Write: Permissions, Wipf and Stock Publishers, 199 W. 8th Ave., Suite 3, Eugene, OR 97401.

Cascade Books
An Imprint of Wipf and Stock Publishers
199 W. 8th Ave., Suite 3
Eugene, OR 97401

www.wipfandstock.com

PAPERBACK ISBN: 978-1-5326-7191-3
HARDCOVER ISBN: 978-1-5326-7192-0
EBOOK ISBN: 978-1-5326-7193-7

Cataloguing-in-Publication data:

Names: Silvas, Anna M., author.

Title: The mystery of Christian marriage through the ages : the Scriptures and the first thousand years / Anna M. Silvas.

Description: Eugene, OR: Cascade Books, 2020 | Includes bibliographical references and index.

Identifiers: ISBN 978-1-5326-7191-3 (paperback) | ISBN 978-1-5326-7192-0 (hardcover) | ISBN 978-1-5326-7193-7 (ebook)

Subjects: LCSH: Marriage—Religious aspects—Catholic Church. | Marriage (Canon law). | Divorce—Religious aspects—Catholic Church.

Classification: BX2250 .S526 2020 (print) | BX2250 (ebook)

Manufactured in the U.S.A.   MAY 8, 2020

*Dedicated to
The memory of the John-Paul II Institute for Marriage and Family,
Melbourne Session, 2001–2018,
And to all my married friends who have borne witness
to me of the Mystery of Christ,
With Marge and Theo, beloved of Christ, my parents, at their head.
I thank you all and bless you before the Lord.*

TABLE OF CONTENTS

Preface and Acknowledgments xi
Abbreviations xiii
Citing Scripture xiv

CHAPTER ONE
In the Beginning 1
    1.1 As it was, is now, and shall be 1
    1.2 Back to the beginning 3
    1.3 The Fall before the Fall 9
    1.4 Enter: the Serpent 9
    1.5 The Children of Cain 12

CHAPTER TWO
The Family: Covenant, Law, and Counsel in the OT 15
    2.1 The Children of Abel 15
    2.2 Covenant 16
    2.3 The Covenant of Sinai 17
    2.4 "House" and family in Israel 18
    2.5 The Father 19
    2.6 The Mother 20
    2.7 The Children 20
    2.8 The household as religious community 21
    2.9 The decay of the family and the undoing of Israel 23
    2.10 Eschatological salvation and the family 24

CHAPTER THREE
The Prophets, the Lord, and Marital Covenant 25
    3.1 Idolatry and sexual sin 25
    3.2 A turning point: the prophet Hosea 27
    3.3 The major prophets 29
    3.4 The Song of Songs 31

CHAPTER FOUR
Retrieving the Truth of Marriage in Israel 34
    4.1 Revisiting the institution of marriage in Israel 34
    4.2 Recovering indissolubility: a beginning is made 35
    4.3 The emergence of vocational virginity 37
    4.4 Who opens the womb? 39
    4.5 The Feminine Persona of Zion 41

CHAPTER FIVE
The Holy Family of Nazareth 45
    5.1 The Threshold Crossed: Annunciation and Visitation 45
    5.2 A Sublime Marriage, Holy Family 47
    5.3 The twelve-year-old in the Temple 51
    5.4 The Holy Family expanded 53
    5.5 The Church, the family household of God 54
    5.6 Family language among Christians 56
    5.7 Recovering the Church as family household 57

CHAPTER SIX
Faithful Marriage and Eschatological Virginity 59
    6.1 Asking the moral questions of the New Testament 59
    6.2 The stricter standards of the Gospel 59
    6.3 The exception clauses in Matthew 60
    6.4 Virginity and lifelong sexual abstinence 65
    6.5 Is there marriage in the Kingdom? 66

CHAPTER SEVEN
Marriage: Analogy, Sacrament, and the End of Time 70
    7.1 Asking the "why" and the "whither" of the NT 70
    7.2 This adulterous generation 70
    7.3 The Bridegroom of Israel is come 71
    7.4 Cana 73
    7.5 Ephesians Five 74
    7.6 Mysterion and Sacramentum 75
    7.7 What of male headship? 77
    7.8 The Eucharist as eschatological wedding feast 79

CHAPTER EIGHT
The Gentile World that Christianity Encountered 82
    8.1 The Church's long pilgrimage of history 82
    8.2 The pan-sexualism of society 83

8.3 Controlling fertility 85
8.4 Human sacrifice and human blood sport 87
8.5 Marriage in Roman law 88
8.6 The family household among the Greeks and the Romans 91
8.7 The philosophers 91
8.8 Pagan civilization: darknesses and half-lights 95

CHAPTER NINE
The Apostolic Fathers and the Apologists 97
    9.1 Asking the Fathers 97
    9.2 The Apostolic Fathers: St Ignatius of Antioch 99
    9.3 The Didache and the Letter of Barnabas 100
    9.4 Hermas 102
    9.5 The Apologists 105
    9.6 Knowing herself to be in the world but not of it 108

CHAPTER TEN
The Early Theologians 110
    10.1 Encratism 110
    10.2 The Church Fathers' response to Encratism 111
    10.3 Tertullian (c. 155–240) 114
    10.4 St Clement of Alexandria (c. 150–216) 116
    10.5 The perils and gains of the 2nd and 3rd centuries 122

CHAPTER ELEVEN
The Cappadocian Fathers 123
    11.1 The story of a family 123
    11.2 The domestic ascetic movement 125
    11.3 St Basil on marriage 129
    11.4 St Gregory the Theologian 132
    11.5 Gregory of Nyssa, Father of Mystical Theology (c. 335–394) 135
    11.6 Epektasis and the elusive Bridegroom 137

CHAPTER TWELVE
St Augustine and the Church in the West 139
    12.1 St Ambrose of Milan (c. 333–397) 139
    12.2 St Augustine (354–430) 142
    12.3 St Augustine: the early years 142
    12.4 St Augustine: On the Good of Marriage 143
    12.5 The Pelagian controversy 145
    12.6 Concupiscence and marital intercourse 148
    12.7 The lasting legacy of St Augustine 150

CHAPTER THIRTEEN
St John Chrysostom and the Christian East 152
 13.1 Beginnings of the estrangement of East and West 152
 13.2 St John Chrysostom (347–407) 153
 13.3 The purpose of marriage 154
 13.4 Marriage, the Incarnation, and the Eucharist 156
 13.5 Marital continence and prayer 157
 13.6 A husband's headship, and the equality of husband and wife 158
 13.6 The family as domestic church 160
 13.7 Divorce and remarriage 161

CHAPTER FOURTEEN
Christian Marriage in Constantinople 500–1200 164
 14.1 Canon Law traditions in West and East 164
 14.2 A 6th century watershed: Dionysius Exiguus and John Scholasticus 164
 14.3 Christian Emperors and Roman law: Justinian 166
 14.4 St Basil's canons on marriage, adultery, and fornication 168
 14.5 Fish rotting from the head 170
 14.6 The witness of the Coptic Church 173
 14.7 Long-term trends between Rome and Constantinople 174

Bibliography 177
Scripture Index 185
General Index 193

PREFACE AND ACKNOWLEDGMENTS

Pursuing a research track at the University of New England, NSW, in the field of Early Christian Studies, I found myself in 2001 invited by a Dominican friar, one Anthony Fisher, to contribute lectures on the Fathers to a historical course on the Catholic Tradition of Marriage and Family at the John Paul II Institute for Marriage and Family, then being established in Melbourne. As the years went by, I was called on to expand my contributions, until by 2012, I was taking the whole course. It allowed me to bring other intellectual interests to bear, above all the desire to understand the genealogy of ideas and events that has led to cultural crisis in Western and world society, and now to the invasion and rending of the church Catholic.

The present book consists in an exhaustive reprocessing and re-researching of less than half of that course, deferring a treatment of events in the Christian West in the second thousand years. Whether this latter has any possibility of being published remains to be seen.

This work is perhaps best understood as the earnest attempt of a passionate believer in Christ and a Catholic, with some credentials in Patristic and ancient language studies, but beyond that of a thoughtful generalist, drawn against her own expectations to dig deep in the field of Christian marriage and human sexuality, in the light of the Nuptial Mystery. In this I was much fortified by the theological anthropology of John Paul II. For me, it was a tremendous thing to grow to see Marriage in the Lord and virginity for the Lord together in a synoptic vision, embraced by the Nuptial Mystery of our first creation and our last end. Praised be Jesus Christ!

I am greatly indebted to years of faith-filled, and intellectually stimulating, and at a deep level *charitable* and cheerful conversations, with my colleagues in the Melbourne Session of the Institute, with Adam Cooper and Conor Sweeney, Anna Krohn and Tracey Rowland, Colin Patterson,

Owen Vyner, the estimable Colonel Toby Hunter and others, and also to valuable insights gained from my own students over the years. Thanks to you all, and in particular to that student, Matthew MacDonald, who in the early years, told me fervently, "You really ought to publish these lectures as a book!" It was the seed of an idea.

I am pleased to see that two colleagues from the University of New England also make appearances in this book: the Romanist, Bronwyn Hopwood, and the Byzantinist, Lynda Garland. Others encouraged over the years, and I mention especially Greg Horsley, Professor of Classics and Ancient History, a fellow-believer and a friend.

Finally, and not the least, I express my warm appreciation for the patience and generosity of my Wipf and Stock collaborators, especially Rodney Clapp and Heather Carraher.

To this task I bring my own particular grounding in the Cappadocian Fathers and a spiritual/theological perspective of the Greek Fathers, and in terms of the West, of the Old Monastic Theology, whose last meteors were Saints Bernard of Clairvaux and Hildegard. And I bring some competencies in Hebrew, Syriac, Latin, and Greek, and in-depth exposure to Jewish studies. More fundamentally, faith in and love of our Lord Jesus Christ, nurtured in prayer, and a conviction that truth, and in particular the core truth about man, does not and will never change, even as we strive to rearticulate ancient truths in the flux and vicissitudes of culture and history. All these are governing elements in my approach.

I hope to engage the thoughtful nonspecialist reader, who is a fellow lover of Christ with me, and who may be scrambling for footholds in the midst of a cultural avalanche. To that end I considered it important to present vital and important passages from the Fathers, rather than sending the reader off to look them up in a thousand scattered sources. And if a reader does not understand Greek or Latin, patience! Let the concrete encounter with text in these languages, even if not immediately understood, be part of the respect we bring to the cause of learning from the great Tradition, which is ultimately the sublime *paradosis* coming down to us from the Father in his Son, the Word, our Lord Jesus Christ.

Finally, my prayer for all readers is, in the words of St Paul:

Grace to all who love our Lord Jesus Christ with undying love (Eph 6:24).

Anna M. Silvas, Easter 2020

ABBREVIATIONS

ANF. *Ante-Nicene Fathers.* General editors Alexander Roberts and James Robertson, revised by A. Cleveland Coxe; original edition, Christian Literature Publishing Co., 1885. Reprinted Peabody, MA: Hendrickson, 1995.

CCC. *Catechism of the Catholic Church.*

CCSL. *Corpus Christianorum Series Latina.* Turnhout: Brepols, 1954.

CSEL. Corpus Scriptorum Ecclesiasticorum Latinorum, a series of critical editions of late antique Latin writers, begun in 1866, now based in the University of Salzburg.

LR. The Longer Rules of St Basil the Great. In Anna M. Silvas, *The Asketikon of St Basil the Great* (Oxford: Oxford University Press, 2005).

NPNF, first ser. *Nicene and Post-Nicene Fathers, First Series.* General editors Philip Schaff and Henry Wace; original edition, Christian Literature Publishing Co., 1886. Reprinted Peabody, MA: Hendrickson, 1995).

NPNF, second ser. *Nicene and Post-Nicene Fathers, Second Series.* General editors Philip Schaff and Henry Wace; original edition, Christian Literature Publishing Co., 1895. Reprinted Peabody, MA: Hendrickson, June 1995.

PG. Migne, *Patrologia Graeca.*

PL. Migne, *Patrologia Latina.*

CITING SCRIPTURE

The RSV has been used generally as a default translation. Even so most scriptural passages and allusions are translated directly from the text at hand. Psalms are mostly quoted in the Grail version. Their numeration is according to the ancient Christian canon of the Septuagint, the Vulgate, and the Peshitta. The numeration of the Masoretic version appears second. "Byz" refers to the Byzantine or Greek liturgical transmission of the Scriptures, often followed by the Greek Fathers.

✠ *In the name of the Father and of the Son and of the Holy Spirit. Amen.*

Chapter One

IN THE BEGINNING

1.1 As it was, is now, and shall be

WE HUMANS FIND OURSELVES traveling in the strange medium of *time*, somewhere between our mysterious origin as creatures outwardly very much like the animals, yet with inward capacities vastly surpassing them, beckoned by something immense. For those lifting their eyes above the necessities, distractions, and struggles of this life, the horizons of this visible world are not nearly enough. Here we seem but "sojourners," itinerant guests for a day. Transience and mortality, even annihilation, overshadow. Pain, sickness, and suffering intrude. Meanwhile conflict, violence, and outrage constantly recrudesce in the human community. Such is the arc of our human existence, stretching from the beginning, on an historical journey, towards eternity.

We begin this book by returning in thought to that beginning of our race, to ponder the "Nuptial Mystery" inscribed in our humanity there. By "nuptial mystery" I mean that strange feature of our creation, our sexuality ordained to communion and life, that unity-in-differentiation encoded in the image of God in which we were created. Who is this transcendent model of all human desiring, imitation, and self-giving? We shall then go on to consider what has become of this Nuptial Mystery now that we are in via, and what draws it beyond history and beyond itself. We will search out the Scriptural word because to us believers in Christ, householders of the Ecclesia, the Bride, the Word of God in the "God-breathed" Scriptures are a fountain of truth and life.

Being children of the Bride, we open the sacred pages in a faith-filled, prayerful, and teachable frame of mind. We situate ourselves not outside and above, but within the dimension of revelation, not abstracted or emancipated from, but participating in the *paradosis* (*traditio*, "handing-on") of the Mystery of Christ from all eternity in the Creation through the incarnation to the *eschaton*, the consummation of the age. We own ourselves very much as *participants* in the story, for the same Spirit of Holiness who breathed upon the human authors is ever at work in the mystery of the Bride, as in our own inmost soul.

Sacred Scripture is forever rereading God's ways with man, forever rehearsing, ruminating, anguishing over, seeking to elucidate more deeply the tenor of God's covenants, often under pressure of severe crises, reverses, and indeed catastrophes. This is the "internal travail"[1] of Scripture and we must taste it deeply in prayer, and enter into it. This "searching out" is true above all of the prophets—not the false prophets, the appeasers, the mollifiers, the deluded and deluding—but the *true* prophets, signs of contradiction in their own age, credentialed by suffering, to whom the Lord discloses his ways with man in *deep unto deep* (Ps 41/42:8), opening in vista upon vista, always pointing beyond and above. Hebrews 1:1–3 and 1 Peter 1:10–12 portray the slow forensic emergence of the divine economy in history leading to Christ. The sublime hymn of Ephesians 1:3–10 marvels at the culminating revelation of "the Mystery" hidden from before all ages. The Gospel of John (cf. John 2:11) is steeped in a profoundly sapiential, "tasting" sense of the God at work in "sacred signs," leading always inward, onward, and upward. It all shows that the layered patristic and liturgical hermeneutic of Scripture is in truth a discipleship of the same vibrant "deep reading" approach of the sacred writers themselves.

At first pass, then, Sacred Scripture has a literal or historical sense, which opens upon fuller and deeper senses: a moral sense, an allegorical or preferably a typological sense, and an anagogical sense.[2] These "senses" correspond to the kinds of questions we might bring to the text.

---

1. Girard, *Things Hidden*, 263.

2. The classic fourfold sense of Scripture is affirmed in Second Vatican Council, *Dei Verbum* no. 12, and CCC nos. 109–19.

The literal asks the immediate "who and what, where and when" of a document in hand. The moral asks "how must we behave then?" The typological asks: "how does this fit into the pattern of salvation history?" The anagogical sense asks: "whither, ultimately, does this lead us?"

These human questionings correspond to the varied ways that the Holy Spirit is ever at work to win us for God, the living God, through epic history and picaresque tales, covenantal literary forms, epideictic commandment and case law, dread theophanies, divine oracles, prophetic appeals, human pleadings full of pathos, warnings, and consolations, poetic metaphors, and apocalyptic images. Through all these varied literary forms found in the Scriptures, the pedagogy of the Spirit is always *anagogical*, which means "leading upward." The Spirit of God, then, leads us onward and upward to ultimate realities, from sin, through redemption and the walk of obedience and the cleaving of prayer, to growth in holiness and finally to perfect union with God, to *what no eye has seen, nor ear heard, nor the heart of man conceived, what God has prepared for those who love him* (1 Cor 2:9).

When we first turn to the Scriptures we find the Word of God addressing us in a complex of stories and narrative histories, whispering the truth to our inmost conscience by the route of our imagination and emotions.

1.2 Back to the beginning

When our Lord Jesus Christ was engaged on the topic of divorce by the Pharisees, his response was: *for your hardness of heart Moses allowed you to divorce your wives, but it was not so from the beginning* (ἀπ' ἀρχῆς Matt 19:8). He the *Logos*, the Word himself who *in the beginning was with God and was God* (John 1:1–2), bids us go back, leaping over all casuistic arguments and cultural formations, to "the beginning," for the truth of God's plan for man and woman.

We make our own then these luminous, numinous words of our Lord: *the beginning*. In the Book of Genesis (in Hebrew *BeReshith*, "in the Beginning") we find two accounts of man's creation. The first is Gen 1:26–28:

> *Then God said, Let us make man in our image, after our likeness, and let them have dominion . . . So God created man in his own image, in the image of God he created him; male and female he*

> *created them. And God blessed them, and God said to them: "Be fruitful and multiply."*[3]

The second, more folkloric account, which names Adam and Eve, is Genesis 2:18–25.

> *Then the Lord God said, "It is not good that the man should be alone; I will make a helper fit for him."*

The Lord creates and presents the man with the beasts of the field and the birds of the air for him to name them, *but,* says Scripture,

> *there was not found a helper fit for him. So the Lord God caused a deep sleep to fall upon the man, and while he slept he took one of his ribs and closed up its place with flesh; and the rib which the Lord God had taken from the man he made into a woman and brought her to the man. Then the man said: "This at last is bone of my bones and flesh of my flesh; she shall be called Woman, because she was taken from Man." Therefore, a man leaves his father and his mother and cleaves to his wife, and they become one flesh. And the man and his wife were both naked, and were not ashamed.* (Gen 2:20–25)

The first creation account reaches its crescendo in three stages: First, there is the creation of the entire world of matter and space, of time and the elements; second, the creation of the widening gradations of life in all its great variety; finally it approaches the summit, the creation of man. At this moment, before proceeding to this culminating act of creation, God, as it were, pauses and enters into himself, for there will be an entirely new level of his creative investment in what he is about to do. This creature whom he is about to create, shall be "the only creature on earth that God willed for its own sake."[4]

For man is created *in the image and according to the likeness of God* (Gen 1:27). This is what differentiates him from the cosmic and animal orders that precede him and lead up to him. We humans were fashioned with a specific affinity to God inscribed in our very being: "by nature, man is related to the Infinite,"[5] man is a "partner of the Absolute."[6] Any

---

3. This account is reprised at Genesis 5:1–2: "*When God created man, he made him in the image of God. Male and female he created them, and he blessed them and named them Man when they were created.*"

4. Second Vatican Council, *Gaudium et Spes* no. 24:3.

5. Pope Benedict XVI, "Dependence on God."

6. See Pope John Paul II, *Man and Woman He Created Them*, Catechesis 6.2, 151.

sort of "humanism," therefore, which would ignore this intrinsic ordination of our nature to God, exclude it from the proposal of what it is to be human, is an anthropological fallacy, a colossal deception. Such a stance can only prove to be, sooner or later, an *anti*-humanism. Accordingly, if we molder in a life of sin, self-interest, and the utilization of others, it is not accurate to describe such behavior as "only human"—no, we are *failing* to be human, we have become *sub*-human.

The *image of God* means that the true model of all man's powers of imaging and desiring and imitation is God, and that this is expressly true for his nuptial constitution. From the human side, the spousal couple are founded in a triangular relationship whose anchoring pivot, whose very lynchpin, is God. From the divine side, what does this indicate?

How much theology, doctrine, and catechesis hang on this *image and likeness of God*. According to the Christian tradition, the "image of God" in which we were created was disclosed in the fullness of time to be God the Word incarnate, Christ himself, of whom St Paul says: *he is the image of the invisible God* (Col 1:15, cf. 2 Cor 4:4).[7] And we know that in

---

John Paul exegetes this from the second creation account, which portrays man's original solitude in relation to the rest of creation, and man as constituted in conscientious relationship to God.

7. "According to Greek Theology—and Ambrose and early Augustine, . . . man is only created *according* to the image of God: he is therefore a copy of the Word, the true Image of God, an image of the Image." (Louth, *The Origins*, 142) Preceded by Philo, Irenaeus was the first Christian writer to distinguish between *image* and *likeness*. (*Adversus Haereses* 5.16.2) God's deifying plan for man is that we attain the divine *likeness* through and in Christ, the Archetypal Image, who is thus both the goal and the way. St Gregory the Theologian, for example, sees our salvation as a process of assimilation to Christ, our growth in an ever more complete *likeness to* the true Image. See Hofer, *Christ in the Life and Teaching of Gregory of Nazianus*, 23–25.

The exposition of man as made in the image of the *Trinity* appears first in Augustine's late work, *de Trinitate*: "For why the *our*, if the Son is the image of the Father alone? But it is on account of the imperfect *likeness*, as we have said, that man is spoken of as *after the image*, and hence *our*, that man might be an image of the Trinity; not equal to the Trinity, as the Son is to the Father, but approaching it, as it is said, by a certain *likeness*, as in things that are distinct there can be a closeness, not however in this case spatially, but by imitation." (*De Trinitate* VII.VI.12, as cited in Louth, *The Origins*) Augustine sees the image of the Trinity in human psychological triads: memory, intellect, and will. It is a view that is focused on man as an individual. Cf. the critique of Augustine on this point by Joseph Cardinal Ratzinger, "Concerning the Notion," especially comments on 447 and at 354n12.

It was the merit of John Paul II to explicate that not only man as an individual subsistence—Adam, say—but precisely as created in twofold form as man and woman (Gen 1:26) and ordained thus to communion of persons and fruitfulness, who is

speaking of Christ we speak of one of the Trinity, of His relationship to the Father, and of our adoptive sonship with Him, into which his saving and redeeming work draws us.

The Hebrew noun for "God," *Elohim*, is singular in number yet plural in form, a feature not shared by other Semitic terms for "God." This peculiarity, together with the divine *we . . . us . . . our* appearing in these texts did not escape the attention of the Fathers. To them, they are proleptic intimations of the Trinity. If we use this as a key to read the text: *in the image of God he created him; male and female he created them* (Gen 1:26), it opens up to us a vista like this: Not only the human individual, but man precisely in the twofold form of male and female, that is, his very constitution as a "nuptial" being, reflects something of the inner life of God, and that *something* is that God is *relational* and *personal*. This Trinitarian interpretation of *the image of God* appears in the Catechism:

> **no.** 1702 The divine image . . . shines forth in the communion of persons, in the likeness of the unity of the divine persons among themselves.

> **no.** 2331 God is love and in himself he lives a mystery of personal loving communion. Creating the human race *in his own image* . . . God inscribed in the humanity of man and woman the vocation and thus the capacity and responsibility, of love and communion. (1 John 4:8, 16)

The second creation account teaches this primordial human call to communion too, but from a different angle and with a different etiology: *It is not good for the man to be alone* (Gen 2:18). This portends man's need to overcome his "original solitude," as Pope John Paul put it, for man finds himself irreducibly "other" than the animals: "incommensurable," finding no match among them.

After God created Eve from the side of Adam, it says, *he brought her to the man* (Gen 2:22). Few the words, great the weight! Here is the "nuptial representation of the bride":[8] the agent joining the two together, is God. The man henceforth cleaves to the woman so that they become *one flesh* (Gen 2:24). This *one flesh* union of one man and one woman, is, in short, monogamy. Moreover, the *one flesh* union also gestures to

---

in this qualified sense the image of the Trinity. See John Paul II, *Man and Woman*, Catechesis 9, and *Mulieris Dignitatem* no. 6–8; Scola, *The Nuptial Mystery*, especially "Human sexuality and the *Imago Dei*," 32–52. Cf. Caldecott, "Male and Female Souls."

8. Elliott, *What God Has Joined*, 7.

the "one flesh" of their child, the fruit of their union. Our Lord takes up this second creation account to teach the indissoluble bond of spouses, because it is God who unites them:

> *"Have you not read that from the beginning He who made them, made them male and female?" And He said, "For this reason a man shall leave his father and mother and be joined to his wife and the two shall become one flesh. So they are no longer two but one. What therefore God has joined together, let not man put asunder."* (Matt 19:4–6, cf. 1 Cor 6:12–17)

Returning to the first account at Genesis 1:27–28, we find that God *blesses* expressly this twofold creation of man as male and female. Such an address he did not accord the sub-human creation. He is therefore configuring human sexual differentiation differently to that of animals. The "place" ordained for human sexuality *in the beginning*, is the nuptial union of one man and one woman. Having blessed their union in *one flesh*, God said to them (*lahem*) (Gen 1:28), that is, he spoke personally to the two, ordaining their union to fruitfulness. The true imprint of *human sexuality*, therefore, is not from below, from the animals, which do have their own kind of blessing (Gen 1:22), but from above, *in the image and according to the likeness of God* (Gen 1:27), as Scola elucidates:

> The affirmation of sexuality as an integral part of the *imago Dei* ... allows us to establish a radical differentiation of human sexuality from animal sexuality, with which it obviously retains solid bio-instinctual connections. Against every Gnostic temptation we must affirm the fully *human*, that is *personal*, character of sexuality.[9]

This divine commission *Be fruitful and multiply* has been called the "creation mandate." It means that the love of man and woman is to be accomplished in a fully human manner, by a *personal, conscientious obedience to a divine call*. Only a freely given response to the God who calls us into being fits the dignity of this new order of creature made *in His image and likeness*. When spouses come together in a way that is open implicitly to fruitfulness, their union is immersed in the streams of the *fountain of life* (Ps 35/36:9), from *the living and true God* (1 Thess 1:9). The spouses' disposition of a humble, childlike openness to a horizon far greater than they, a divine horizon, allows them to participate in the superabundant love of God who brings forth creation, brings forth *life*.

---

9. Scola, *The Nuptial Mystery*, 10.

Such a nuptial affection of the human mind and heart is well pleasing to God; it sanctifies his name, whether or not a child comes of this union. That is his affair. Here is the impetus of all else Scripture will have to say to the idea of setting out to sterilize the marital act.

The creation mandate is honored in the liturgy of marriage. Before proceeding to the mutual consent, the couple are asked: *Will you accept children lovingly from God and bring them up according to the law of Christ and his Church?* Without this professed openness to the gift and the responsibility of children the sacrament cannot proceed; if this intention was verifiably absent from the outset, the marriage is null and void. In the life in Christ, marriage was never about setting up a snug convenient twosome on our own or the world's terms—the secular image of marriage today—but about a man and a woman giving themselves to each other on God's terms to *increase* as a family.

When he had finished the creation of man as male and female and given them his first commands, *God saw everything that he had made, and behold, it was very good* (Gen 1:31). Whereas after each of the days of creation God found it *good*, after the creation of man as *male and female in his image and according to his likeness*, he found it *very good*. Founding this human nuptial mystery, therefore, was like the culminating delight of the divine work of creation.

Finally, Adam and Eve are said to have been *naked without shame* (Gen 2:25). Since in our original innocence the body was translucent to the spirit, and the unity of the *two-in-one-flesh* transparent to the Creator, what possible shame could come of visible nakedness to each other?

The notes of scriptural anthropology which we have been considering from the Genesis accounts might be summed up as follows:

- Human beings were ordained, in the first place and in a manner specific to them, as the image and likeness of God. The vocation Godward is therefore primordially and fundamentally and intrinsically *human*.

- Our constitution in twofold form, male and female—the "nuptial mystery"—is of God's making; inscribed with the *image of God*, it is *very good*.

- It is God who brings the woman and the man together so that they become *two-in-one-flesh*. The marriage of one man and one woman is of God's joining, and may not be dissolved by man.

- The nuptial mystery expressed in marital union is ordained by God to *fruitfulness;* so disseminating *the image of God* by participating in the self-giving and life-giving character of the life-giving love that God *is.*

1.3 The Fall before the Fall

So it was, then, *in the beginning.* The book of Genesis, however, has more to tell us of the fate of human sexuality. Enter the Serpent.

But before we go down that path, let us first ponder the Fall before the Fall. The Scriptures attest over and over again the existence of non-human, intelligent, personal beings who are not of this spatiotemporal order. These "purely noetic creatures," as the Greek Fathers would say, we commonly call "angels." Some are ministers of God and helpers to man; some decidedly not. In a modality we cannot imagine, a "yes" or "no" to God was put to the freedom of each of these spirits. Some responded "yes" and became the hosts of the divine glory; some, however, took the route of "no." This "no" to God by a portion of the angels constitutes the Fall before the Fall. From this cohort of dark angels, an evil *paradosis* (handing-over, *traditio*) of envy passed over to the nascent human race. So the book of Wisdom attests. After graphically portraying the pathology of envy and the cruel vengeance it exacts of all whose way of life it finds a provocation, Wisdom traces the genealogy of this envy much further back:

> Thus they reasoned, but they were led astray,
> For their own wickedness blinded them,
> And they did not know the mysteries of God,
> Nor hoped for the wages of holiness,
> Nor discerned a reward for blameless souls.
> For God created man for incorruption,
> And made him the image of his own eternity,
> But through the devil's envy, death entered the world,
> And they who are of his party do experience it. (Wis 2:21–24)

1.4 Enter: the Serpent

How then did the evil *paradosis* between the worlds come about? We turn to the one privileged resource of revelation we are given, Genesis 3, for the utter gravity and seriousness of what is told there. Let us then immerse ourselves deeply in the earliest moments of human existence. This story is *our* story, our *drama*.

The Antagonist meets Eve in the guise of the Serpent (Gen 3:1–7). He engages a friendly discussion with her about God and his intentions. God, you see, is already "objectified." She reports the words of the command not to eat of the fruit of this particular tree, *lest you die* (Gen 3:3). He retorts: *No, you will not die!* Which is to imply that God is a liar. This is a proleptic jolt to her, but he acts swiftly to soothe it. Sounding eerily like a master of higher consciousness, he taps a truth written in her inmost being by the Creator: *likeness to God* (3:5). Here is the paradigm of all wicked cunning: simulate cordiality, put your finger on a truth, something with which your target has an affinity, and go from there. So he does not begin by tempting Eve to *manifest* evil, but to the lofty prospect of *likeness to God* instead. Around this aspiration of her mind and heart he weaves sympathetic "questions," until at last he injects the full-bore lie: the command given to her was not about love and self-gift—as if the gift and task ever set before the first humans were not a return of steadfast love and truth for steadfast love and truth. Such was the original and good emulation: the imitation of God. No! The Serpent lowers Eve's thoughts to the parameters of his own envy: the *real* motive of God's command is *rivalry*! It's all about *power*! Stealthily he foments her suspicion and fans her resentment. What he is doing is insinuating himself as Eve's model, and to that end getting her to expel God from that shrine of her soul. Here is the turning point of the human tragedy: "Humankind is never the victim of God; God is always the victim of humankind."[10] She finds the reasoning persuasive. That she should assert her "right" to compete with God first appears attractive, then possible, *surely* justifiable, finally *demanded*. At last, mesmerized, she yields. Eve imitates the Serpent.

Let no one say these are "primitive" documents! These stories are vividly prophetic and truthful! Our ancient Baptismal vows remember the truth: it is not so much *obvious* evil that we must refuse, but Satan's *pomps,* his masquerades, feints and stratagems, the clever blur of truths, half-truths, and lies, to which our Lord bade us be *wise as serpents and*

---

10. Girard, *I see Satan*, 191.

innocent as doves (Matt 10:16). God grant us that *innocence as doves* which is *wiser than serpents*, which knows that for us humans, all, ultimately, must come down to a "yes" or "no" to God.

Yet one last line of defense remained: Adam. Scripture notes that throughout this elegant theological discussion between the Serpent and Eve, Adam was *with her* or *by her side* (Gen 3:6). He could have, *should* have been alert to "clear and present danger," acted vigorously to rescue Eve, countered the poison of false emulation she was imbibing, with the older and deeper medicine of the imitation of God. But no. He did not intervene. He said and did nothing. Reckless of what truly made for their nuptial unity, forgetting the primacy of God which was ever its safeguard, ignoring their mutual ordination to God that was ever its *meaning*, he emulates her desire and falls in with her proposal. Adam too, imitates the Serpent. In this descent into the vortex, his reckless oblivion of God is tragic beyond measure. The Serpent's conquest is complete.

Now God our Creator loves our human freedom. This was the great risk of a God who is *not* "all about power." Freedom is the mark of his fashioning us as *persons* in his sight, both a gift and a *task*. He respected it with the angels, he respects it with us. He will never *force* anyone's freedom. The voice of the Lord calls out to us, that we only make a personal return of steadfast love and faithfulness for his steadfast love and faithfulness. The corollary of this freedom is that we bear our own choices and acts. Human responsibility God does not abrogate. Often our reward or our punishment, in this life and in the next, is to get what we wanted and asked for—with all the consequences attending that choice. This teaching of Scripture has been called the Law of Sowing and Reaping. St Paul expressed it as: *Do not be deceived; God is not mocked, for whatever a man sows that he will also reap* (Gal 6:7). The prophet Hosea says: *they sow the wind and they shall reap the whirlwind* (Hos 8:7). You want a God-free life—or at least a relationship with him configured to your own specifications? Right. This is what it looks like. Having expelled God as their only true life-giving model, Adam and Eve now enter the realm of necessity, reaping a whirlwind for themselves and their offspring: exile from Paradise, suffering and toil, bodily death, above all the loss of *original integrity* or *innocence*, that sweet good order of the human person, in which all our powers—the inner senses, intellect, will, memory, the vital passions and emotions, the bodily senses—are in right accord with each other and disposed implicitly to divine grace. In the Fall, the human condition became warped: we lost our transparency to God and that ready self-command that was our original birthright and our God-glorifying vocation.

"Once the primacy of God is lost, everything becomes idolatry"—so my colleague Conor Sweeney, and he is right. Adam and Eve's grab for autonomy from God affects their sexuality. They begin objectifying each other, absent the divine transparency: *Then the eyes of both were opened and they knew that they were naked and they sewed fig leaves together and made themselves aprons* (Gen 3:7). Alien elements of self-consciousness and suspicion, of furtiveness and calculation, enter into their capacity to be naked to each another, naked to themselves, and—most important of all—naked to God: *and the man and his wife hid from the presence of the* LORD *God among the trees of the Garden* (Gen 3:8).

Other consequences for human sexuality follow, learned especially from the words addressed to Eve: *I will greatly multiply your pain in childbearing; in pain shall you bring forth children, yet your desire shall be for your husband, and he shall rule over you* (Gen 3:16). The phrase, *your desire shall be for your husband and he shall rule over you,* should give us pause. It means that a disturbance has entered into God's original plan for the relations between man and woman. Instead of the mutual *two-in-one-flesh,* an alien inequity now tears and gnaws at their relationship, and it is the woman who is especially vulnerable to it. Thus, a greater or lesser degree of man's domination of woman, and even some emotional weakness in woman that colludes with her own intimidation, whether in marriage or in the general relations of the sexes, is historically all too patent. Alas, it has sometimes entwined itself in our religious traditions. We need to grasp very clearly that any exploitation, any scapegoating of woman by man, is a symptom of our fallen condition, a deviation from the Creator's original plan, a mark of sin in our nature which we must recognize, from which we need to be redeemed.[11]

It seems as if it is a dire lookout for woman in particular. Nevertheless, there is a seed of hope for her in the sentence pronounced upon the Serpent: *I will put enmity between you and the woman, and between your seed and her seed; he shall bruise your head and you shall bruise his heel* (Gen 3:15). This so-called *proto-evangelium* is the antiphon to the entire saga of salvation history to follow. It forecasts all human history as a dramatic contest with evil, a struggle concerning especially the woman, yet bearing a mysterious promise of victory to come—at cost.

---

11. I rely upon Pope John Paul II for this exegesis, *Mulieris dignitatem* nos. 9, 10, 24.

1.5 The Children of Cain

Scripture depicts the ever widening and tragic consequences of human sin following the exile from the Garden. They explode in the deeds of Adam and Eve's first-born son, Cain. *And when they were in the field, Cain rose up against his brother Abel and killed him . . . And the* LORD *said, "What have you done? The voice of your brother's blood is crying out to me from the ground."* (Gen 4:8,10).

Cain, his brother's murderer and accursed of God, is said to have founded a "city" (Gen 4:17). "City" in Greek is *polis,* whence *politeia* and *politics*, and in Latin *civitas,* whence *civilis* (citizen) and *civilization.* The children of Cain, then, invent the "civilization" of fallen man. Let us call it the City of Man: a *politeia* of managed violence at best, ever devising stratagems to quell violence through deploying further violence, in an endless cycle of ambiguous symmetries. What else can *the mark of Cain* (Gen 4:16) be, but the offensive defense of pragmatic vengeance? And the violence ever seethes and breeds, as civilizations slowly rise, peak, and ignominiously decay.

In this City of Man, one of the earliest manifestations of the disorder between man and woman is the appearance of polygyny, in which a single man takes several wives. It means that the Creator's plan for the *one-flesh* union of one husband and one wife is broken. The first named polygynist is Lamech, of Cain's lineage (Gen 4:10). Scripture constantly exposes the strongest link between sexual greed and violence. Accordingly, Lamech is soon found boasting to his two wives Adah and Zillah, of his boundless capacity for murderous ultra-vengeance.

Another deterioration is concubinage, i.e., having "sub-wives" of slave status, as for example Abraham and Hagar in Gen 16:1–4. Abraham had received the divine promise that his descendants would be *as many as the stars of heaven* (Gen 15:5–6), yet Sarah, his wife, continued childless. The years went by, testing them greatly in patience. The ruse with Hagar, one might say, was an attempt to manipulate reproductive outcomes. The results were baleful indeed: rivalry between Sarah and Hagar, rupture in the household, enmity between the descendants of the two sons, Isaac and Ishmael. Ishmael is the putative progenitor of Arabian tribes, with all that that suggests of the enmity of blood brothers that has simmering for thousands of years.

The book of Genesis exposes the destructive consequences for the family of violating the human covenant with God. Every one of Israel's foes, each hostile nation or tribe is traced back to some sexual sin leading to a rupture within the family and to social ruin. The sins of parents in the sexual realm affect the lives of their children, and their children's children. Even the great patriarchal families are, all of them, in one way or another sinful and "dysfunctional." There is scarcely a major figure in salvation history unscathed by sexual sin. What is true of Genesis continues throughout the history of Israel, to mention only King David. Long lists of alarming exemplars from Scripture could easily be drawn up.

Scripture relentlessly exposes the fact that dark riddles plague the human heart, that a malevolent power is ever at work to drag us down, apt to insinuate itself in even the best of our aspirations. The *mystery of lawlessness* (2 Thess 2:7) erupts from generation to generation, to the fearful bloodying of human history. It is a bleak, indeed a tragic picture, and the scriptural narrative is set to become darker yet. Yet we shall see that, the Lord having *lifted us up and thrown us down* (Ps 101/102:10), never abandons us without the hope of his salvation.

Chapter Two

THE FAMILY: COVENANT, LAW, AND COUNSEL IN THE OT

2.1 The Children of Abel

As THE SPIRIT OF God once hovered over the waters of primeval chaos for the work of creation, so now He hovers over lost and disoriented man for the work of reclaim, if He can find any to respond to him. And He does find them! In the midst of the worsening depravity, the *anamnesis* (remembrance) of God springs up like tender shoots from the arid ground of humanity, in one individual or another. Their response brings a distant hope to human lineage. The sense of the lost likeness to God stirs; a Godward yearning dares to revive.

The first to respond are Adam and Eve's descendants through Seth, not Cain. Seth is born for the murdered Abel, as his own mother declares: *"God has appointed for me another child instead of Abel, for Cain slew him." To Seth also a son was born, and he called his name Enosh. At that time men began to call upon the name of the* LORD (Gen 4:25–26). We might call Seth's lineage the Children of Abel, meaning, of course, Abel's children in spirit. The Children of Abel are all who share in the disposition of him of whom it was said: *And the* LORD *had regard for Abel and for his offering* (Gen 4:5). And so it goes from generation to generation, until Christ comes as the crown of Abel's offering and of his innocent blood, and that of all his spiritual kin, *from the foundation of the world* (Luke 11:49–52, Heb 12:24).

A little later it is famously said of one of Seth's descendants: *Enoch walked with God; and was no more, for God took him* (Gen 5:24). Now one of Enoch's descendants is Noah, and so we arrive at the line of covenant bearers.

2.2 Covenant

Covenant is one of the governing ideas of Scripture. An older English word for *covenant* is *testament*. Both translate διαθήκη, used in the Septuagint for the Hebrew *berith*. This usage continues in the Greek New Testament, above all at that supreme moment, when Our Lord on the eve of his Passion takes up the *blood of the Covenant* of Exodus 24:8 and the promise of the *New Covenant* in Jeremiah 31:31, and enacts them in his own Blood (Luke 22:20). Thus the Sacred Scriptures compass the Old and the New "Testaments," that is, *covenants*.

In the ancient Near East, a covenant was a treaty establishing a binding alliance between two parties, sometimes of equal, sometimes of unequal status. The "cutting" of a covenant comprised certain formal elements: historical prologue, stipulations, oaths and imprecations, and ritual enactment. The precise forms varied with the different Near Eastern cultures. The Assyrians and Egyptians were more concerned with the exercise of power and a unilateral imposition of terms, whereas the Hittites were more interested in *relationship* and the use of historical preamble in order to persuade to a plan of common action. I once heard a Hittite scribe quoted to say: "Read in the tablets the tale of blood!" One can recognize the same idea in our scriptural narratives. These Hittite treaties of the second millennium BC offer the most convincing antecedents of the scriptural idea of "covenant," because with the Hittites, a covenant established a relationship based on *prior history*. It seems that the inspired authors put to theological use a contemporary political, legal, and literary instrument to articulate the framework for God's relationship with the human race in general (Noah), and with his chosen people in particular (Abraham).

At this point then we are asking the moral question of Scripture: how are we to *walk with God* in this domain of human sexuality, marriage, and family? The covenant tradition answers this primarily in the form of moral instructions: the commandments that are the covenant provisos of the covenant; whereas moral reflection and reasoned counsel is the manner of the later wisdom writers.

2.3 The Covenant of Sinai

Scripture presents a succession of covenants through which God attempts to anchor a relationship with man that will call him back from his runaway depravity to the reassurance of living in accordance with the divine plan. While more could be said of the covenants made with Noah and with Abraham, let us move on quickly to the Sinaitic or Mosaic covenant.

The Covenant of Sinai, begins, as all covenants, with God's will to save, his gratuitous initiative, his intervention in human history. Thus the prologue of the Ten Commandments begins: *I am the* LORD *your God who brought you out of the land of Egypt, out of the house of bondage* (Exod 20:2). The Lord establishes his claim to covenant loyalty through his prior acts of salvation in favor of the people. This antecedent history, this *anamnesis* of his mighty acts, speaks to the understanding of the people, inviting their avowal. Then they hear the covenant stipulations of their Divine benefactor, which are proposed at first in the form of apodeictic, that is, declaratory and prescriptive law.

The core of the many different levels of commandments in the Torah are the "Ten Words," or Ten Commandments, which are in fact presented twice. The first few commandments teach the primacy of allegiance to God above all else, of the *justice* we owe to our creator and benefactor. They underscore our creation *in the image of God*, the truth about man that he is ordered, *intrinsically,* to God.

The commandments then turn to man's social relations. God's very first concern in this sphere is revealed to be: *Honor your father and your mother* (Exod 20:12). Piety towards God means piety towards those through whom God created us. Eventually the truth comes home to Israel that God the Creator and Redeemer is also "Father," and that the role our parents have towards us is some echo of the transcendent Fatherhood of God. Man's filial relationship to God was already being learned in Israel before the plenitude of its disclosure in the Incarnate Son.

Two commandments address marriage and human sexuality expressly: *You shall not commit adultery* (Exod 20:14), and, embedded in the tenth: *You call not covet your neighbor's wife* (Exod 20:17). These inculcate the exclusivity of marriage, and underscore adultery as a wronging of the *third* person, a transgressive emulation of our neighbor, from whom the spouse is snatched. We want what our neighbor has, and we will have it, no matter how forbidden it may be. This tenth commandment is about the disciplining of desire itself, curing it by re-blocking it on the original good emulation, the imitation of God. So we arrive again at the first commandment: the primacy of God for the healthy constitution of the human being, of our desiring and of our sexuality, and of our whole social existence. The church has traditionally seen in these commandments all that concerns the integrity of marriage and the right ordering of our human sexuality, that is, the virtue and call to chastity.

The Ten Commandments embody moral truths transcending all historical periods and cultures. Follow-up commandments and ordinances in the Mosaic law there are aplenty, but often these are on a secondary or tertiary level, presented in the form of case law. Some more than others have to be interpreted to their context. Much of the case law on sex, marriage, and family is found in the so-called Code of Holiness of Leviticus 17—26, where extensive laws of ritual purity hedge about the bodily processes connected with sex and childbirth (Lev 15:16–18, 19–30, 18:19, 23; 20:13; 22:4; cf. Deut 27:20), the kinship ties within which marriage cannot be conducted (Lev 18:6–18; 20:11–14, 17, 19–21), homosexual practices (Lev 18:22), homosexual prostitution (Deut 23:18), bestiality (Lev 18:23), child sacrifice (Lev 19:23), and cult prostitution (Deut 23:17).

It is worth pondering the fact that spouses observing the law of Leviticus 18:19 will be practicing regular periods of abstinence. Whatever we may think of the designation of menstruation as "unclean," spouses are trained by this obedience to observe a kind of salutary Sabbath in their marital relations, which has the potential of increasing their mutual respect by encoding the primacy of God into their very bodily lives. This is a true training in mutual discipline and marital chastity.

Deuteronomy 24:1–3 mentions in passing the custom of divorce; it is solely a husband's prerogative, and the right to remarry is part of it (Deut 24:1, 3).

2.4 "House" and family in Israel

The most common word for "family" in Hebrew is *bayit,* meaning "house" (Gen 24:38; 46.31), deriving from the verb *banah,* "to build." The words for son, *ben,* and daughter, *bat* (shortened from *bantah*), also derive from *banah*. In the Hebrew idiom, then, to found a family is to *build a house* (Deut 25:10, Pss 126/127:1, 3–5; 127/128:3). The Greek word for household is οἰκία. Its related field includes οἰκιακός and οἰκεῖος. These all have to do with close kinship, familiar relationship, membership of the same household. Another Hebrew word, *mishpahah*, refers to the extended family, "kindred" and "clan" (Gen 12:3; 24:38, 40; 28:14). The Greek equivalent is πατριά (cf. Eph 3:15). One could make a rich word study of the soteriological and theological resonances of these terms throughout the Scriptures. The family in Israel comprised husband and wife and children—but also, as in much of the Near East and the ancient world, close stem or collateral kin in residence, concubines, hired servants (Gen 14:14; 17.12–13), slaves and even sojourners, guests who came under the shelter of their hosts during their stay.

2.5 The Father

The family in Scripture is inherently patriarchal. Our disposition is one of faith, and we need to keep the ideological fads of our time at a distance, if we are to be free to learn the perennial scriptural truths about the father. The significance of patriarchy, redounding to the good of women and of children, is that it puts responsibility for family in the center of men's lives. Fatherhood is the vocation, par excellence, of every man. The truth of it recalls a young man from the slide to reckless promiscuity, from the shabby use of women, from alienation from the children he begets, and from the hazardous honor to be had in the competitive world of male gangs, cabals, and predatory mobs, where he can stay safely frozen in emotional adolescence forever. Such is fallen, feral masculinity. The call to fatherhood, to mature manhood, is part of its cure, and crucial to the well-being of the family, the first cell of all human society.

In the Scriptures, therefore, the father is head of the family, its principle of authority and of ownership of property. He bestows his name on the family. Since he himself is obedient to the covenant and accountable to God, his power is not arbitrary, but is ruled by the fear of the Lord. He both provides materially for his family, and provides moral leadership. He commands (Gen 50:16; Jer 35:6–10; Prov 6:20), teaches (Gen 18:19; Exod 12:26–27; 13:8, 14–15; Deut 6:7; Prov 1:8; 17:6), corrects (Gen 37:10), loves his family (Gen 25:28; 37:4; 44:20), trusts in a faithful wife (Prov 31:11), has compassion on his children in imitation of God's compassion (Ps 102/103:13), and delights in their uprightness (Prov 23:25, Jer 47:3). In early Israelite times, he exercised certain priestly roles, such as sacrifice. He remained responsible for certain observances, such as circumcision (Gen 17:37), and for the religious nurturance of his children (Deut

1:31; Job 1:5; Hos 11:1–3). Finally, a father's blessing on his children was held to be ratified by God, and powerful in its effects (cf. Gen 27).

2.6 The Mother

By her husband's side, the wife and mother possessed her own particular honor and authority within the family. In a way she is the heart of it: *your wife will be like a fruitful vine in the heart of your house* (Ps 127/128:3). She loves her children (Gen 25:28; Isa 49:15; Prov 4:3) and comforts them, which images God's comforting of Israel (Isa 66:13); she deserves their love and respect in return. As the diligent mistress and manager of the household she wins great esteem, as in the praise accorded the *good woman*, the faithful wife in Proverbs 31. If her husband dies, and no sons are of age, she acts as head of the household (2 Kgs 8:1–6).

She has an office of counsel to her husband, and of teaching and of moral instruction to her children, especially in their earlier years (Prov 1:8). There is a long honor roll of influential, proactive mothers in Scripture: the matriarch Sarah (Gen 21:10–12), Rebecca (Gen 27:11–17), Leah (Gen 30:16), Rachel (Gen 31:34), the wife of Manoah (Judg 13:23), the mother of Micah (Judg 17:2–6), Hannah (1 Sam 1:22–23), and the mother of the Maccabee martyrs (2 Macc 7), whose greatest gift to her sons was to point them to the primacy of faith in God, beyond all the terrors of torture and death.

A woman attained no higher role in ancient Israel than that of *Gevirah*, the Queen Mother (1 Kgs 2:19; 14:21; 15:13; 2 Chr 15:16). This scriptural archetype comes to its singular flowering in the Christian dispensation with Mary, called *blessed* by all generations (Luke 1:48), the all holy *Theotókos*, God-bearer, and Queen of Heaven.

2.7 The Children

Since family descent is through the male line, the arrival of a first son was much longed for. The first-born son, the *bekhor*, held a status next to his father. The *bekhor* belonged to the Lord as a "first-fruits" and was "redeemed" by sacrifice (Exod 13:13). He himself exercises a quasi-paternal role towards his younger siblings. Nevertheless, one of the themes of Scripture is the not infrequent failure of the first-born son, and his being supplanted by a younger male sibling. Daughters remain under the special care of their mothers; it is her father's prerogative to dispose of his daughter's hand in marriage, which was treated as her transfer from one "house" to another "house."

Hebrew and Aramaic had no specific term for "cousin," as does English. Hence the term "brother" is used for relatives in the extended family, e.g. nephews (Gen 13:8; 14:14), fellow members of the same tribe (Lev 21:10), and others with a claim (Deut 2:4, 8; 23:8). Brotherly solidarity is often extolled (e.g. Prov 17:17), as for example that beautiful line in the psalm: *How good and how pleasant it is when brothers dwell in unity* (Ps 132/133:1). In thinking about sisters, one cannot but remark on the outstanding example of sisterly initiative in Moses' elder sister, presumably Miriam. Thanks to her quick wit (Exod 2:7), their mother Jochebed (Exod 2:9) was taken into the pay of Pharaoh's daughter to nurse and rear her own child.

2.8 The household as religious community

The household in Israel was called to be a religious community, the first cell of the covenant people of God. But before we go into that, a huge difference between the society of ancient Israel and ours should be pointed out. The ancient cultures did not know a sharp separation between the sacred and the secular, between religious and cultic life on the one hand, and domestic, civil, and everyday life on the other—the sort of mental split that has long become normal in liberal Western thinking today.

Piety towards God is the warp and woof of family life. This is evidenced in a complex of ways: the father and mother are the moral teachers of their children. There are ceremonies that have their proper setting in the family home: the weekly welcoming of the Sabbath, for example. The Passover was observed with a domestic liturgy. Every Holy Thursday we hear detailed prescriptions in Exodus 12, for the carrying out of the commemorative ritual in each local household. The catechesis of children is essential. *And when your children say to you, What do you mean by this service? you shall say, "It is the Passover of the* LORD, *for he passed over the houses of the people of Israel in Egypt when he slew the Egyptians but spared our houses"* (Exod 12:26–27; cf. Ps 77:3–7).

Domestic piety is enshrined in the core of the *Shema*, the core confession of Israel, the verbal icon of Jewish piety:

> *Hear O Israel: the* LORD *our God is the one* LORD; *and you shall love the* LORD *your God with all your heart, and with all your soul, and with all your might. And these words which I command you this day be upon your heart; and you shall teach them diligently to your children, and shall talk of them when you sit in your house, and when you walk by the way, and when you lie down, and when you rise. And you shall bind them as a sign upon your hand, and they shall be as frontlets between your eyes. And you shall write them on the doorposts of your house and on your gates.* (Deut 6:4–9)

This loftiest statement of Israel's piety, re-expressing the first few of the ten commandments in positive form, and which our Lord designated the *first* commandment (Matt 12:29–30), is taught to the children at home. The practice of covenant remembrance sanctifies the name of the Lord in the family. Such a disposition is summed up in one word: the Hebrew *hesed* (steadfast love/covenant loyal love), the Greek εὐσέβεια (godly reverence), and the Latin *pietas,* or "piety." Other synonyms come to mind, the *yir'at Adonai* (e.g. Prov 1:7), that holy fear which is sovereign awe and remembrance of the Lord—but then if we go on with word studies there will never be an end of it.

The later wisdom literature of the Bible dwells on family relations and has some wonderful passages to offer. The very format of these books is often that of a father, or sometimes of a mother, teaching his or her son: *Hear, my son, your father's instruction, and reject not your mother's teaching* (Prov 1:8; cf. 3:11–12; 6:20–22; 13:1; 22:15; 23:13–14; 29:17), and: *Listen to me your father, O children* (Sir 3:1).

Reflecting the image of God as Father (Deut 1:31, 32:6, Hos 11:1; Isa 64:8; Mal 1:6; 2:10), a father's conduct towards his children is a mirror of God's conduct towards us: *Know then in your heart that as a man disciplines his son, the* LORD *God disciplines you* (Deut 8:5; see also Prov 3:12). A father must not neglect his duty to teach his children: *Discipline your son while there is hope* (Prov 19:8; see also 13:24; 29:17).

Children for their part are told this: *With all your heart honor your father, and do not forget the birth pangs of your mother. Remember that through your parents you were born; and what can you give back to them in return for their gift to you?* (Sir 7:23–28 at 27–28; cf. Prov 1:8; 19:26; 30:11; Tob 4:3–4).

The wisdom writers are sometimes more concerned for the behavior of adult children towards their aged parents, than for children who are still minors. Adult children are not called always to *obey* their parents, but, in the stresses and strains of family relationships, always to pay them practical *honor*, and never to belittle them. It is a profound, humbling, and beautiful idea that the fulfilment of respect towards one's parents, perhaps in trying circumstances, may serve as an atonement for one's own sins before the Lord. That is what the book of Sirach teaches us: deep implicit respect for our parents *especially* in the diminishments of their old age:

> For the LORD honored the father above the children, and he confirmed the right of the mother over her sons. Whoever honors his father atones for sins, and whoever glorifies his mother is like one who lays up treasure . . . O son, help your father in his old age, and do not grieve him as long as he lives; even if he is lacking in understanding, show him forbearance; in all your strength do not despise him. For kindness to a father will not be forgotten, and against your sins it will be credited to you; in the day of affliction it will be remembered in your favor. (Sir 3:2–3, 12–14)

2.9 The decay of the family and the undoing of Israel

In the context of the effects of the Fall, especially on human sexuality and on family life, we have seen that the commandments of the Mosaic covenant were intended as a restoration of the right order, God's order, for family life.

Notwithstanding the Lord's saving acts on behalf of Israel, the privilege of the covenants and the Law-giving, the prophets and wisdom writers have often to decry the deterioration of family life, decline in respect for parents and the proliferation of sexual sins (Jer 3:1–4; Ezek 18:6; 22:7; Mic 7:6, Prov 20:20). They read these disorders and corruptions in the family as the unravelling of the covenant, presaging the dissolution of Israel. The prophet Ezekiel indicts Jerusalem for systematically undoing the Holiness code of Leviticus 17–26, and the consequences shall surely follow:

> Behold the princes of Israel in you, everyone according to his power, have been bent on shedding blood. Father and mother are treated with contempt in you; the sojourner suffers extortion in your midst; the fatherless and the widow are wronged in you . . . in you men uncover their father's nakedness [incest]; in you

> they humble women who are unclean in their impurity [in their monthly periods]. One commits abomination with his neighbor's wife; another lewdly defiles his daughter-in-law; another in you defiles his sister his father's daughter . . . I will scatter you among the nations and disperse you through the countries, and I will consume the filthiness out of you. (Ezek 22:6–7, 10–11, 15)

2.10 Eschatological salvation and the family

The experience of the family, positively and negatively, ran so deep in Israel and so resonated with the inspired authors, that they extend family imagery to the nations of Israel and Judah, and to Israel in her covenant relationship with God. When the prophets turn from excoriation to hope, they often portray, in terms of family language, the coming salvation of the Lord after catastrophe and exile. The day of the Lord's salvation will mean the renewal of families, the rapprochement of parents and children, the restored fidelity of husbands and wives. Each of these salutary family images is then applied to the relationship of Israel and the Lord. In the very chapter of Jeremiah in which he announces the coming New Covenant, the prophet speaks of the God of all the families of Israel: *At that time, says the* LORD, *I will be the God of all the families of Israel [mishpehot yisrael], and they shall be my people* (Jer 31:1).

A few verses later, the prophet applies the image of father and son to God and Israel: *for I am a father to Israel and Ephraim is my first-born . . . therefore my heart yearns for him; I will surely have mercy on him, says the* LORD (Jer 31:9).

A later prophet, Micah, agonizes over all aspects of marriage and family as they apply to the salvation history of Israel. In his prophecy, referenced at Luke 1:17, he envisages the eschatological day of salvation as the restoration of ravaged family bonds, the healing of the wounds of sin that proliferate through the generations, which is so much a theme of the Scriptures. The Day of the Lord will mean the reconciliation of wounded, broken, and ravaged families.

> *Behold, I will send you Elijah the prophet before the great and terrible day of the* LORD *comes. And he will turn the hearts of fathers towards their children and hearts of children towards their fathers, lest I come and smite the land with a curse.* (Mic 4:5)

Chapter Three

THE PROPHETS, THE LORD, AND MARITAL COVENANT

3.1 Idolatry and sexual sin

EARLY ISRAEL WAS A theocracy administered by religious cult and precept, presided over by a series of charismatic "judges." Such is the story of the books of Joshua and Judges. It was not long, however, before the people craved to emulate the surrounding nations. They wanted to have their own king and court and royal army. The first book of Samuel reveals strong ambivalences surrounding the institution of monarchy in Israel. Such fears were well founded. Scripture completes a remarkable circle between this prophetic wariness of monarchy, and the kind of kingdom in which Christ is king, which owes nothing to emulation of anything in this world (John 18:36–37).

The Israelite monarchy had only reached as far as the third king, Solomon, when it precipitated an avalanche of idolatry. The imitation of the surrounding nations became imitation of their religious cults too. In Solomon's case, idolatrous syncretism went hand in glove with his outrageous polygamies (1 Kgs 11:1–8), a moral deterioration that did not escape the notice of later wisdom writers: *But you laid your loins beside women, and through your body you were brought into subjection. You put a stain upon your honor and defiled your posterity* (Sir 47:19–20).

Playing the harlot, or, *whoring after other gods* is a recurring scriptural idiom (cf. Exod 34:12–16; Num 25:1–3; Ps 105/106:39)! No mere literary figure, however, it played out in concrete practice. In the surrounding nations, the religious cult was deeply mired in sexual instinctualism. Sacred prostitution had an ancient history in Mesopotamian cultures, going as far back as the Sumerians and the cult of the goddess Inana. In Israel the great lure was the cult of the Canaanite god of the storm and the weather, Baal, and his consort Asherah, goddess of fertility, of the same lineage as Ashtarte and the Babylonian Ishtar. Worship melded into imitative magic: the use of cult prostitutes, they thought, promoted agricultural fertility. Exposing perfectly the link between sexual depravity and violence, the cosmogonic pair, Baal and Asherah, was complemented by Moloch/Molech, a voracious god to whom the surplus human product of cultic fornications were *passed through the fire* (cf. Lev 20:1–5). They masked the horror of their deeds by "devoting" the babies as sacrifices (Jer 19:4–5, Ezek 16:20–21). With what other sophistries today do we lie to ourselves about the same horror?

It was the burden of the true prophets to recall Israel and Judah from this intoxicating brew of religious syncretism, sexual promiscuity, and human sacrifice. They had a hard and failing battle of it. Kings, priests, Levites, and false prophets abetted the corruption, even to importing the iconography of Baalism into the Lord's Temple (Ezek 8:9–12). The filth was not finally scourged until implacable war, catastrophe, and exile came ringing down first on the northern kingdom and then on the southern (cf. 2 Chr 36:14–21).

The prophets constantly decry these cosmogonic gods invested with all the traits of corrupted human sexuality, and the soaking of religious cult in instinctual sexualism. Yet Israel succumbs to the lure over and over again: *Lift up your eyes to the bare heights* [the cultic "high places"] *and see! Where have you not been lain with? . . . You have polluted the land with your vile harlotry* (Jer 3:2; cf. Ezek 23:5–8).

Here is the germ of a ruling idea: if instinctual sexualism mediates idolatry, then . . . idolatry itself mediates fornication, mediates adultery. Israel had to learn again and again that the God of Abraham and Isaac and Jacob is wholly *other* than these sexualized pagan gods. Worship of the Lord cannot be alloyed with the magic cults of natural forces. The living and true God is *holy*; and to worship him means to walk with him in holy conduct. *Get among the rocks, hide in the dust, before the terror of the Lord, at the glory of his majesty! . . . Holy, holy, holy is the LORD of Hosts!* (Isa 2:9–10; 6:3). This is why the Israelites must distinguish themselves from the surrounding nations, separate themselves, seek purity: *Be holy, because I the Lord your God, am holy* (Lev 19:2). Satinover wonderfully distills the crucial issues:

> Monotheistic worship leads *away from the violent, hedonistic, and orgiastic.* Because instincts are creaturely and not divine, they must not be elevated as final arbiters of individual and social mores. In other words, instincts are not worshipped. The history of Israel as laid out in the Old Testament is in large part the two-thousand-year-old struggle of the worship of the one Lord against the various forms of pagan instinct worship that dominated the ancient Near East. Supremely it is the story of the fight of God against Baal, the god of sacred sexuality—heterosexual, homosexual, and bestial; against his sacred consort Anath/Astarte/Ashtoreth, the virgin-whore who copulates and conceives, but does not give birth; and against Molech, the god to whom the unwanted offspring of these practices were sacrificed.[1]

How can we treat this central lesson of Israel's history as something that happened *back then,* millennia ago! Another circle, an evil one this time, is completed: The lessons apply more than ever *now.* Andrew Comiskey nails the perennial relevance:

> What does Israel's spiritual and sexual idolatry have to do with us today? *Plenty.* Whenever anyone, Christian or not, yields his body to another for erotic gratification outside the heterosexual context, he makes a sacrifice to Baal. The principle of perversion is alive and well. We bow down to it whenever we engage in sexual immorality. We may not mouth prayers to Baal or to Ashteroth, but we worship them with every illicit orgasm, each immoral fantasy, each pornographic watch we keep, each seductive, controlling gesture.[2]

3.2 A turning point: the prophet Hosea

The ministry of the prophet Hosea, in eighth-century northern Israel, was a watershed in the prophetic tradition, for it was he who made an epochal transposition from the imagery of *whoring after other gods,* to the imagery of Israel as pledged to one husband, the Lord. His prophetic reading of the Lord's relationship with Israel in terms of spousal imagery

---

1. Satinover, *Homosexuality*, 234.
2. Comiskey, *Pursuing Sexual Wholeness*, 100.

opened up vistas. Some will speak of its use as poetic metaphor, and others as theological analogy. Whichever it is, this nuptial key shafts through to the core of our human constitution. To grasp the breakthrough being made here, let us hear what a Jewish commentator expresses so succinctly and so well, even to using the Catholic language of "the sacrament of marriage" for the Hebrew idiom of "sanctification":

> From the Judeo-Christian perspective, sexuality—an aspect of nature—cannot itself be "sacramental." It partakes of sacramental reality and is thereby elevated (sanctified) only in the context of the "sacrament of *marriage*." Sacramental sexuality, on the other hand, is the very essence of pagan worship.[3]

In short, human sexuality is redeemed to God *only* in the covenant of marriage. The prophet Hosea excoriates the sinful folly that the cult of instinctual sex could mediate any contact between man and the divine: *The spirit of harlotry is in them, and they know not the LORD* (Hos 5:4). What the prophet proposes instead is *marital covenant*.

In the church's teaching on the divine inspiration of the Scriptures, the Holy Spirit does not override the personal character of the sacred authors, but plays their human intelligence and sensibilities like a poet. Accordingly, Hosea articulated these tremendous ideas around his own painful marriage to Gomer, "an Israelite girl who had been initiated into the fertility rites of the Canaanite worship of Baal,"[4] who even as his wife continued as a harlot of the Baals (Hos 1:2). Hosea suffered the sting of her wantonness. The Spirit of God hovered over the appalled state of the husband. He read the whole affair in a deeper light—this was nothing but the reality of Israel's own recurring faithlessness towards the Lord. Indeed, Hosea's personal trauma and the Lord's trial with Israel turned on the same cult of Baalism. Hosea likened Israel's infidelity to the rupture of the closest of human bonds, that of husband and wife. His divorce of Gomer in turn became Israel's chastisement by destruction and exile.

Hosea then turns from using spousal language negatively to using it positively. Ignoring—and mark this—*ignoring* the ban on remarrying a divorced wife who has since been "defiled" by another man (Deut 24:1–4; cf. Jer 3:1), he will take her back, despite her many defilements. Through this staggering act of marital forgiveness, he wins his wife at

---

3. Satinover, *Homosexuality*, 241. The author uses "nature" and "natural" here to mean human nature as affected by the Fall.

4. Schillebeeckx, *Marriage*, 36.

last to spousal fidelity. He sees this miraculous change as the Lord's "rebetrothal" of Israel in a future day of hope, a day bearing all the hallmarks of a new marital covenant. In the following famous passage, Hosea 2:14-20, the Lord foretells the conversion of the harlot Israel from the cult of idolatrous, instinctual sex denoted by *Baal*, to the true covenant of marriage with the Lord, denoted by *husband*:

> *Behold, I will allure her and bring her into the wilderness and speak tenderly to her. And there I will give to her her vineyards, and make the Valley of Achor a door of hope. And there she shall answer me as in the days of her youth, as at the time when she came out of the land of Egypt. And in that day, says the* LORD, *you will call me "my Husband," and no longer call me "my Baal." For I will remove the names of the Baals from her mouth, and they shall be mentioned by name no more. And I will make for you a covenant on that day with the beasts of the field, the birds of the air, and the creeping things of the ground, and I will abolish the bow, the sword and war from the land. And I will betroth you to me in righteousness and in justice, in steadfast love, and in mercy. I will betroth you to me in faithfulness; and you shall know the* LORD. (Hos 2:14-20)

Since an ancient idiom for marital union is *dahat*, or "knowledge" as in *Adam knew his wife Eve* (Gen 4:1), *knowing the Lord* here codes the consummation of the spousal covenant between God and man. Coming to *know the* LORD through covenant fidelity, through exclusive and steadfast love, is something so *whole* and hallowing, it is as the consummation of a marital covenant. As the prophets go on, this tentative spring of holy "knowing" in Israel, becomes a floodtide meant to engulf the whole earth:

> *And the earth shall be filled with the knowledge of the glory of God, as the waters that cover the sea* (Hab 2:14)

3.3 The major prophets

Hosea is, as it were, the father of the Major Prophets, for each of these in their turn take up the great breakthrough of the spousal analogy. As if ringing out the bell of salvation, again and again they proclaim the themes of covenant, marriage, exclusive faithfulness, and "knowing," as in Isaiah 49:18, 23; 54:1-10; 55:3; 60:16; 62:4-5; Ezek 16:5-32; 23:1-49; Jer 2:1-12; 3:1-14, 20-25; 31:31-34. Here, for example, is the prophet Isaiah (or Deutero-Isaiah) speaking of the Lord as husband:

> *For your Maker is your husband, the* LORD *of Hosts is his name; and the Holy One of Israel is your redeemer, the God of the whole earth he is called . . . and as the bridegroom rejoices over the bride, so shall your God rejoice over you* (Isa 54:5–6, 62:5).

Ezekiel graphically depicts spousal election and betrothal as the making of a covenant. The theme here is that the Lord chooses Israel not for anything she could offer to him of her own, but precisely in her weakness and littleness.

> *And when I passed by you, and saw you weltering in your blood, I said to you in your blood, "Live, and grow up like a plant of the field." And you grew up and became tall and arrived at full maidenhood: your breasts were formed and your hair had grown; yet you were naked and bare. When I passed by you again and looked upon you, behold, you were at the age for love; and I spread my skirt over you and covered your nakedness; yea, I plighted my troth to you and entered into a covenant with you and you became mine. Then I bathed you with water and washed off your blood from you, and anointed you with oil. I clothed you also with embroidered cloth and shod you with leather; I swathed you in fine linen and covered you with silk. And I decked you with ornaments and put bracelets on your arms and a chain on your neck. And I put a ring on your nose and earrings in your ears and upon your head a beautiful crown.* (Ezek 16:6–14)

In the prophet's portrayal, Israel's original state was one of insignificance, abandonment, and total abjection. All Israel's beauty comes from the Lord's sovereign election of her. His choice alone endows her with all she has of worth. Later, St Paul references this theme from Ezekiel in Ephesians 5, to describe the relationship of Christ and his Bride the church.

We are led at last to another watershed moment. As Hosea had spoken of the Lord's projected *re*-betrothal of Israel in terms of a new marital covenant, and Ezekiel described the original election as a betrothal, so now through the prophet Jeremiah, the Lord announces a future *New Covenant*, a covenant which is to be consummated in a new and universal "knowing" of the Lord:

> *Behold, the days are coming, says the Lord, when I will make a new covenant with the house of Israel and the house of Judah, not like the covenant which they broke, though I was their husband, says the Lord. But this is the covenant I will make with the house*

of Israel after those days, says the LORD: *I will put my law within them, and I will be their God and they shall be my people. And no longer shall each man teach his neighbor and each his brother, saying "Know the* LORD." *for they shall all know me, from the least of them to the greatest, says the* LORD. (Jer 31:31–34)

3.4 The Song of Songs

The rise of spousal imagery in the prophetic discourse culminates in a book unique in the entire canon of Scripture: the Song of Songs, composed of a series of passionate appeals between bride and groom, glowing with ardor and sensuousness. In a sense, the Song is a midrash on Adam's cry of recognition and delight in the Garden of Eden, when he first beheld the bride whom the Lord God had brought to him:

This at last is flesh of my flesh, and bone of my bones! She shall be called Woman, because she was taken out of man. (Gen 2:23)

The prophetic disclosure of nuptial love as a privileged figure of the covenant between God and Israel surely guided the mind either of the inspired author, and/or those who included these love songs in the scriptural canon when they included the prophets in the late post-exilic period and first century AD.[5] The earliest recorded rabbis were already reading the Song in this transposed key.[6]

In such a way of reading it, the Song becomes the promise of a longed-for consummation in the future when Israel will no longer be

---

5. See the exegesis of the Song in relation to Genesis by John Paul II, *Man and Woman*, Catecheses 108–13, 548–92. The footnotes survey the views of "scientific" biblical criticism, which is dismissive of any mystical hermeneutic. One of the more satisfactory statements appears in a note to Catechesis 108:3: "D. Lys observes that the content of the Song of Songs is at the same time sexual and sacred. When one prescinds from the second characteristic, one ends up treating the Canticle as a purely secular erotic composition; and when one ignores the first, one falls into allegorism. It is only by putting these two aspects together that one can read the book in the right way" (551).

6. "All [the ages of] the whole world are not the equal of the day when the Song of Songs was given to Israel. All the Scriptures are holy: but the Song of Songs is the Holy of Holies." (Rabbi Akiva, Order Taharoth, Yadayim III:5, in *Mishnayoth*, vol. 6, 764.) Akiva bases his praise on its anagogical sense as confirmed by another saying attributed to him: "He who warbles the Song of Songs in a banquet-hall, treating it as a (secular) love-song has no portion in the world that is to come." (Sanhedrin 12:10, in *Tosefta*, vol. 4: Neziqin, 237; cf. Babylonian Talmud, Sanhedrin 101a.)

unfaithful to the Lord. For in the Song, *eros* must surpass itself, must learn the accents of the divine *hesed we' emeth*, steadfast love and truth.[7] Then Israel's faithfulness will hold, even as the Bride's does, when the Lord God, as the Bridegroom, seems to have vanished and is nowhere to be found. The dispositions of the Bride shall then have become so purified and steadfast, that even in the crucible of privation she will no more turn aside to another. The experience of absence, contradiction, suffering, shall only lead to a redoubling of her fidelity, for *Blessed are those who do not see and yet believe* (John 20:29), says the Lord, and *Blessed is he who is not scandalized in me* (Matt 11:6). These enigmatic passages of the Bridegroom's *absence* (Song 3:1–4, 5:6–9), which have so inspired the apophatic theologians, virgins, and mystics over the centuries, are surely the key to the deeper *theological* import of the Song.

One becomes a little impatient with those who rebuke the language of *eros* as something "Hellenic" and alien to the Hebrew and Christian concept of God and man. They must reckon with the fact that all the notes of *eros* are here in the intense love of man and woman. The nuptial accents of Israel's covenant with God, explored by the prophets and hovering about the Song of Songs, opened up a vein of yearning for intimacy with God in the deepest wells of Israel's piety. Psalm 62/63, for example, breathes the air of the Song.[8] Here are all its intense yearnings, and even its bodily imagery, but now trained wholly and purely upon God: the search for him in one's bed at night, the watching at dawn, the pining of the flesh, the yearning *to behold your glory,*[9] the *clinging fast* of the soul to God, and even the embrace *in the shadow of your wings, your right hand holding me fast*.

Let us then bring the Platonic "divine beauty" as tribute to the Hebrew "glory of God." The transcendent glory of God we shall see as a

---

7. ". . . the frequent refrains that speak of the search full of longing, and of the spouses' reciprocal rediscovery. This brings them joy and calm, and at the same time seems to lead them to a new search, a continual search. One has the impression that *in reaching each other*, in experiencing closeness to each other, *they ceaselessly continue to tend toward something*: they yield to the call of something that goes beyond the transitory content and seems to surpass the limits of *eros*. . . . In the Song of Songs, human *eros* reveals the face of *love* ever in search and, as it were, *never satisfied*. The echo of this restlessness runs through the verses of the poem." (John Paul II, *Man and Woman*, Catechesis 112:1, 4)

8. Cf. other psalms of divine intimacy: 15/16, 25/26, 41/42, 83/84, 90/91, 138/139.

9. This, if realized by participation in the Temple liturgy, will consist of the beholding of veils and thresholds in an awe-inducing hierophanic liturgical framework.

mystery inspiring both fear and great joy (Matt 28:8), dread and profoundest attraction. On the one hand, the severe lessons of God's consummate holiness must be learnt. This is a threshold of greatest peril, and yet, and yet . . . Moses' resurgent longing, despite all the privileges he has already received: *Show me your glory I beg you* (Exod 33:18), and the enigmatic response he receives from the Lord, are opened, through the witness of the holy prophets, to all who venture to walk an interior journey like his.

Chapter Four

RETRIEVING THE TRUTH OF MARRIAGE IN ISRAEL

4.1 Revisiting the institution of marriage in Israel

THERE IS NO DOUBT that the prophets, in portraying the relationship of the Lord and Israel in the terms of a marital covenant, cast a reflective glow on the institution of marriage itself, which led by degrees to a rediscovery of primal truths about marriage and the remediation of serious defects in its practice.

Significantly, it renewed the understanding of marriage as a *covenant*; not simply a legal transaction between families, or the getting of a wife by a man, but as a deeply held bond between two persons, a man and a woman, calling for all the qualities of loyal love and faithfulness in imitation of the God who encompasses the two spouses in his Mystery.

Moreover, the marital covenant as explored by the prophets had no cogency except in terms of monogamy: the exclusive espousal of one man and one woman. *You shall not play the harlot, or belong to another man, so will I also be to you* (Hos 3:3), says Hosea to Gomer, matching the exclusive fidelity of the wife with that of the husband, a rather new emphasis. Accordingly, the same period that saw prophetic exploration of spousal imagery, from the later pre-exilic prophets onwards, saw also the disappearance of polygyny in Israel. A striking confirmation that this was so was the practice of the Hasmonean kings in the last two centuries BC. Whatever else may be said of their conduct, these Jewish kings never did return to the appalling polygamies of the earlier kings of Israel.

The warmest testimony to the spirit of faithful, exclusive monogamy in the late post-exilic period is the book of Tobit. Here we find an unmistakably interiorized and spiritualized understanding of marriage. Tobit 8:4–8 presents the wedding night of Tobias and Sarah in the light of a fully religious spirit, with the bride and groom wholly disposed to Godward, expressing perfectly the "triangular" relationship of marriage. It is almost as if we have returned to marriage as God had intended it to be before the Fall. Their prayer before consummation has a liturgical quality, calling to mind the Creator's plan for man and woman *in the beginning*. It is a favorite reading at weddings, especially when bride and groom are of genuine faith and deep conviction:

> *When the door was shut and the two were alone, Tobias got up from the bed and said, "Sister, get up and let us pray that the Lord may have mercy upon us." And Tobias began, "Blessed art Thou, O God of our fathers, and blessed be Thy holy and glorious name forever. Let the heavens and all Thy creatures bless Thee. Thou madest Adam and gave him Eve as his wife as a helper and support. From them the race of mankind has sprung. Thou didst say, 'It is not good that the man should be alone; let us make a helper for him like himself.' And now, O Lord, I am not taking this sister of mine because of lust, but with sincerity. Grant that I may find mercy and may grow old together with her." And she said with him, "Amen."*

4.2 Recovering indissolubility: a beginning is made

With the recovery of monogamy, the next step was to recover the unbreakable *one flesh* union of *the beginning*. The renewed sense of the interior qualities of marriage led in some quarters to a rethinking of the custom of divorce. Both Hosea and Isaiah had ignored the Mosaic law when speaking of the Lord's *remarriage* of Israel though she had prostituted herself with many lovers and been divorced. The redemptive love of the Lord would prevail even over divorce:

> *Is the wife of one's youth to be cast off, says your God? For a brief moment I abandoned you, but with immense love I will take you back* (Isa 54:6–7).

Here is the germ of another remediation of marriage, and the prophet Malachi above all bears witness to it. He is alarmed at the spread of adultery and divorce among the priests serving the temple after the return from exile; such practices profane the covenant with Levi. Seeing the marriage covenant between husband and wife and the covenant between the Lord and Israel in a single vision, he cries out that the Lord "hates" divorce. We notice too his feeling for womankind, above all the repudiated wife. So many themes—divine fatherhood, mutual fidelity of spouses and the spirit of *life*, family bonds and covenant—converge in the burning proclamation of Malachi:

> *Have we not all one father? Has not one God created us? Then why are we faithless to one another, profaning the covenant of our fathers? Judah has been faithless, and abomination has been committed in Israel and in Jerusalem; for Judah has profaned the sanctuary of the* Lord, *which he loves, and has married the daughter of a foreign god . . . You cover the* Lord's *altar with tears, with weeping and groaning because he no longer regards the offering or accepts it with favor at your hand. You ask, "Why does he not?" Because the* Lord *was witness to the covenant between you and the wife of your youth, to whom you have been faithless, though she is your companion and your wife by covenant. Has not the one God made and sustained us for the spirit of life? And what does he desire? Godly offspring. So take heed to yourselves, and let none be faithless to the wife of his youth. For I hate divorce, says the* Lord *the God of Israel . . .* (Mal 2:10–11, 13–16)

This blazing indictment of divorce was never admitted for a moment by the rabbinic party, the preceptors of the Oral Law. They walked as ever in halakhic disputes over the *'ervat dabhar* and the technicalities of divorce law. The baton of the prophetic rebuke, however, *was* taken up by another contemporary form of Judaism, the Essenes, who staunchly repudiated marital repudiation.[1] The reason is that in the spectrum of late Judaisms, the Essenes were those who cleaved most intensely to the tradition of the prophets, and above all, to its eschatological tenor. Here then was one form of late Judaism that fully recovered the indissolubility of covenantal marriage.

---

1. Among the Qumranis the "statutes for the king," which applied also to commoners, prohibit both polygamy and divorce. From the Temple Scroll, the text 11QTemple 57:17–19 reads: "And he shall not take in addition to her another wife, for she alone shall be with him all the days of her life; and if she dies, he shall take for himself another (wife)." (Fitzmyer, "The Matthaean Divorce," 215) "Also striking is the identical attitude towards divorce, which both the Damascus Document (CD 4:20) and Jesus (Mark 10:2–9) reject (against common Jewish practice)." (Davies et al., eds., *The Complete World*, 202)

4.3 The emergence of vocational virginity

So then, having tracked the pattern of salvation history of Israel so far, have we come full circle at last? Have we come back again to Eden again, in the understanding of marriage and family? In a certain sense, yes, as far as the noble domestic spirituality of the book of Tobit goes. But in late post-exilic Israel, something more was stirring: the emergence of virginity for the Lord as a life-long vocation.

The early Old Testament shows the highest esteem for virginity, but strictly as a dispositive preparation for marriage. The Mosaic Law set a premium on the virginity of the bride, making much of its physical verification. The proof of virginity, called the *bettulim*, from the Hebrew word for virgin, *betulah*, on the night of consummation, became an important feature of the Jewish ritual of marriage. It was the triumphant testimony to the pre-nuptial chastity of the bride.

In this perspective, virginity has its value not as a way of life sufficient in itself, but precisely as a bearing of *insufficiency*, of a very real *incompletion*, in the patient waiting for a fulfillment yet to come. The worth of virginity was in reserving oneself for the joyous day of consummated marriage. As the book of Sirach says: *A patient man will endure until the right moment, and then joy will burst forth for him* (Sir 1:23). The Song directs the discipline of pre-nuptial chastity to one's future spouse: *my choicest fruits . . . I have laid up for you, my beloved* (Song 7:13). So in general we can say that virginity is a state of incompletion that reaches in hope to the future, a reserving of oneself for the spousal union that is yet to come. This core dynamic of virginity never loses its validity, all the more so when virginity for the Lord begins to be embraced as a life-long vocation. For of a truth, the patient bearing of privation, of a state of poverty that looks for its completion in the Day of the Lord, is near to the heart of humility and prayer.

Initially, vocational virginity is a rare and sporadic occurrence linked with the prophetic charism. Nowhere is a husband or children recorded for the prophetess Miriam, sister of Moses. She was regarded by Christians, though not in later rabbinic midrash, as the founder of the virginal life.[2] Prophets such as Elijah and Elisha clearly lived an itinerant, unmarried lifestyle for the Lord.

---

2. E.g., "Mariam, the sister of Aaron who inaugurated this achievement," St Gregory of Nyssa, *On Virginity*, 19.

With the prophet Jeremiah the divine summons to virginity first becomes explicit. *The word of the* Lord *came to me: You shall not take a wife and you shall not have sons and daughters in this place* (Jer 16:1–2). Jeremiah's virginity was intended to bear witness to the vanity of Israel's earthly hopes in the face of impending catastrophe. Here already is the germ of that eschatological tension that would inspire the virginity of later times. The expectant waiting of virginity is prolonged until a deliverance that the Lord alone shall give, when and as he knows how—but it could be any moment now, and we must be ready. It is surely not insignificant that this virgin prophet was the first to announce the coming *new covenant*, a covenant no longer written in the *flesh*, but in the *heart*.

Prophetic virginity grew slowly in the soil of Judaism as the centuries unfolded, until in the last two centuries before Christ, life-long virginity or continence was known and devoutly practiced by both men and women in one strand of the Judaism of the time: the Essenes,[3] who were to be found in Qumran, the "Essene Quarter" in Jerusalem, and dotted throughout Judea. There was something very akin to them in the Greek-speaking Jewish diaspora: the *Therapeutae* of Egypt described by Philo of Alexandria in his *De Vita Contemplativa*. Philo, a contemporary of our Lord, says that these Jewish monks and nuns, or "philosophers" as he calls them, were quite widespread, found in every *nome* of Egypt. Finally we arrive at John the Baptist, the virgin desert prophet—followed by our Lord Jesus himself, virginal for the profoundest of spousal reasons, as we shall see.

As fasting from food is not because food is a bad thing, so also sexual abstinence is not because the marital embrace of husband and wife is a bad thing, but it does have to do with stripping oneself, effacing oneself, emptying oneself before the advent of something enormous, something utterly transcendent and perilous: the manifestation of God. The hope motivating the choice of life-long continence or sexual abstinence had several track-heads in Scripture: eschatological, liturgical, and even martial. Continence was mandated as an immediate preparation for theophany (Exod 19:15), priestly liturgical service (Exod 19:22; 1 Sam

---

3. They began as the *Hassideans*, "the pious ones" of 1 Maccabees 2:42, who resisted the increasingly worldly and political leadership of the Maccabees, and above all the arrogation of the High Priesthood by Jonathan in 152 BC. Keeping themselves aloof from what they saw as the compromised priesthood and Temple cult in Jerusalem, they pursued a highly apocalyptic version of Judaism, with headquarters in the Judean wilderness above the Dead Sea.

21:4; Luke 1:8, 23), and holy warfare (1 Sam 21:5; 2 Sam 11:9–11). To practice such continence was a form of "sanctifying" or "consecrating" oneself for the perilous approach to the All Holy. The prophets and the Essenes took this to the next level by adopting sexual abstinence as a lifelong stance before God, reserving themselves as combatants ever at the ready for the impending Day of the Lord.

The Falashas, the historical Jews of Ethiopia, followed an ancient pre-rabbinic form of Judaism, innocent of the Oral Law, Tannaitic literature, and the Talmud. Compare the Ethiopian Jew in Acts 8:27–34, and notice his scriptural focus. The Falashas had monks and nuns who were held in high esteem by their fellow Jews. Some have supposed that this Jewish monasticism was due to Christian influence. Say rather it was a *Jewish* phenomenon of two thousand years vintage, from the Therapeutae of Egypt, surviving through the sheer antiquity and isolation of Ethiopia.

While the Essenes espoused vocational virginity, neither of the two strands of Judaism we often meet in the Gospels, the Pharisees and the Sadducees, held any brief for it *at all*. Now, apart from the Nazarenes or Christians, the only other form of Judaism to survive the fall of Jerusalem in AD 70—or the Bar Kochba Revolt in AD 132 at the outside—was the rabbinic party, i.e. the Pharisees. We need to grasp this spectrum of experimental Judaisms up to that historical watershed, each testing a claim to the continuing tradition of ancient Israel, lest we uncritically retroject into the Judaism of the Hellenistic and Roman periods the premises and practices of that single strand that stamped its character, almost exclusively, upon historical Judaism thereafter.

Thus, while the virginal motherhood and ever-virginity of Mary are new and unique and pivotal in salvation history, it must be affirmed that virginity as a possible life-choice was most certainly practiced in the contemporary Judaism of her time. Accordingly, vocational virginity for the Lord is *not* to be thought of as only appearing with the event of Christ, but rather as preparing the ground for it. A long time in gestation, the seeds of eschatological virginity quietly sprouted in the Israel of the late Hellenistic and Roman eras, and the fairest flower of that stock was Mary of Nazareth.

4.4 Who opens the womb?

Searching the Scriptures on the topic of contraception commences with the creation mandate: *be fruitful* (Gen 1:28), which straightaway immerses the union of spouses in *the fountain of life* (Ps 35/36:9) cascading down from *God, the living God* (Ps 83/84:2). Transparency to God is therefore central to their bodily union, as to their entire marital covenant. They who imagine that Scripture has nothing to say to the idea of manipulating the sterility of the marital embrace are shown to be inattentive.

To learn the truth, we must purify ourselves from a secular mind-set and allow Scripture to form the question in us in its own way: *who opens the womb*? Once we attune ourselves to the scriptural idiom, a rich seam of teaching begins to disclose itself to the reader.

The sacred pages answer that question consistently and repeatedly: it is not the husband, but *God* who opens or shuts the womb; *God* who bestows or withholds the conceiving of a child from any particular marital act. The whole sense of this teaching is already contained in the first testimony of human motherhood, when Eve exclaims in wonder: *I have acquired a man from the* LORD (Gen 4:1).[4] It is learnt with particular clarity from the story of Rachel. When she appealed desperately to her husband *Give me children or I shall die!* (Gen 30:1), Jacob is rattled, and protests to her: *Am I in the place of God, who has withheld from you the fruit of the womb?* (Gen 30:2). Many vicissitudes had to pass, before, as Scripture significantly puts it: *God hearkened to her and opened her womb* (Gen 30:22). In the book of Ruth it is the same: *So Boaz took Ruth and she became his wife; and he went into her, and the* LORD *gave her conception and she bore a son* (Ruth 4:13)—which neatly conveys the "triangular" relationship of marriage, between God and husband and wife. As one more testimony that sovereignty over life in the womb belongs to God alone, let us have that exclamation of the psalmist to the Lord:

> *It was you created my being,*
> *Knit me together in my mother's womb.*
> *I thank you for the wonder of my being,*
> *For the wonders of all your creation.*

---

4. "In Eve, as in every woman and every couple who contemplate the mystery of generation, there is a clear feeling that the newborn child is not a 'thing' belonging to the two parents, but is in immediate strict dependence upon God. This means that the mystery of human conception contains within itself the insertion of the human being's *procreative* power within the *creative* power of God." (Scola, *The Nuptial Mystery*, 75)

Already you knew my soul,
My body held no secret from you,
When I was being fashioned in secret,
And molded in the depths of the earth. (Ps 138/139:13–15)

All this bears on the language we use to describe the role of parents in bringing life into the world: they "*procreate*," not *create*—that is God's work. In giving themselves to each other, they lend themselves to God's sovereign purpose. Note the semantic shift in public discourse, as we hear of the "creation" of embryos in IVF laboratories. The meaning of this is, in Jacob's language, that the *place of God* has been usurped.

Here then is the context of the story of Onan. Called upon to fulfill his levirate duty by raising up a son for his dead brother, he shirked it by means of *coitus interruptus*, a contraceptive expedient. *What he did was displeasing to the* LORD *and he slew him also* (Gen 38:9–10). Revisionists would have it that Onan's fault lay only in defrauding his brother of issue, not in his contraceptive act itself. But if so, why such drastic punishment? Deuteronomy 25:5–10 prescribes the penalty for a man who refuses his levirate duty, and it is far short of death. What *was* a capital offense, however, was blasphemy (Exod 20:7; Lev 24:11–16, 23), that is, an act of *hubris* against the divine prerogative, or in Jacob's terms, *usurping God's place*. By manipulating the sterility of this union, Onan arrogated its issue to his own choice; he appointed himself a lock-keeper of *the fountain of life* (Ps 35/36:9). Seen in this way, to deliberately secure the sterility of marital union bears a kinship with blasphemy, because it *usurps God's place*. Since Scripture everywhere attests that opening the womb is God's work alone, the *fear of the Lord*, that is, the sovereign respect for his primacy, acting in *justice* towards God, belongs to the inmost form of marital union.

A closely related theme is that of the barren woman made fruitful by God's gift and in God's own time, as the Psalmist puts it: *He gives the barren woman a home, making her the joyful mother of children* (Ps 112/113:9). How many prophets were born of mothers who had suffered the humiliation of barrenness until Lord's intervention! It was preeminently true of the matriarch Sarah. The long years of childlessness endured until she bore Isaac show that Sarah's motherhood, so iconic in salvation history, was contingent on God's promise, on God's working, not on man's doing.

4.5 The Feminine Persona of Zion

We have traced how the prophets' lofty use of spousal imagery initiated a gradual recovery of truths about marriage itself. It also opened up a better feeling for womankind. It is as if the nuptial vision released a new intuition in the prophets. They began to develop the use of a feminine persona for Israel, for Jerusalem, for Zion. They seem to be fascinated with this feminine spectacle, playing it from this aspect and that, like so many facets of a luminous jewel. More and more they reveal a joyful sense of the feminine and the role it might yet have in the saving purpose of God. We saw their excoriating use of *harlot* and *adulteress* and *faithless*. But now an opposing field of words comes into view: *virgin* and *daughter* and *mother*. A verbal tapestry of noble feminine imagery builds up through their oracles: *virgin of Israel*, a very early one from Amos (5:2); *daughter of Zion* (Zeph 3:14; Zech 9:9; Joel 2:21); the *virgin Israel*, (Jer 8:13); *virgin daughter of Zion* (Isa 23:22); *daughter of my people* (Jer 4:11); *virgin daughter of Judah* (Lam 1:15); *daughter of Jerusalem* (Zeph 3:14).

The image of Israel or Jerusalem personified as *virgin* and *daughter*, is of a young woman preparing for her betrothal, or, conversely, bereft of marital joy (Lamentations). But if the daughter of Zion is a virgin, she is also mysteriously a *mother*. The feminine gender of the word for "city," in both Hebrew and Greek, comes wonderfully into play in explicating the mystery:

> *The streams of a river give joy to the city of God*
> *The Most High has sanctified his tabernacle.*[5]
> *God is in the midst of her; she shall not be shaken,*
> *God will help her at the dawning of the day.* (Ps 45/46:5–6)[6]

Here is the answer that the unfolding of salvation history gives to the fraught, raddled City of Man instituted by the children of Cain (Gen 4:17): the beckoning, coming City of God, the universal mother of all the nations, to those who give themselves to God:

> *And Zion shall be called "Mother,"*
> *For all shall be her children* (Ps 86/87:5).

---

5. Translating from the Septuagint, which is followed by the Latin Vulgate. The Masoretic text reads with difficulty: "(the) holy of tabernacles of the Most High."

6. See also Pss 47/48; 121/122; 124/125. In the latter psalm, an interesting inversion of imagery occurs; instead of the city "indwelt" by the Holy Place, the Lord encompasses the city.

The long, intensely messianic book of Isaiah ends on the joyful note of the eschatological motherhood of the City of God:

> *Shall a land be born in one day? Shall a nation be brought forth in a moment? For as soon as Zion was in labor, she brought forth her sons. Shall I bring to the birth and not cause to bring forth? says the* LORD. *Shall I who cause to bring forth shut the womb? says your God. Rejoice with Jerusalem and be glad for her, all you who loved her . . . that you may suckle and be satisfied with her consoling breasts; that you may drink deeply in delight from the abundance of her glory . . . As one whom his mother comforts, so will I comfort you; and you shall be comforted in Jerusalem. You shall see, and your heart shall rejoice.* (Isa 66:8–14)

These goodly feminine personifications open up the brightest vistas of eschatological salvation, of long-deferred ingathering and homecoming at last. This is what the Day of the Lord will mean: a day of joyful deliverance when all the scattered children of Israel shall return—and more than that: in the grand universalist thinking of the prophets, all "the nations" who were once enemies, shall also stream to the ingathering (cf. Isa 2:2; 43:5–7; Ps 21/22:27–28).

The feminine, the bridal, and the maternal evoked in the prophets a sense of "indwelling," and understandably so, which they apply above all to the divine indwelling, when the Lord shall come to "tabernacle" in the midst of Zion. Here, the 'cloud', 'tabernacle', and 'glory of the Lord' of Ex 40:34–35 converge on the feminine figure of Zion:

> *Sing and rejoice, O daughter of Zion, for lo I come and I will dwell in the midst of you* [lit: tabernacle in your midst]. *And many nations shall join themselves to the* LORD *that day, and shall be my people; and I will dwell* [tabernacle] *in the midst of you, and you shall know that the* LORD *of Hosts has sent me to you. And the* LORD *will inherit Judah as his portion in the Holy Land, and will again choose Jerusalem. Be silent, all flesh, before the* LORD, *for he has roused himself from his holy dwelling place.* (Zech 2:10–13; cf. Zeph 3:14–17)

This is the way the prophetic tide is running—and running strongly. The startling synoptic of "virgin" and "mother" culminates in the third century BC when Jewish translators of Isaiah 7:14 rendered it precisely and expressly as: *the virgin (parthenos) shall conceive and bear a son, and shall call his name "God-is-with-us."*

If one has been sensitive to the gradual revelation and the anagogical leading of the Scriptures, particularly to the ways the prophets are ever anguishing over the fearful crises of Israel's covenant with the Lord, and reinvestigating its terms and deepening the understanding of it, and seeing it all as leading to something new and more splendid to come, one would have caught strong currents of expectancy. Something divinely immense is brewing, and the God-breathed prophets intuited it, though they could not see it in all its outlines. In the end we find their daring, inspired cry to God: *O that you would tear the heavens and come down!* (Isa 64:1). For indeed, something truly wonderful, truly astonishing, is about to happen!

> *Blessed are the eyes that see what you see, for I tell you that many prophets and kings desired to see what you see, and did not see it, and to hear what you hear, and did not hear it.* (Luke 10:23–24)

Chapter Five

THE HOLY FAMILY OF NAZARETH

5.1 The Threshold Crossed: Annunciation and Visitation

WE ENDED OUR SURVEY of marriage and family in the Scriptures thus far in the company of the prophets of Israel. It was their use of marriage as the figure of the covenant relationship between the Lord and Israel that helped renew the appreciation of marriage itself. With Israel as the betrothed bride of the Lord in mind, we found ourselves increasingly drawn to the feminine persona of Zion/Jerusalem, as *virgin*, as *mother*, as the designated precinct of the divine indwelling.

We now stand at the threshold of the New and Everlasting Covenant. In the school of the prophets we gained a sense of the profound continuity of God's covenants in Israel of old, and the culminating Covenant to be revealed in Christ. Yes, there is continuity, assuredly, yet also a tremendous irruption of the "New." But it begins so very quietly, unobtrusively, and hiddenly.

The first words of the fourth Gospel are the same as those which open the Book of Genesis in the Septuagint: Ἐν ἀρχῇ: *in the beginning*. It was a new beginning and a new creation for us, the *regeneration* of the human race when the *Word became flesh and dwelt [tabernacled] among us, full of grace and truth, enabling all who receive him . . . to become children of God, born not of blood, or of the will of the flesh, or the will of man, but of God* (John 1:1, 14, 12–13). It is hard to miss Zechariah's prophecy in this culminating epiphany of divine indwelling.

When we turn to the human context in which God the Word tabernacled among us, we find two women and two men: the women are the barren woman Elizabeth, and the virgin Mary of Nazareth, and the men are Zechariah priest of Jerusalem, and Joseph of the house of David.

The Gospel of Luke sets the Annunciation in a precise narrative sequence: *In the sixth month*—that is, of Elizabeth's conception of the child who will one day be as the Elijah who was to return, *turning the hearts of the fathers to their children and the disobedient to the wisdom of the just, to make ready for the Lord a people prepared* (Luke 1:17). Elizabeth is the classic, scriptural barren woman made fruitful, after long humbling years, through the Lord's intervention.

Mary, however, is something new, both the *virgin daughter of Israel*, and the *Zion who as soon as she travailed brought forth, before her pain came upon her, was delivered of a son* (Isa 66:8). Now, both "virgin" and "mother" converge this time, not in poetic metaphor only, but in living flesh and blood, and the overshadowing, and the tabernacling, and the divine indwelling.

In the exchange between Mary and the angel Gabriel, all the tangle of Eve's disobedience is unraveled backwards till it reaches Mary's response of obedience: *Be it done unto me according to your word*. Mary is revealed as *the woman* of the proto-evangelium, whose seed (and mark that word), will crush the head of the serpent. Elizabeth's greeting, *blessed is the fruit of your womb* (Luke 1:42), is like a deferral of honor, a *paradosis* from all the scriptural *barren women made fruitful*, to the still more wonderful intervention of the Lord's grace: the *virgin made mother*. Mary experiences a surge of joy, and as Eve, the *mother of all the living* once exclaimed *I have gotten a man with the help of the Lord* (Gen 4:1), so now the new Eve exclaims: *The Almighty has done great things to me* (Luke 1:49).

Before the Annunciation, Mary is described as *betrothed to a man whose name was Joseph, of the house of David*. Joseph had already been "factored in," of set purpose. Precisely in that interval when he and Mary had been "sanctified" to each other in betrothal, God, as it were, stepped in. On the continuities and distinctions between Jewish betrothal and marriage, Blackman explains:

> In Talmudic times[1] . . . there were two stages preceding wedded life: (1) *eirusin* and (2) *nissuin* or *knisa* . . . *Eirusin* was the betrothal ceremony, and comprised the *qidushin* (sanctification,

---

1. This includes the "Tannaitic" era, i.e. first century BC to third century AD.

consecration), whereby the woman was wife except in regard to sexual intercourse and some pecuniary modifications. *Nissuin* or *knisah* [the *home-taking*] was the actual marriage, the actual physical union of the man and the wife, and was preceded by the bride receiving the document *ktuvah, marriage contract.*[2]

5.2 A Sublime Marriage, Holy Family

As the Scriptures begin with the story of a family—Adam and Eve and their sons Cain, Abel, and Seth—so the New Covenant begins with a family: Joseph, Mary, and the child Jesus. In this family, all the ills that have torn at even the best of families through salvation history are undone. The Matthaean genealogy notes disreputable moments in the Davidic lineage of *Joseph the husband of Mary of whom Jesus was born*: Tamar acting the harlot with her father-in-law, Rahab the harlot of Jericho, Bathsheba wife of the murdered Uriah—and there are sorry names among the males like Rehoboam and Manasseh, yes, and Solomon too. Ancestors so highlighted say that Christ, on coming into the world, bore all the lamentable history of sexual sins before him, dissolved its poison, and, as the theophany of the *mercy promised to our fathers, to Abraham and to his seed forever* (Luke 2:54–55), transmuted it to the good.

For that saying, *Christ redeemed us from the curse* (Gal 3:13), is in a sense manifested in this entire family. In this sacred domestic precinct, with Jesus its center, all the effects of sin that ever came upon human families, before or since, are undone; all the historic ills between man and woman, and between parents and children perish beyond its outer pale. It is like the anticipative first cell of *God's household, the church of the living God* (1 Tim 3:14; 1 Pet 4:17).

> At the culmination of the history of salvation, when God reveals his love for humanity through the gift of the Word, it is precisely *the marriage of Mary and Joseph* that brings to realization in full "freedom" the spousal "gift of self" in receiving and expressing such a love. In this great undertaking which is *the making all things new* in Christ (Rev 21:5), marriage—it too is purified and renewed—becomes a new reality, a sacrament of the New Covenant. We see that at the beginning of the New Testament, as at the beginning of the Old, there is a married couple. But whereas Adam and Eve were the source of evil which was unleashed on

---

2. With Hebrew terms transcribed from *Mishnayoth* Volume II, *Order Nashim*, 19.

the world, Joseph and Mary are the summit from which holiness spread all over the earth. The Savior began the work of salvation by this virginal and holy union, wherein is manifested his all-powerful will to *purify and sanctify the family*—that sanctuary of love and cradle of life.[3]

Mary and Joseph's marriage is sometimes glibly dismissed as a model for husband and wife, because Mary and Joseph didn't "have sex"—that's when we are at least fortunate enough to have Mary's ever-virginity acknowledged—and pardon the crass language. But they did not forgo the marital embrace because there was something unworthy of such between husband and wife. No Encratism or Manichaeism need apply here! How then shall we account for their renunciation of bodily union?

Both were long apprenticed in docility to the Holy Spirit. Mary, as the great Church Father says, "had been purified beforehand in soul and body by the Spirit"[4]—in the very moment of her being conceived, the Church affirms. But the Gospel of Matthew describes Joseph as *the just man,* and shows the prompt and filial quality of his obedience to God, in this holy equation, the masculine complement of Mary's obedience. "The faith of Mary meets the faith of Joseph."[5] In their marriage, Joseph made the gift of his manhood to Mary, and Mary of her womanhood to Joseph, as is the part of spouses to do. But for Joseph, how to dispose himself to this womanhood entrusted to him, so signally touched by God as to be with child without knowing man, and a child of such fearful election? Then surely, there were the confidences Mary shared with Joseph in the privacy of their home once they were married, and their prayer to God together. The sanctifying and strengthening effect of these intimacies of mind and heart on him must have been very great indeed. In the case of this marriage therefore the only fitting response that Joseph could make was not to think of bodily consummation with Mary, not until she had given birth (Matt 1:24), not *ever*. That he *could* act in this way flowed from his obedient acceptance of the intervention of God in his nascent marriage (Matt 1:20), and his profound reverence for the divine seal set upon his betrothed. All that Adam lost by forsaking the primacy of God

---

3. St John Paul II, *Guardian,* no. 7.

4. St Gregory the Theologian, Oration 38.13, PG 36 325B. Jeremiah and John the Baptist were sanctified in their mother's wombs for their calling. Mary's calling was loftier by far. They were great prophets of the Word, she the virginal "poet" of the Word, conceiving that very Word in her womb and bringing Him forth in the flesh.

5. St John Paul II, *Guardian,* no. 4.

in his nuptial unity with Eve, Joseph gained in his nuptial unity with Mary: reverence for that primacy was the stamp and stay of their union.

The marriage of Joseph and Mary nevertheless carried through the internal logic of earthly marriage, even as it far surpassed it. All the potential of womanhood in Mary, now pregnant with the Divine Word, was already flowering far beyond any promise of earthly union. Joseph grasped this by obedient faith in God, so that her continuing virginity and his own, was his spousal gift to his wife. Their virginal gift of self, each to the other, came of the same "freedom of the gift" that dignifies the act of marital union itself. "The good of offspring?" The fruitfulness of this sublime marriage hardly needs further comment.

Courtesy, I submit, is the specifically masculine note of Joseph's spousal love, even *chivalry*. Grasping God's dispensation for his life, he accepted that the Messiah would not be the fruit of *his* loins—and that there would be no fruit of his loins anyway. In this disposition of self-abnegation, his personal share in the spirit of *kenosis*, he put forth all his energies as a servant of God's saving *oikonomia*. The life-long courtesy of his own virginal abstinence with which he adorned Mary and the Mystery of Christ, reserved in him a vibrant *tonos* to Godward in this life, until it attained its end in an unspeakable glory of intimacy beyond the walls of this world.[6]

In such dispositions Joseph lived a domestic life with the woman who, in the words of the Song, would be forever for him *my sister, my bride* (Song 4:9). But if they forbore the act of marital union, they did not renounce their manhood and womanhood. Far from it! For God sought a true *man*, the *just man*, to match Mary, the *woman*, take the child and his mother into his house, give them his name and protection, give the name "Jesus" to the child, and do for Mary's son what she herself, for all her excellences, could not do: be for him a shelter of manhood and fatherhood, with all that says of patterning the Fatherhood of God. As Mary had the unique gift of motherhood without the act of marital union, so

---

6. "Obviously, Christ does not now deny to Joseph that intimacy, reverence and very high honor which he gave him on earth as a son to a father. Rather we must say that in heaven Christ completes and perfects all that he gave in Nazareth. Now we can see how fittingly the last summoning words of the Lord apply to Joseph: *Enter into the joy of your Lord*. For even though the joy of eternal happiness does enter into the soul of a man, the Lord prefers to say to Joseph: *Enter into joy*, his intention being that the words should bear for us a spiritual meaning: they convey not only that this holy man possesses an inward joy, but also that it surrounds him and it engulfs him like an infinite abyss." (St Bernadine of Siena, sermon, Feast of St Joseph, Office of Readings)

the virginal Joseph became a father too, even in the high terms of salvation history. For it pleased God that the *paradosis* of the messianic title "son of David" (Ps 88/89:26–37) should descend to Jesus through Joseph. A great Church Father persuades to the reality of Joseph's fatherhood of Jesus:

> The *Son of Mary* is also Joseph's son by virtue of the marriage bond that unites them: "By reason of their faithful marriage *both of them* deserve to be called Christ's parents, not only his mother, but also his father, who was a parent in the same way that he was the mother's spouse: *in mind*, not in body." In this marriage none of the goods of marriage were lacking: "In Christ's parents all the goods of marriage were realized—offspring, fidelity, the sacrament: the *offspring* being the Lord Jesus himself, *fidelity*, since there was no adultery, the *sacrament*, since there was no divorce."[7]

The Most High intended, therefore, that Mary be fully a woman, and Joseph fully a man, and that they be so for each other and for the child given to their care. Thus, though they forever remained virgins, Joseph's part in this domestic *perichoresis* confirms the Scripture: *male and female he created them* (Gen 1:27), twice affirmed from our Lord's own lips (Mark 10:6; Matt 19:4). This husband and this wife are what God determined for the human upbringing of his own incarnate Son. We do well to keep this in mind when we see the effects of the unraveling roles of man and woman, of father and mother, on children in our society today—the divorce industry, the chaos of the "gender agenda," and the severe toll on the young, and especially boys, of the lack of a father.

Episodes of the Gospels show the sovereign freedom and respect with which our Lord related to women. His chaste masculinity is in so profound a poise, that in his calm ambience women are liberated to be their better selves. He *who knew what was in man* (John 2:25; cf. Ps 43/44:21) sees women "in all the peace and tranquility of the interior gaze."[8] He regards them from within the Garden of Eden, as it were, and

---

7. St John Paul II, *Guardian*, no. 7. John Paul cites St Augustine, *De Nuptiis et Concupiscentia* I.11, 12: PL 44, 421; and I:11, 13: PL 44, 421, and he references Augustine's *De consensu evangelistarum* II:1, 2: PL 34, 1071; *Contra Faustum*, III:2: PL 42, 214; *Contra Iulianum*, V:12, 46: PL 44, 810. To Augustine, like Ambrose, the marriage bond is established in the act of consent, not by consummation. The seal of the marriage is the child, which comes about in the normal course of events through marital union, but in this case by a unique divine intervention. See also Lienhard, *St Joseph*, 3.

8. John Paul II, *Man and Woman*, Catechesis 13.1, 178.

for a moment draws them there. In this serene "look" of Jesus, disturbed and troubled women return to themselves, or find themselves for the first time.[9] So limpid is his purity that in his humble, all-seeing gaze they recover their chastity, their mental sanity, and their spiritual health. For a moment, with him, they find the courage to be naked to God, and it cures everything. Think of our Lord's gentle but forensic dialogue with the Samaritan woman at the well (John 4), the sinful woman who covered his feet with her tears and kisses as he reclined at table (Luke 7:38), the woman with the incurable bleeding (Mark 5:25–34), the woman taken in adultery (John 8:9–11), Mary of Bethany sitting at his feet hanging on his every word (Luke 10:38–42), his affection for her sister Martha (John 11:20–28), that woman—John names her as Mary of Bethany—who in the profoundest of symbolic gestures, broke the vessel of most precious nard, and poured it upon his head, anointing him for his burial (Mark 14:3), the devoted band of women who followed him from Galilee and dared to stand for him on Golgotha, and Mary Magdalene *from whom he had driven out seven demons* (Mark 16:9) clasping his feet in another Garden in the holiest dawn. He is the God the Word incarnate, but since he did not spurn *to subject himself* (Luke 2:51) to his own creatures and learn from them in his human nature, perhaps it is not too much to say that behind the luminous chastity of our Lord, we see the traces, writ far larger, of Joseph's own redeemed masculine sexuality, his plenitude of chastity and charity and chivalry towards Mary his wife, and the lived testimony of manliness he gave to the boy he cherished as a father.

5.3 The twelve-year-old in the Temple

After the infancy narratives, the only episode of the family life of Joseph, Mary, and Jesus told us in the Gospels is the losing and the finding of Jesus in Jerusalem, when he was twelve years old. Mary voiced Joseph's and her distress at not having been able to find him: *Behold, your father and I have been looking for you anxiously* (Luke 2:48). Jesus replies: *How is it that you sought me? Did you not know that I must be in my Father's house?*

---

9. Jesus' gaze works for men too! In a stanza of his *Aeterne Rerum Conditor*, St Ambrose wonderfully captures the effect of Jesus' "look" on Peter (Luke 22:61): *Jesu labantes respice, et nos videndo corrige; si respicis labes cadunt, fletuque culpa solvitur.* "Jesus, look on us who are falling, and by your seeing us, correct us; if you would look on us, our lapses fall away, and our faults by weeping are dispelled." (Ambrose, Hymn I, *Hymni [Hymns]*, PL 16:1409)

(Luke 2:49) That is the RSV translation, somewhat interpretive. ὅτι ἐν τοῖς τοῦ πατρός μου δεῖ με εἶναι is the Greek; literally: "that I must be in/among the things of my Father," or "must be about my Father's affairs." This twelve-year-old, then, knows very well who his unique and ineffable Father is, and names him as he will do so throughout the Gospels, *my Father*. From the juxtaposition of Mary's *your father*, referring to Joseph, and Jesus' *my Father*, referring to God, we surely have here a gentle but firm correction of his mother's terms of reference.

This twelve-year-old is therefore in complete possession of his identity. He is at the threshold of puberty. He is well apprised of human sexuality and marriage. He understands his mother's virginity and knows its import for himself. He is at the age when he assumes religious responsibility, enacted in the bar mitzvah at which Joseph would be his sponsor as his legal, civil, and religious father. The "note" of the moment, then, is that now the boy Jesus affirms his identity and insists on it to his own mother and foster father. All this highlights the freedom of his return to Nazareth and his "subjecting himself" to them, and his continuing to share their domestic life for another uneventful eighteen years or so. Slowness, silence, hiddenness. Indeed, it should give us pause that the God the Word Incarnate lived most of his earthly life "in the interior quiet of ordinary domestic life" as Scott Hahn has beautifully put it.[10]

He went down with them to Nazareth and was obedient [or *subjected himself*] *to them* (Luke 2:51). There is a riddle here prickling all our earthbound notions of rank and honor, so affected are we by the Fall and the regime of the City of Man. He who was of *infinitely* greater dignity, *subjected himself* to two mere human beings, his creatures. Of these two, she, the *Theotókos*, "God-bearer," respected as head of the family one of lesser election than either her son or herself. Think of the divine gesture of courtesy to Joseph, that Jesus should leave his infancy behind calling this mere man "abba." The absence of envy and rancor and ego, an internal transfiguration of "rank," are the inscape of this sublime family, and it all turns on the secret humility of God—even to *kenosis*—inaccessible to the mind of this world.

The domestic prayer life of the three surely ushered into ever deeper abysses from then on. Can we imagine what it was to Mary and Joseph to stand facing towards Jerusalem together according to Jewish practice,[11] to

---

10. This is remembered from a tape long ago. It is traceable online in a lecture, "The Holy Family: a Model for the Catholic Home," at http://zuserver2.star.ucl.ac.uk/~vgg/rc/aplgtc/hahn/m6/hfm.html.

11. Think of the implications! If Jesus *set his face to go to Jerusalem* (Lk 10:51), he was practicing it for years beforehand in this bodily gesture of prayer with Joseph and

chant the psalms and Scripture portions in their home, with such a one as this standing between them in the flesh, raising his hands and voice along with theirs, year in, year out? The Word of God! Daily Mary and Joseph lived in closest proximity to *the Mystery hidden before ages and generations* (Col 1:26), the glory of the divine presence now *tabernacled* (cf. John 1:14) beneath their roof, and they were not burnt.[12] Meanwhile, Mary, as was her way, *kept all these words in her heart* (Luke 2:51)—from whom alone, surely, derives this precious, long pondered memory recorded in the Gospel.

5.4 The Holy Family expanded

Other incidents of apparent corrections of his mother occur during our Lord's public ministry. All are aimed at expanding the borders of the earthly family life that they once knew, around his own eternal Sonship of the Father. It was as if Jesus were applying to Mary the prophet Isaiah's words: *Enlarge the space of your tent, and let the curtains of your habitations be stretched out* (Isa 54:2). So he forms her to the widening scope of her own motherhood in the new order which he is inaugurating, where he, the Only-Begotten, shall be the *first-born of many brethren* (Heb 1:6). We can apply our old word *anagogical* to his manner with her: Our Lord was leading his own mother onward and upward.

> While he was still speaking to the people, behold, his mother and his brothers stood outside, asking to speak to him. But he replied to the man who told him, "Who *is my mother, and who* are *my brothers?" And stretching out his hand toward his disciples, he said, "Here are my mother and my brothers! For whoever does the will of my Father in heaven is my brother and sister and mother."* (Matt 12:46–50)

Our Lord institutes a new order of kinship in the new order of salvation, and it is not one of racial or physical descent. As to Mary's position in this new order of things: no mere creature ever did *the will of my Father in heaven* as did she, so she already qualifies to be called "the mother of Jesus" on this criterion—preeminently. By his use of family language, our Lord gathers all his disciples into unity in him, a family that acknowledges one father, *his* Father, in which all share kinship with him as his *brothers* and *sisters*. What Jesus had in mind for Mary is fully revealed when the *hour* finally arrives. She had *taken her stand*—in the

---

Mary. In facing towards Jerusalem with him, they were not unlike Aaron and Hur holding up the arms of Moses *until the going down of the sun* (cf. Exod 17:9–12).

12. Cf. St John Paul II, *Guardian*, no. 25.

Greek it is a strong pluperfect verb—by the cross of her son. *When Jesus saw his mother and the disciple whom he loved standing near, he said to his mother, "Woman, behold your son!" Then he said to the disciple, "Behold your mother!"* (John 19:25–27). No one who has assimilated the accents of the fourth Gospel will miss the resonances here. Jesus addresses Mary by the eschatological title, "Woman," referencing the "Woman" of the *proto-evangelium*, and the "Woman" at the wedding feast of Cana. On one level she, a widow about to be left childless in this world, is entrusted to a male relative. On another, he entrusts this one disciple, and with him all the Lord's disciples, to her as their mother. God's appointments for his family are now all finally in place: There is in this family one Father, who is in heaven; one first-born son, the Son of God, who is the eldest of many brothers and sisters; and there is a flesh and blood woman, *the* woman, mother of the incarnate Son, the perfectly obedient disciple, who is now designated as the eschatological *mother of all the living*.

At Pentecost a few weeks later, we find Mary in her role as spiritual mother of all the disciples. *All these with one accord devoted themselves to prayer, together with the women and with Mary the mother of Jesus* (Acts 2:14). The scenes of the Annunciation and of Pentecost mirror each other. The disciples pray with her who had been overshadowed by the power of the Most High (cf. Luke 1:35), the Holy Spirit. She had led the way, and now in her company, all were *filled with the Holy Spirit* (Acts 2:4). As the unique Mother, she was at the birth of the church, the brethren of Jesus, the household of God.

5.5 The Church, the family household of God

The New Testament is full of the idea of the church as the family household of God. But first let St Paul give us the theological dynamic behind it:

> *But when the time had fully come, God sent forth his Son, born of a woman, born under the Law, to redeem those who were under the Law, so that we might receive adoption as sons. And because you are sons, God has sent the Spirit of his Son into our hearts, crying "Abba! Father!" So through God you are no longer a slave but a son, and if a son then an heir* (Gal 4:47), *for* [as he explains a little earlier] *in Christ Jesus you are all sons of God through faith.* (Gal 3:26)

The Letter to the Hebrews applies the well-pondered family language of the Scriptures to our new status in Christ. We become not only sons in the Son, but even *the assembly of the first-born*, with all the scriptural resonances that attach to that privileged title (cf. Heb 12:23).

In the Johannine stream the favorite term is "children." *See what love the Father has given us that we should be called children of God, and so we are* (1 John 3:1). This harks back to the prologue of the Gospel of John, which it is affirmed that our new kinship in Christ is not based on physical descent (John 1:12–13).

Turning to the language used of the church herself, St Paul expressly speaks of *the household of God* (ἐν οἴκῳ θεοῦ), *the church of the living God, the pillar and bulwark of the truth* (1 Tim 3:15). The Greek nouns οἶκος and οἰκία and the adjective οἰκεῖος denote not only "house," but also "household," "family," and "home." If someone is οἰκεῖος it means he is a fellow householder, a member of the family, a *familiaris*, to use the Latin equivalent. Fellow believers are described as οἰκεῖοι in Galatians 6:10, *do good to all, and especially to those who are of the household of the faith,* and in Ephesians 2:19 *you are no longer strangers and sojourners, but you are fellow citizens* (συμπολῖται) *of the saints and members of the household of God* (οἰκεῖοι θεοῦ).

What else but the church living in fraternity as a common household can account for the terms used to describe the earliest church in Jerusalem?

> *Now the company of believers were of one heart and soul, and no one said that any of the things which he possessed was his own, but they held everything in common. And with great power the Apostles gave their witness to the resurrection of the Lord Jesus, and great grace was upon them all. There was not a needy one among them, for as many as were possessors of lands or houses sold them, and brought the proceeds of what was sold and laid it at the Apostle's feet; and distribution was made to each as any had need.* (Acts 4:32–35)

The church as family household figures prominently in the opening and closing greetings of the Epistles, which offer precious glimpses into the internal life and domestic character of the early church. We see a constant reciprocation between the wider church as the universal household of God, and family households as local "cells" of the church, as it were—quite literally "house churches," domestic churches, which host apostolic preaching and the celebration of the Eucharist. It is often hard to know where one type of household begins and the other leaves off.

As Martha had once welcomed our Lord Jesus into her home at Bethany, so too, in the early church, local households welcomed the apostles and became a base camp for the spread of the church in that locality. Women were notably "proactive" in ecclesial hospitality and are named gratefully. In mothering the apostles and church workers, they mothered the early church. This was exactly how the church first established a beachhead on European soil (Acts 16:14–15). Other episodes in the Acts show whole households following their master or mistress in receiving baptism, and then offering the hospitality of their household for the propagation of the church in that local area.

The Lord's Day and the Eucharist, of course, could not be observed in synagogues. That meant that believers frequently came together for the Liturgy and catechesis in family households. In the last chapter of Romans Paul salutes old friends, a married couple who were a great team in the advancement of the church: *Greet Prisca and Aquila, my fellow workers in Christ Jesus, who risked their necks for my life, to whom not only I, but also all the churches of the Gentiles give thanks; greet also the church in their house* (Rom 16:3–4).

What is obvious here is a great spirit of collaboration between men and women and between the faithful and their elders in Christ, without upset to the apostolic and sacramental constitution of the church—rather in service of it. The key to understanding this is surely the early church's consciousness of being a new kinship *in Christ*, a sense of all being brothers and sisters in the one common household of the faith, in which the apostles are warmly and gratefully received and acknowledged as spiritual fathers and elder brothers.

5.6 Family language among Christians

The address Christians use to each other are those of family relationships: brother, sister, father, and mother. Thus Paul instructs Timothy as a new bishop: *Do not rebuke an older man but exhort him as you would a father; treat younger men like brothers, older women like mothers, younger women like sisters* (1 Tim 5:2).

The body of fellow Christians is often simply called *the brothers*, ἀδέλφοι, which in Greek sounds little different to ἀδέλφαι, "sisters," and in its generic sense includes them anyway. St Peter refers to the church as the ἀδελφότης, the brotherhood, or fraternity, which is completely inclusive of females. The Apostle Paul addresses a male fellow worker in the gospel or even a junior disciple as "brother," for example: *Onesimus, a faithful and beloved brother* (Col 4:9), and a female fellow worker in the Gospel as "sister," as in, *I commend you to Phoebe our sister* (Rom 16:1). We even catch him referring to an older woman as his "mother": *Greet Rufus, eminent in the Lord, also his mother and mine* (Rom 16:13).

The apostles were fathers in this household of the faith. In the earliest stratum of the New Testament writings we find: *like a father with his children, we exhorted each one of you and encouraged you* (1 Thess 2:11). Again and again in the first letter, St John calls his addressees *My little children* (1 John 2:1), echoing the risen Lord on the shore of the lake of Galilee: *Children, have you caught any fish?* (John 21:5). St Paul even uses maternal imagery on occasion, as did our Lord when he likened himself to a hen gathering her brood under her wings. No one who reads the farewell of the church at Ephesus to Paul (Acts 20:36–38) can mistake the spontaneous and tenderly felt paternal and filial bonds between him and the Christians of Ephesus. This is the apostolic origin of Bishops as fathers. A candidate about to be ordained a bishop, is addressed: *you are chosen by the Father to rule over his family . . . As a father and a brother love all those whom God places in your care . . . in the name of the Father whose image you personify in the Church.*

5.7 Recovering the church as family household

All this offers some perspectives in the present historical plight of Christianity. Many are the models and images applied to the church: kingdom, flock, vine, "people of God," *the Body of Christ,* and *the Bride,* which we shall have cause to revisit. The term "hierarchy" did not appear till the sixth century.[13] Perhaps the model we most need to recover is that of the family *Household of God,* inserted totally in our Lord's own sonship to his Father, to which the Spirit breathed upon us by Jesus gathers us. St John Paul II himself affirmed: "the Church can and ought to take on a more homelike or family dimension, developing a more human and fraternal style of relationships."[14]

For the true inner face of the Bride owes precious little to the power constructs of this world. Our Lord's prophetic action at the Last Supper

---

13. In the *Ecclesiastical Hierarchies* of Pseudo-Dionysius (early sixth century). He appropriated the language of "hierarchy" from the stream of Neoplatonism coming through Proclus and Iamblichus.

14. St John Paul II, *Familiaris Consortio* no. 64.

shows us the way, when he, *the Lord and Master* (John 13:14), divested himself, bent down, and washed the feet of his disciples. In this Master of ours was no vestige of *respect of persons*, or *men-pleasing*. We *who are obedient to the truth*, are all equally *children of obedience* together (1 Pet 1:14,22)—the *great* no less than the little.

In the overwrought era of hyper-modernity, the church could be returning perforce to something like her original condition in this world, that of a small diaspora in an uncomprehending and hostile environment. The destructive anti-civilization, the civilization of death looming all around us is in piteous need of our *witness* to Christ and him crucified. It may be that in an increasingly tense era, as the church's former historical ways of doing things strain to breaking point, and as many of the favors she sought for from the world and thought to rely upon, are stripped from her,[15] and, if she consents to soberly and painfully resort herself as to the Truth—perhaps even *repents*—we shall again see something like the house churches of our first beginning as Christians, in which bishops, now social outcasts, discover anew "the precious gift of apostolic folly"[16] (cf. 1 Cor 4:9–13), becoming itinerant fathers of the universal Household of the Faith threading together a network of local house churches, many of these hosted by flesh and blood families, the flower of Christian marriage and seedbeds of Christian witness. Reduced again to a *little flock* (Luke 12:32), we children of the church shall have to learn again the spirit of the martyrs who knew when the sword of the Word called them to resist the blandishments of this world *absolutely*. And we want to see among us again the heirs of the martyrs, the desert ascetics and virgins, those *watchers* on the boundaries, striving to live out their allegiance to Christ alone in advance outposts in this world of the world that is to come.

15. "The future of the Church can and will issue from those whose roots are deep and who live from the pure fullness of their faith . . . From the crisis of today the Church of tomorrow will emerge—a Church that has lost much. She will become small and will have to start afresh more or less from the beginning. She will no longer be able to inhabit many of the edifices she built in prosperity. As the number of her adherents diminishes, so she will lose many of her social privileges . . . As a small society, she will make much bigger demands on her members . . . The Church will be a more spiritual Church, not presuming upon a political mandate, flirting as little with the Left as with the Right. It will be hard going for the Church, for the process of crystallization and clarification will cost her much valuable energy. It will make her poor and cause her to become the Church of the meek." From a Christmas day broadcast of 1969 of Joseph Ratzinger, *Faith and the Future*, 116–18.

16. Saward, *Perfect Fools*, 197.

Chapter Six

FAITHFUL MARRIAGE AND ESCHATOLOGICAL VIRGINITY

6.1 Asking the moral questions of the New Testament

WE NOW TURN OUR attention to several important New Testament texts concerning the moral standards of marriage. As God's word in the Old Testament was conveyed first in the events of narrative history, then in the moral instructions of the commandments, followed by the counsels of the wisdom writers, then through the poetic metaphors of the prophets and so on to greater depths and heights, so with the New Testament: having begun with the events of salvation history, we now ask the moral questions of Scripture.

6.2 The stricter standards of the gospel

Liberal theologians, as we are all too aware, claim that the principles of morality in the Scriptures and church teaching must be "adapted," usually a euphemism for "dispensed with," because, so the spiel goes, these principles are historically and culturally conditioned, and no longer "speak" to modern social circumstances, because humankind today is so very different from what it was, and "truth" anyway is a fluid thing, always *evolving*, which we now euphemize with another corrupted word as: "development." To this is added an emotive appeal: only by taking this more "pastoral" or accommodating view can we truly be "merciful" and "non-judgmental" and "inclusive"—like the Jesus of the Gospels, they say.

Yet when we look at our Lord's words and deeds in the Gospels, we find that the standards of marital chastity and sexual morality, so far from being watered down, are in fact affirmed by him in much stricter form. It is true above all in the passages on divorce and remarriage and adultery. The only kind of "abrogation" we hear is that our Lord abrogates the idea of accommodation to easier social customs.

In the Gospel of Mark (10:2–12) the Pharisees press our Lord on the permissibility of divorce. Having elicited from them the Mosaic grounds for the practice, Jesus did not deny that it was so, but, declaring Moses' command a concession to the hardness of hearts, points instead to *the beginning of creation*. He demonstrates the divine institution of marriage and its indissolubility from the Genesis text on the *two in one flesh*. Afterwards, in the house, he is pressed further by the disciples. He confirms what he has just said without the least mitigation and makes a declarative statement of case law, lest there be any doubt: *Whoever divorces his wife and marries another, commits adultery against her; and if she divorces her husband and marries another, she commits adultery* (Mark 10:11).

Earlier in Matthew our Lord makes another austere statement of case law, in which he goes to the core of the issue of human sexuality and chastity: the adultery of the heart, the interior act of libidinous desire: *You have heard that it was said, "You shall not commit adultery," But I say to you, everyone who looks on a woman lustfully has already committed adultery with her in his heart* (Matt 5:28).

It is perfectly clear then: this mild, compassionate, and non-judgmental Jesus of the Gospels in fact raises the moral standard of marriage to a loftier and more demanding level. As we go on, we will seek a deeper insight into the *why* of this strictness, which is so violently antipathetic to secular modernity.

6.3 The exception clauses in Matthew

In Matthew 5:31–32 at 32, and 19:3–9 at 8, two so-called "exception clauses," or really phrases, qualify the dominical prohibition of divorce and remarriage. The location of our Lord's dispute with the Rabbis is significant. Jesus is staying across the Jordan (cf. Matt 19:1; Mark 10:1), the scene of John's ministry, ended by his public rebuke of Herod's adultery with his brother's wife. Here, in this prophetic place, our Lord upholds the witness of his holy forerunner, teaching the divine institution of indissoluble marriage, and making no mistake about what constitutes adultery.

The subtext of the encounter is rabbinic jurisprudence, the disputes over *halakhah* by the preceptors of the Oral Law. In the Torah, divorce is only mentioned passingly, in the conditional clause of a case law. The vague grounds given for divorce are that *he has found some indecency in her* (Deut 24:1-4 at 1). The rabbis around the turn of the eras wrangled over interpreting this *something indecent ('ervat dabhar)*. Early in the third century AD, the Mishnah redacted these oral debates laconically. Some of them go back to our Lord's time. Dealing with the grounds for divorce are the Tractates *Yevamot* ("levirate marriages") and specially *Gittin* (after *Get*, "bill" or "writ" of divorce), in the order *Nashim* ("Women"). *Gittin* redacts a dispute on the grounds for divorce between the *Beit Shammai*[1] and the *Beit Hillel*, two traditions of rabbinic jurisprudence, the Shammai school tending to strictness, the Hillel, to a liberal accommodation.

> Beit Shammai say, "a man may not divorce his wife unless he has found in her something improper, as it is said *because he has found something unseemly in her* (Deut 24:1)." But Beit Hillel say, "even if she spoilt a dish for him, as it is said *because he has found something unseemly in her* (Deut 24:1)." Rabbi Akiva says, "even if he finds another more attractive, as it is said, *then it comes to pass if she find no favor in his eyes*" (Deut 24:1).[2]

The Beit Shammai understood the phrase "something improper/ unseemly" to mean sexual impropriety or unchastity, but Beit Hillel widened its connotations. Finally, Rabbi Akiva, of the Beit Hillel in the second century AD, goes further. Mark the fact that his judgment reflects a post-Christian situation. If he is consciously rebutting the known position of Christians and Essenes, who rule out divorce and remarriage altogether, it is a witness to the practice of the early church.

With these rabbinic disputes in mind, let us consider again the two qualifying phrases. First, Matthew 5:32: ἐγὼ δὲ λέγω ὑμῖν ὅτι πᾶς ὁ ἀπολύων τὴν γυναῖκα αὐτοῦ παρεκτὸς λόγου πορνείας ποιεῖ αὐτὴν μοιχευθῆναι, literally "apart from the word of fornication." Then, Matthew

---

1. See Huizinga, "Marriage and the Matthaean Jesus."

2. *Gittin* 9.9, translation slightly adapted from *Mishnayoth* Volume II *Order Nashim*, 444. Cf. also *Gittin* 90a (vol 2, 38) and *Yevamot* 112b in *Tosefta* vol. 2.

19:9: ὃς ἂν ἀπολύσῃ τὴν γυναῖκα αὐτοῦ μὴ ἐπὶ πορνείᾳ καὶ γαμήσῃ ἄλλην μοιχᾶται, literally "except for fornication."

A word about the Greek terms. The noun for "adultery," μοιχεία, refers in this period to sexual relations between a husband and a married woman not his wife, or between a wife and any man not her husband. The noun πορνεία on the other hand, at this period, denotes sexual licentiousness in general, well conveyed by the English "unchastity." The relation of πορνεία to μοιχεία therefore is as generic to specific: μοιχεία is πορνεία that offends directly against marriage. The strict separation of the two terms, as if πορνεία, *in the Graeco-Roman-Jewish world in the first century*, denotes only sexual relations between the unmarried, and μοιχεία that at least one of the paramours is married, is not verifiable for the period we are dealing with.

How are the ways that the Matthaean "exception clauses" have been interpreted?

First, the way the early Fathers of the church dealt with them, and is continued in the Catholic Church to this day. They understood the verb ἀπολύων, meaning literally to "let go," "send away," or "dismiss," to authorize only *separation*, which might or might not involve legal divorce, and πορνεία, in this case, as marital unfaithfulness. They interpret this Matthaean text to say that a separation of husband and wife was only permissible—indeed they would insist, *required*—if one of them continues in unrepentant adultery, and that any attempted remarriage by either party was adultery.

A second, more recent and still orthodox interpretation reads "adultery" and "fornication" as mutually exclusive terms—which, as argued above, is anachronistic. So it will be interpreted that πορνεία does not reference adultery but some form of sexual relationship that is not in fact marriage at all: e.g., consanguinity or an illicit degree of kinship, etc., or deceitfully undeclared prenuptial intercourse, or mere cohabitation, that might nullify a supposed or reputed marriage null and void. In this view, the Matthaean text permits "divorce" and remarriage, because it is not a matter of a real marriage to begin with. A query however: Jewish *halakhah* already distinguished between divorce and a declaration that a putative marriage was not really a marriage *from its inception*. There were no grounds for dispute between the rabbis and Jesus on what rendered a supposed marriage null and void.

A third interpretation, which appeared much later in Christian history, reads ἀπολύων as "divorce" in its full sense, i.e. the dissolution of a *real* marriage with a right to remarry; and πορνεία, in this case, as adultery. On this view, the Matthaean text permits divorce *and remarriage* if one of the spouses is guilty of adultery. This, however, is nothing else than the position of the Beit Shammai. Such an understanding is completely absent elsewhere in the NT and in the earliest thinking of the church. And predictably, once one ground is admitted, soon there are two or three other grounds that cannot be denied, and then there are five or six, and so it goes. One ends up flocking with the rabbis in their disputes of the possible nuances of *'ervat dabhar*. Are we to imagine that this was our Lord's intent: "I am taking a position on this, and I am for the Beit Shammai?" No indeed!

The internal evidence of the Gospel of Matthew itself is against the granting of any exception. The disciple's dismayed reply, *If such is the case of a man with his wife, it is not expedient to marry* (Matt 19:10), scarcely suggests they have just heard our Lord offering them a loophole. No, they have just heard one of his hard sayings. The New Testament elsewhere is entirely innocent of any dominical permission for remarriage. When Paul expressly reports *the Lord's* teaching in Romans 7:2-3 and 1 Corinthians 7:10-11—and he is writing earlier than the final redaction of the Gospel—this is the position: no divorce *and remarriage* in the lifetime of one's lawful spouse is possible that does not constitute adultery.

These then are three interpretations. But how to account for the qualifying phrases in Matthew that are not found in the parallel texts of the other synoptic Gospels and Paul? A part of the answer may lie in its redaction. Comparison of textual parallels in Mark, Luke, and even John on occasion, shows that the Matthaean final editor often added interpretive glosses.[3]

Still, Matthew's text remains inspired canonical Scripture, and we respect it as such. So, allowing that the dominical affirmation of indissolubility stands, why then, we ask, might these phrases have been added? We are here in the realm of educated guesses. Did it have something to do with the audience the final editor had in view, perhaps in the 70s of the first century?

---

3. E.g., the addition of *for repentance* in Matthew 3:11 v. Mark 1:8; Luke 3:16; John 1:26; the two extra petitions in the Our Father, Matthew 6:10, 13 v. Luke 11:2-4; the added qualifiers in the Beatitudes, Matthew 5:3, 6 v. Luke 6:20-21; the extra epithet in Peter's confession, Matthew 16:16 v. Mark 8:29; Luke 9:20; the added phrase in Matthew 13:12 v. Mark 4:25; Luke 8:18; the addition of the mother ass in Matthew 21:2, assimilating the accompanying Zechariah prophecy, against all *three* other Gospels. On Matthew's glosses see Fitzmyer, "The Matthaean Divorce Texts," 208-11.

If one thinks of a *Jewish-Christian* audience, two explanations suggest themselves. First, that the *porneia* assimilates the *'ervhat dabhar* of Deuteronomy 24:1 in the sense of some prior unseemliness that renders the marriage not a marriage at all. But we have already fairly scotched that view. Another attractive view, however, argued by Bruce Vawter in 1954,[4] is that these "exception phrases" are rhetorically "preteritive," that is, they act to exclude the term *porneia* from consideration altogether. To our Lord's rabbinic interlocutors, the qualifying interjection would signal: "I have no intention whatever of entering into your disputes about the *'ervhat dabhar*." It is doubtful that textual criticism would back up this reading. Nevertheless, in my view, this does accurately capture our Lord's mind, and with it, the Christian tradition.

Another possibility is that the *porneia* phrases address *Gentiles* entering the Israel of Jesus the Christ, Gentiles who find themselves in situations that do not meet the criteria of marriage either in civil law, or *in the Lord*. Graeco-Roman society knew a range of sexual liaisons that fell short of *matrimonium*, more of which in a later chapter. In Christian history, one thinks of the case of St Augustine and his *de facto* marriage (cohabitation) with the sadly unnamed mother of his son, or the case of Emperor Lothair II and his *freidelehe* (cohabitation) with Waldrada, and his *muntehe* (full legal marriage) with Theutberga, of which more later. So, in this view, the phrases would not be about the grounds for nullity of a putative marriage, but about various cohabitation arrangements of Gentiles newly arrived to the faith of Christ.

Before we leave this issue, let us revisit the additional verse that appears in Mark, but not in Matthew: *and if she divorces her husband and marries another, she commits adultery* (Mark 10:12). In Rabbinic Judaism divorce is a husband's prerogative alone. Mark's text proclaims a revolutionary new element in our Lord's teaching: the absolute parity of the sexual and marital standards expected of men and of women. Our Lord allows no quarter whatever to a double standard, one for men, and one for women, so often found in legal and social codes, pagan and Jewish, and even tolerated in some periods of Christian history, according to which the same order of sexual sin was thought less serious in a man than in a woman. It bears repeating: the Gospel teaches absolute parity in the moral truth to be lived by both men and women.

---

4. Vawter, "The Divorce clauses."

6.4 Virginity and lifelong sexual abstinence

The course of the Gospel itself delivers us to the dominical teaching on virginity or perpetual continence for the kingdom:

> *The disciples said to him, "If such is the case of a man with his wife, it is not expedient to marry." But he said to them, "Not all men can receive this saying, but only those to whom it is given. For there are eunuchs who have been so from birth, and there are eunuchs who have been made eunuchs by men, and there are eunuchs who have made themselves eunuchs for the sake of the kingdom of heaven. He who is able to receive this, let him receive it."* (Matt 19:10–12)

Often in hearing this Gospel we "pale out" the unsavory term *eunuch* and vaguely hear "celibate" instead. Perhaps we should allow the weight of our Lord's choice of term. A eunuch is someone castrated, with life-long impotence and privation his lot thereby. If the prophet Isaiah meant a very great deal to our Lord—as is certainly the case—then his words are surely echoing behind our Lord's:

> *let not the eunuch say, "Behold, I am a withered tree." For thus says the* LORD: *"to the eunuchs who keep my sabbaths, who choose what pleases me, and hold fast my covenant, I will give in my house . . . a monument and a name better than sons and daughters; I will give them an everlasting name which shall not be cut off."*(Isa 56:4–5)

To be unmarried *for the sake of the kingdom* therefore retains the tentative aspect of virginity we saw in ancient Israel: it is a state of human incompletion, having no value in itself except as a testimony of self-reservation looking to the day of consummation. In Isaiah, the eunuch is exhorted to humbly sustain his privation through the whole of his life for a fulfillment that the Lord alone will give. This is his consolation: stay faithful to my covenant, put your hopes in me beyond this life, and what I will do and be for you shall far outweigh all that you have so sorrowfully lost or never known upon the earth. Our Lord is saying the same, only now he applies it to all who *willingly* renounce marriage and children in view of the kingdom.

A wide range of people might rightly be called *eunuchs for the sake of the kingdom of heaven*: those with a broken marriage behind them, especially in the worst case of abandoned spouses; faithful widows and widowers; those who, for all their yearnings never did find a spouse and a domestic hearth; those burdened mentally, emotionally, or physically; those afflicted with some lack from birth; those who experience same-sex attraction. All, insofar as they set their heart on steadfast love for our Lord, bearing their loneliness humbly and courageously with him and in him, are, through their adoption in baptism, and the seal of the Spirit, and the Lord's flesh and blood, deservedly considered *eunuchs for the sake of the kingdom of heaven*. The Catechism, no. 1658, applies a beautiful passage from *Familiaris Consortio* no. 85, to such as these:

> *We must also remember the great number of single persons who, because of the particular circumstances in which they have to live—often not of their own choosing—are especially close to Jesus' heart and therefore deserve the special affection and active solicitude of the Church, specially of pastors. Many remain without a human family, often due to conditions of poverty. Some live their situation in the spirit of the Beatitudes, serving God and neighbor in exemplary fashion. The doors of homes, the "domestic churches," and of the great family which is the Church must be open to all of them. "No one is without a family in this world: the Church is a home and a family for everyone, especially those who 'labor and are heavily laden.'"*

6.5 Is there marriage in the Kingdom?

This Gospel episode of the rich young man who went away sad at the Lord's invitation to radical dispossession, concludes in Luke's version: *Peter began to say to him, "Lo, we have left everything and followed you"* (Mark 10:23–28). Our Lord's reply in Luke is:

> *Amen I say to you, there is no man who has left house or wife or brothers or parents or children for the sake of the kingdom of God, who will not receive manifold more in this time, and in the age to come eternal life.* (Luke 18:29–30)

Or wife? Are we to ascribe this, as do some commentators, to the *ascetic impulse* of the New Testament? Indeed it is *ascesis*, a training of our aspirations to the highest perspectives of the world to come. It does not mean a repudiation of marriage and family. Is the Lord who blessed bride and groom through his presence at their wedding at Cana and gave them the best wine, who consoled all parents when he took Jairus and his wife in with him to cure their little daughter (Mark 5:40), who insistently welcomed children—*let the children come to me... for to such belongs the kingdom of God* (Mark 10:14), who invoked the duty of filial piety against the casuistries of the rabbis (Matt 15:1–9), and made a mother's joy after giving birth *because a child is born into the world* (John 16:21) the image of paschal joy—is he likely to be condemning marriage and childbearing?

To our Lord, marriage and family are "signs" on this earth of the eternal life to which he points everyone: that is, our becoming sons in him, the only begotten Son of the Father. If the family lives, or in its honest weakness *strives* to live this upward calling, it prepares its members for this affiliation in Christ to the heavenly Father. Hence, the earthly family, insofar as it is closed in on itself, has no absolute value at all. It is true when it looks to the Father, *from whom every family, in heaven or on earth takes its name* (Eph 3:14). This truth of transcendence at the heart of the life in Christ, is by no means excused in the case of husband and wife. The *left ... a wife* of the Gospel means that this most intimate of human relations too is predicated on the primacy of God.

The hard sayings of our Lord are sharp reminders that God alone is the luminous model of our human life, and that all else—and expressly the family—exists for us only in relation to this truth. The earthly family that renders itself opaque to the transcendent proves itself a scandal to Godward faith. In such a crisis, the gospel will appear not as a word of peace but of strife, as in another of our Lord's hard sayings:

> *Do not think that I have come to bring peace on earth; I have not come to bring peace but a sword. For I have come to set a man against his father, and a daughter against her mother ... and a man's foes will be those of his own household. He who loves father or mother more than me is not worthy of me ... and he who does not take his cross and follow me is not worthy of me.* (Matt 10:34–38, cf. Luke 12:51–53; 14:26–27)

We find a similar tension in St Paul. In 1 Corinthians 7 he speaks of the married life. After see-sawing between affirmations of the good of marriage and suggesting something better in being devotedly unmarried for the Lord, he finally downs tools, as it were, and comes clean:

> *I mean, brethren, the appointed time has grown very short; from now on, let those who have wives live as though they had none, and those who mourn as though they were not mourning, and those who rejoice as though they were not rejoicing ... and those*

> *who deal with the world as if they had no dealings with it, for the fashion of this world is passing away.* (1 Cor 7:29–31)

In short, this earthly order in every age is tentative, contingent, waiting on that Day of the Lord that will come down on every human being on the face of the earth: *for we have here no lasting city, but we look for the one in the life that is to come* (Heb 13:14). This pressing on to heavenly realities is the touchstone of eschatological virginity. St Paul, who had just been warning Christian husbands and wives against prolonged abstinence, does not suddenly bid them adopt it permanently, but he *is* saying that the married too must live their union in this same eschatological vision of faith and hope that inspires Christian life-long virginity. The married and the unmarried for the Lord are both on the same spiritual trajectory.

There is yet another hard saying in regard to marriage and virginity:

> *Jesus said to them, "The sons of this age marry and are given in marriage; but those who are accounted worthy to attain to that age and to the resurrection from the dead neither marry nor are given in marriage, for they cannot die anymore, because they are equal to angels and are sons of God, being sons of the resurrection."* (Luke 20:34–36)

In our Lord's perspective, human sexuality as lived out in marriage is a reality belonging to the "in-between" time of the dimension of history, to Paul's *fashion of this world which* is *passing away*. In the life that is to come, in the Resurrection, there is no marriage. Our state there will be the same as the angels in heaven—not "like," mind you, but the *same*, or *equal to*, that is what the Greek text says—ἰσάγγελοι. The nuptial mystery of our first creation was intended to imitate *God's image and likeness* through our capacity for love and loyalty and generous fruitfulness. For most of us this is refracted in the union of flesh and spirit in the life of marriage, family, and society. But as each of us passes beyond the veil of death into eternity, this earthly manner of refracting the divine mystery disappears as we participate through Christ in the communion of the Holy Trinity in the most direct, immediate, and fullest way possible to us while remaining creatures, that is, the same state as the angels.

The Fathers of the church applied this Gospel teaching to dedicated virginity in *this* life: The virgin anticipates in his or her own flesh the world that is to come. To live *devotedly* unmarried for the Lord, therefore, is not a "sacrament" of heaven on earth, because it is already heaven on earth, through faith. The virgin who *cleaves undistractedly to the Lord alone* (1 Cor 7:35) keeps fresh in the church a living awareness of the end to which the *mysterion* of marriage itself is ordered: the eschatological Wedding of the Lamb. Through a direct purchase on our common end, she beckons Christian spouses from any slide to this-worldliness in the living out of their marriage. Those who are married in the Lord pattern to those who are unmarried for the Lord the character of nuptial love, the covenant of a mutual love that is unique, personal, exclusive, and, being disposed to the Transcendent, life-giving, affective and effective in body, mind, and spirit, the flower of our human vocation as we have given account of it from the beginning, which virgins too must live out and realize. Thus something of the inner pattern of each way of life is refracted in the other. The poetry of the Song is for both: *With my body I Thee worship*! By their faithful sacramental witness married believers call their unmarried brethren to watch the living out of their virginity, lest it end in effete bachelorhood or spinsterhood, dissipated in distractions, busy sidelines, or adulterous compensations, because virginity was given you for *holy desire,* and to make progress in it. The warmth of virginity for the Lord comes from the ardor of its nuptial character, trained and led by faith to the Bridegroom on the cross. Absent this nuptial mainspring, all is anemic, insipid, *as salt that has lost its savor* (Matt 5:13). Meanwhile the humble, faithful, and loving virgin is a beacon to his or her married brethren of their transcendent destiny beyond this world, and even of their growth toward eschatological "virginity" in a way: that fruition of unspeakable joy in God and in one another, beyond death in eternity, when we shall all be as the angels, gathered forever as one in Christ, immersed in the aureole of God's infinite purity and holiness, loving God face to face and, in that sublime Communion of Persons, loving each other, person to person, heart to heart.

Chapter Seven

MARRIAGE: ANALOGY, SACRAMENT, AND THE END OF TIME

7.1 Asking the "why" and the "whither" of the NT

THUS FAR, IN THE New Testament, we have sought the truth about marriage and family in the events of the Incarnation, in the holy family of Nazareth and in the gradual expansion of that family as the church through our adoption in Christ as the children of the Father. We then turned to the expressly moral teaching of the New Testament: especially to the re-establishment of marriage in its original indissolubility by our Lord. The high standard of marital fidelity he taught led to the question of virginity for the kingdom. It is now time to ask the "why" and "whither" questions of the New Testament, and that means probing the use of marriage as a sublime analogy.

7.2 This adulterous generation

Our Lord, like the prophets, equates faithlessness and adultery:

> *An evil and adulterous generation seeks for a sign, but no sign shall be given it except the sign of the prophet Jonah* (Matt 12:39; 16:4), . . . *Whoever is ashamed of me and of my words in this adulterous and sinful generation, of him will the Son of man also be ashamed when he comes in the glory of his Father with the holy angels.* (Mark 8:38)

There is little question of the involvement of Roman-era Judaism in the licentious cultic practices of eight centuries and more before. But many are the ways in which *the heart which is more devious than anything and desperately sick* (Jer 17:9), can install idols for itself. Our Lord calls the infidelity of the Israel of his day "adultery," not for its external idols and cults, but for the constricting schemas of the mind that ensured complete deafness to the Word, the Bridegroom of Israel, when he comes at last: *He came to his own and his own received him not* (John 1:11). Israel, in these impervious leaders, is unbelieving all over again: *O Jerusalem, Jerusalem, killing the prophets and stoning those who are sent to you. How often I would have gathered your children together as a hen gathers her chicks under her wings, but you would not* (Luke 13:34).

7.3 The Bridegroom of Israel is come

It seems that the holy prophet, John the Baptist, son of Zechariah and Elizabeth, was the first to announce the coming of Christ the Bridegroom. Remembering that the apostle and evangelist John, "the beloved disciple," was first a disciple of the Baptist, we meet the theme very early in his Gospel where the holy Forerunner deprecates himself as merely *the friend of the Bridegroom*:

> You yourselves bear me witness that I said, I am not the Christ, but have been sent before him. He who has the bride is the Bridegroom; the friend of the Bridegroom who stands and hears him rejoices greatly at the Bridegroom's voice; therefore this joy of mine is now full. He must increase, but I must decrease. (John 3:28–30)

Mark 2:18–19 confirms the Johannine linkage of the Bridegroom theme with John the Baptist. Jesus, in conversation with John's disciples, owns himself as the Bridegroom. *Then the disciples of John came to him, saying, "Why do we and the Pharisees fast, but your disciples do not fast?"* And Jesus replies: *"Can the wedding guests fast while the Bridegroom is with them?"* He employs a prophetic, symbolic idiom already known to them from their teacher, who in turn was but tapping the nuptial imagery of the prophets.

It is possible to see John's baptism in a nuptial light. Today, in Qumran, one can see the relics of the *mikva'oth*, the baths of ritual purification used by the Essenes. Likewise there were *mikva'oth* down on the outer reaches of the Temple mount in Jerusalem. Each pilgrim, according to need, immersed himself—the practice is called *tevilah*—in a *mikveh* or bath of running water, to be purified from a range of prescribed ritual uncleanesses, before ascending to participate in the liturgy above.[1] Ev-

---

1. Prescriptions for the use of the *mikveh* are discussed at length in tractate

ery bride, too, immersed herself in the waters of the *mikveh* as she approached her wedding day.

John, in *preparing for the Lord a people fit for Him* (Luke 1:17), reconfigured the *tevilah*: it is not the array of extrinsic ritual uncleannesses from which you must be cleansed, but from your *intrinsic* moral uncleannesses, your sins (cf. Mark 7:20–23). In transposing the *tevilah* as a baptism of repentance for sins, and administering it to all suppliant comers in the streams of the Jordan, the *Friend of the Bridegroom* was preparing the Bride to meet the Bridegroom of Israel when he came.

He must increase, but I must decrease! One cannot but be awed at the spirit of *kenosis* by which John was truly the "forerunner" of the One who *emptied himself* (Phil 2:13). John was so very promptly aware of what he *was not*—he repeats this self-negation like a refrain of prayer—if only he might defer to *Him Who Is*, that is, to true divine Being. In the end, this interiorly stripped man, this virgin ascetic, this acme of apocalyptic and messianic fervor, died for no other cause than the sanctity of marriage, his head an adulterous king's chit to a dancing girl's show—in symbol, all that is suborned and corrupted in human sexuality. Let us ponder the enigmas of John's exodus, how he was rated by this world's elite, and how by the Word of God: *the greatest born of women*.

Jesus in turn uses the nuptial mystery in his parables, where he likens the kingdom to a wedding feast. *The kingdom of heaven may be compared to a king who made a wedding feast for his son* (Matt 22:2). The king, clearly, is God, and the Son, whose wedding it is, is Christ himself; we hear the great eschatological invitation ringing down the ages of history: *Come to the Wedding!* (Matt 22:4).

In Matthew 25:1–12 our Lord tells of ten virgins awaiting the Bridegroom's arrival at the wedding feast.

> *As the bridegroom was delayed, they all slumbered and slept. But at midnight there was a cry, "Behold the Bridegroom comes, go out to meet him!" . . . [T]he Bridegroom came and those who were ready went in with him to the marriage feast.*

Like the prophets and John the Baptist before him, Jesus uses the wedding to figure the final denouement of the relationship between God and man. The covenant of God and Israel of old converges in him who has come to espouse his Church in his *hour* upon the cross.

Mikva'ot of the Seder *Taharot* ("Purities"). It contains ten chapters, comprising eighty-three paragraphs in all. Cf. also the tractates *Niddah* ("The menstruant") and *Zabim* ("They who suffer a flux").

Let us linger with the forerunner one last time. Just as we saw the child Jesus subjecting himself to Joseph and learning from him as he humanly matured, so Jesus fortified his own obedience from the witness of his humble forerunner. He weighed the import to him of John's execution. He must withdraw into solitude and be before his Father in prayer (Matt 14:12–23). As his own hour drew nigh, *he departed again to the far side of the Jordan where John had once been baptizing*—and had indeed baptized him—*and there he abode* (John 10:40). That charged Johannine verb: *abode*: this is a pilgrimage and a retreat. In his night hours of prayer before his Father in this place, he remembers the days of John's ministry long gone by, and faces before his Father *the baptism he has yet to undergo* (Mark 10:38). Then, as the hour draws nearer, he crosses the Jordan, leaves the Jordan valley for the last time, and climbs towards Jerusalem, *for it cannot be that a prophet should perish outside Jerusalem* (Luke 13:33).

7.4 Cana

Nuptial symbolism and apocalyptic tones pervade Jesus' presence at this wedding, where he worked his first "sign" (John 2:1–11). The wedding is presented as if three days after the Lord's baptism at John's hands. It is the character of John's gospel always to move from concrete "sign" to the higher spiritual reality signified and then back again. This *perichoresis* of sign and signified, of visible and invisible, of flesh and spirit, is our Lord's way in the other Gospels; but in the Gospel of John it is distilled and intensified. In keeping with the anagogical tenor of the Scriptures, that pedagogy of the breath of God who through the course of sacred history leads man *onward* and *upward*, so are all our Lord's words and acts in the Gospel of John. Unremittingly he hints at, discloses ,and calls to a higher plane, to *spirit and truth*. But it is also an essential feature of this most "spiritual" of the Gospels never to lose purchase of the concrete sign, to be ever returning to the material, the tangible and the visible and "seeing" it anew in the light of its true meaning from on high.

Jesus, then, comes to the wedding with his new disciples, and his mother Mary is also a guest. The wine for the feast runs out, and at his mother's discrete insistence, he changes the jars full of water for the Jewish rites of purification into wine, the *good wine*, usually kept till the last. *This, the first of his signs, Jesus did at Cana in Galilee, and he manifested his glory* (John 2:11). All the elements of the story, therefore, have an import for his mission. Every word resonates.

She to whom he once subjected himself, now, after his baptism, authorizes him as his mother, launching him away from herself on his public mission. Jesus addresses her as "Woman" in connection with his eschatological "Hour," as an idea known to her. We note too that the human author of the narrative was present then at Cana, and also beside Mary when that Hour came.

On one level, Our Lord hallows the earthly marriage of this particular husband and wife through his presence: indeed, his own phrase, *the Bridegroom is with them* (Mark 2:19) is singularly apposite to these spouses. He blesses their wedding by an overflowing supply of good wine: a double gesture, operative on both mundane and metaphorical levels because it is called the first of his *signs*. It is an event of the *New—Behold, I make all things new* (Rev 21:5), here figured as the transition from the water of the old rites which has now run out, to the superabundant good wine of the Gospel. It is a gesture to the love of man and woman itself, raising the water of all that is natural and earthly in marriage to a participation in divine realities. It is a pointer to the coming eucharistic mystery through the change of the elements and the *good wine* itself.

Finally the wedding at Cana foreshadows the Lord's own espousal of his church when his *hour* shall come.

> *Now before the Passover, when Jesus knew that his hour had come to depart out of this world to the Father, having loved those who were his own in the world, he loved them to the end* (John 13:1).

It will be the hour of his glorification when he shall be lifted up on the cross and the water and blood shall flow from his pierced side, which is gathered up, memorialized, and communicated in the eucharistic banquet, anticipated in the *sign*, in the *best wine* poured out at the wedding banquet.

7.5 Ephesians 5

Ephesians is of pivotal importance for the Mystery of Christian marriage. Here, Paul expressly identifies Christ's Bride as the church when he says that marriage as *a great mystery, and I mean in reference to Christ and his Church*:

> *Be subject to one another out of reverence for Christ. Wives, be subject to your husbands, as to the Lord. For the husband is the head of the wife as Christ is the head of the Church his body, and he himself is her Savior. As the Church is subject to Christ, so let wives also be subject in everything to their husbands. Husbands,*

> love your wives, as Christ loved the Church and gave himself up for her, that he might sanctify her, having cleansed her by the washing of water with the word, that he might present the Church to himself in splendor, without spot or wrinkle or any such thing, that she might be holy and without blemish. Even so husbands should love their wives as their own bodies. He who loves his wife loves himself. For no man ever hates his own flesh, but nourishes and cherishes it, as Christ does the Church, because we are members of his body. For this reason a man shall leave his father and mother and be joined to his wife and the two shall become one flesh. This is a great mystery, and I am saying that it refers to Christ and his Church. (Eph 5:21–33)

Paul draws on the prophet Ezekiel 16 and cites Genesis 2:24, even as he transposes the traditional spousal imagery of the prophets into a fully Christian key. The Lord God the Bridegroom and Jerusalem the Bride, are become Christ Jesus the Bridegroom and the church the Bride. Paul rereads the relationship of husband and wife in Christ in the light of the bridal language already owned by our Lord himself. To him, marriage in Christ is invested with a tremendous richness of meaning. How profound and indissoluble is the union of Christ and his church! Just so the union of a husband and wife *in Christ* is profound and indissoluble, for they are immersed in the marriage of Christ and his church! Throughout the passage Paul weaves so closely between human marriage and the union of Christ and the church, it is difficult to distinguish which dimension he is referring to—and that is exactly how it should be.

7.6 Mysterion and Sacramentum

Paul's use of μυστήριον here, while not technically equivalent to what came to be defined as "sacrament," is nevertheless the *fons et origo* of that sense of sacramentality which ever surrounded Christian Marriage in the mind of the church.[2] The sense of the English word *mystery* can be a little pallid, suggesting something baffling, unknown, or puzzling. In the ancient Greek culture, μυστήριον and its cognates—and we might add also in the Syriac speaking tradition, *raza*—retains a full "liturgical" register, denoting an initiation through sacred rites into divine secrets. In Paul, the Mystery *par excellence* of all mysteries is Christ: that *mystery hidden for ages and generations but now made manifest to his saints . . . this mystery*

---

2. On the semantic and theological history of the terms *mystery* and *sacrament*, see the long excursus in John Paul II, *Man and Woman*, 489–90n88.

which is Christ among you, your hope of glory (Col 1:26–27). Among the Greek Fathers, a *mystagogue* is not a speaker who somehow mystifies or obfuscates his topic, or someone who introduces you to "mysticism," but one who expounds the inner meaning of the sacred Liturgy.

Ancient Latin translators rendered *mysterion* as "sacramentum." A *sacramentum* was the oath of allegiance taken by a new soldier at his enlistment. Eventually it referred to any pact or rite conferring a *sacred* character on an undertaking. The common element between the Greek and the Latin terms was the note of a socially witnessed ritual initiation. So then, marriage in Christ is both a *sacramentum*, a solemn oath-taking over which God Himself yearns, a *mysterion* or a liturgical initiation, a "sacred sign" that reveals to its participants and in its participants something of the secrets of God, which Paul refers to the espousal of Christ and his Bride the church.

St Paul borrows from Ezekiel the imagery of Israel found by the Lord God prostrate in helplessness and transformed and prepared for marriage solely through his merciful, redemptive love. So in the Christian dispensation, Jesus Christ finds the church in weakness and cleanses her by the washing of water with the word and prepares her to be presented to himself in splendor. Christ's love for his church is wholly unmerited; it is precisely his redeeming "love" that makes her "lovely," his "grace" that makes her "grace-filled." Christ Jesus went to his Passion bearing not only the rejection of the leaders of Israel, but also the weakness and cowardice of most of his own disciples at that hour; he knew fully that this was how it would be with many who would be called by his name. Yet he still chose the Bride and called her and loved her and gave his life for her. Therefore, an abiding love of the church, perhaps all the more in the contradictions of her apparent weakness and debility, acquires the accents of Christ's own redemptive spousal love for his Bride. This is truly to put on the *phronesis*, the mind of Christ. The washing, the cleansing, will go on till the End.

This idea of Ephesians that Christ finds his church in *weakness*, and transforms her, has its bearing on Christian marriage, for bride and bridegroom too, espouse each other in weakness. Each marries a fallible and sinful human being. By pledging themselves to each other for life and putting on the mind of Christ, they undertake to grow together to human and spiritual maturity. "All husbands and wives are called in marriage to holiness," John Paul II says in *Familiaris Consortio* no. 34, meaning that marriage is set before spouses as a journey of moral and spiritual progress, a progress that demands awareness of sin, a sincere commitment to observe the moral law and the ministry of reconciliation. It must also be kept in mind that conjugal intimacy involves the wills of two persons, who are however called to harmonize their mentality and behavior: this requires much patience, understanding and time.

7.7 What of male headship?

Another aspect of the Ephesians passage concerns the issue of a husband's headship and a wife's subordination. Is the wife to be *subordinate* to the husband? One observes in all the teaching of Pope John Paul II a conspicuous absence of the language of subordination, matched instead by a determined language of mutuality and reciprocity. In *Mulieris Dignitatem* he uses the first account of the creation of man in Genesis, with its simple parity of male and female, as a hermeneutic key to interpreting the second creation account, so that all the "help" to man that the woman represents, is held to operate *reciprocally*. The Apostle Paul himself prefaces his Ephesians passage on spouses with a remarkable statement of mutual subordination: *Be subject to one another out of reverence for Christ*. If we take this as a kind of antiphon, a hermeneutic key to all that follows, the Ephesians text will not be understood one-sidedly, as if the husband were somehow the principal of his wife's *spiritual* life. In fact, the husband is just as much a child of the church as is his wife, as dependent on the ministrations of Christ's saving grace to and through his church. He, like her, participates in the "femininity" of the church in relation to Christ the head. The same is to be said of every ordained priest. Certainly, at the altar, they stand as the figure of Christ the Bridegroom to his church. But they too are children of the church, participating in her espousals to the Lord.[3]

---

3. "In a way, every Christian is also believed to be a bride of God's Word, a mother of Christ, his daughter and sister, at once virginal and fruitful. These words are used in a universal sense of the Church, in a special sense of Mary, in a particular sense of the individual Christian." (Isaac of Stella [c. 1100–c. 1170], Sermon, the Office of Readings for Saturday of the Second Week of Advent.)

"Every soul that believes—that soul both conceives and gives birth to the Word of God and recognizes his works. Let the soul of Mary be in each one of you, to *magnify the Lord*. Let the spirit of Mary be in each one of you, to *rejoice in God*. According to the flesh only one woman can be the mother of Christ, but in the world of faith Christ is the fruit of all of us. For every soul can receive the Word of God if only it is pure and preserves itself in chastity and modesty. The soul that has been able to reach this state *magnifies the Lord* just as Mary did and *rejoices in God its Savior* just like her." (St Ambrose, *Commentary on the Gospel of Luke*, the Office of Readings, 21st December.)

That said, I think there is some issue, not, let us say, of subordination, but of order. Is there "subordination" in the Holy Trinity? The smelting of church dogma in the crucible of the fourth-century theological debates came to a firm conclusion: there is no "subordination" of the divine Persons, but perfect co-equality in dignity. We do not use 'hierarchy' here, lest it give entry to Arianism. But there is *order*, for the Son is the *only-begotten* of the Father who is the ἀρχή (source) of the Son, and, not without the Son, of the Holy Spirit, the seal and *pleroma* of their relation.

> The Father is the principle, the originating starting-point of the Son, as is a human of the being of his child—and is so in such wise that all earthly fatherhood is but a defective copy of the eternal generation of the Word.[4]

Thus the Divine Persons, their distinct *hypostases,* are not known from their *nature*, but only from their *relations*. And that should arrest us deeply, very deeply. All possibility of personhood, of the capacity to love, descends from the relations of the Divine Persons in the inner life of God who is love (1 John 4:8, 16),[5] and is realized supremely when the *Father draws us* (John 6:44) to the Son *in the Holy Spirit* (1 Cor 12:3), to become his *adopted sons through Jesus Christ* (Eph 1:5).

Moreover, we can take another cue from the economy of salvation. It was no arbitrary matter that God the Word, who in his divine personhood had no sex, took flesh in the womb of Mary as a male. So much that is sacramental, symbolic, and in terms of salvation history *dramatic*, is distilled in this incarnation of the Word as a *man*. He is the eternally foreseen New Adam (cf. 1 Cor 15:45; Rom 5:14–15), recapitulating the nuptial mystery of our human constitution, and everything embedded in it: Adam as *son of God* (Luke 3:38), now writ far larger as *the* Son from all eternity, now disclosing truly the Father, now come as the Bridegroom to espouse the Bride.

Hence there is an *order* in marriage and the family, as indeed there is in the church herself, where indeed everyone is a *first-born* and co-equal in dignity, all looking to Christ as head. A man fulfills his specific role as husband and father as head of the family in the pattern of Christ.[6] He is

---

4. Nichols, *Criticising the Critic,* 77.

5. Cf. the seminal work on personhood and the Trinity, Zizioulas, *Being as Communion.* See also the wonderful synthesis in Ratzinger, "Concerning the Notion of Person in Theology."

6. "God exalted Christ over all things to be the Head of the Church for her sake. Christ's headship is the pattern to which the husband's headship is conformed in a typological manner, the earthly marriage relationship displaying an unseen heavenly reality." Winger, "Ephesians 5:21b–33, The Gospel in God's Order," in Winger *Ephesians,* 605.

therefore *auctor* ("who makes things grow," whence *auctoritas,* "authority"), who actuates motherhood through loving his wife, and continues the mystery in his steadfast moral and spiritual shielding of mother and children.[7] The man through faithfulness in his role sets the woman free to fulfil her role as wife and mother at the inner face of life and family, without confusion or equivocation. All is assumed into *Christ and him crucified*, and irrigated and given life by the water and the blood flowing from his pierced side into their souls and bodies.

7.8 The Eucharist as eschatological wedding feast

The New Testament has other ways of pointing Christian marriage onward and upward. We saw Christian marriage described as the *mysterion* of Christ's union with his spouse the church. But the church has the Sacrament of Sacraments, the Eucharist, which Scripture presents to us as the foretaste of the wedding feast at the end of time in the kingdom. In the Eucharist therefore we discern the mystery of marriage in its highest spiritual terms: that of the marital covenant between God and man, between Christ and the Bride.

In the words which our Lord uses to institute the Eucharist, he gathers into one all the themes of covenant, new covenant, eternal covenant, and marital covenant from the Old Testament. His words, *This cup is the new covenant in my blood* (1 Cor 11:25), assume and transform Moses' words over the sacrifice that ratified the Covenant of Sinai, *Behold the blood of the Covenant* (Exod 24:8), the *everlasting covenant* promised in the prophet Isaiah (Isa 55:3), and the coming *new covenant* announced in the prophet Jeremiah (31:31).

But this new covenant is a *nuptial covenant*. In the very passage of Jeremiah announcing the *new covenant* appropriated by Jesus, God is spoken of as *their husband* (Jer 31:32). Our Lord Jesus Christ therefore came to his *hour* as the Bridegroom of the New Covenant foretold by the prophets: *With desire I have desired to eat this Passover with you before I suffer; for I tell you I shall not eat of it until it is fulfilled in the kingdom of God* (Luke 22:15–16).

There are other notes of marital imagery: Compare Adam's declaration of Eve, *this is bone of my bone and flesh of my flesh* (Gen 2:23) and the words, *unless you eat of the flesh of the Son of Man* (John 6:53). As

---

7. I am indebted to conversations with my colleague Conor Sweeney for stirring my thinking on this topic. See now Sweeney and Trainor, *The Politics of Conjugal Love*.

marriage is the *one flesh* union of husband and wife, so the sacrificial banquet of the New Covenant is a *one flesh* union between Christ and his faithful. The church sees the sanctity of both sacraments marriage and Eucharist in profoundest relation to each other: the Eucharist is the sacrament of spousal love between Christ and the church.

In the Synoptic Gospels the Eucharist is provisional. It is an advance made to us now of a fulfillment that will only come at the end of time. The Eucharist is presented as the New Covenant partly realized, but partly not yet. It is an *earnest*, a foretaste of what is to come when *all is made new* (2 Cor 5:17; Rev 21:5). Our Lord leaves the eucharistic mystery to his church as "way-bread" for the long pilgrimage of history, signifying its eschatological fulfilment under the image of a banquet: *I assign to you, as my Father assigned to me, a kingdom, that you may eat and drink at my table in my kingdom* (Luke 22:29–30).

So we progress from earthly marriage to spousal analogy to eucharistic Mystery to eschatological consummation, when all sacraments will pass into eternal life, when we shall be *partakers* of *the divine nature* (2 Pet 1:4).

The Gospel of John comprehends it slightly differently. Here the sacramental and the eschatological converge in an *interiorized eschatology*. This is the Johannine vision of the Eucharist: to partake of our Lord's flesh and blood here is to partake even *now* of that union with him which we shall enjoy in eternity:

> *he who eats my flesh and drinks my blood has eternal life, and I will raise him up on the last day. For my flesh is food indeed, and my blood is drink indeed. He who eats my flesh and drinks my blood abides in me and I in him.* (John 6:54–56)

The last book of the scriptural canon, the Apocalypse, concerns itself precisely with that *eschaton*. In these visions Christ is presented under the figure of *the Lamb*, the Lamb of God hailed by John the Baptist, the all-propitiatory innocent sufferer, the *Lamb slain since the foundation of the world* (Rev 13:18). The age-long war with evil announced at our banishment from the Garden of Eden is finally over. After the fearful tribulations of human history, through rivers of blood and slaughter, we mysteriously arrive again where we first began. *And he who sat upon the throne said, "Behold I make all things new"* (Rev 21:5). We find ourselves *eating of the tree of life which is in the paradise of God* (Rev 2:7). In that paradise, we discover the end of salvation history is the celebration of a marriage—not a marriage of one man and one woman, but the eternal espousal of Christ and the redeemed in which the human race is restored and raised up forever:

> *Alleluia! For the Lord our God the Almighty reigns. Let us rejoice and exult and give him the glory, for the marriage of the Lamb has come, and his Bride has made herself ready . . . And the Angel said to me, "Write this: Blessed are those who are invited to the marriage supper of the Lamb."* (Rev 19:6–7, 9)

How many scriptural themes are rippling through these words: marriage covenant, sacrifice, wedding feast, eucharistic Mystery, and eschatological banquet! And how significant that, of all the Mysteries of the church, just two are left luminously shining at the consummation of the age: marriage and the Eucharist, the sacraments, as it were, of the Beginning and of the End.

Here at the end, the scriptural theme of the "city" reappears for the last time. This city too has a feminine persona, just as we saw with the prophets: it is the City of God, the answer to the fraught, dark city of man inaugurated by the children of Cain. And, feminine as she is, the holy city is revealed as a Bride:

> *Then I saw a new heaven and a new earth, for the first heaven and the first earth had passed away, and the sea was no more. And I saw the holy city, the new Jerusalem, coming down out of heaven from God, prepared as a bride adorned for her husband* (Rev 21:2); her spouse is the Lamb: *Come and I will show you the Bride, the wife of the Lamb.* (Rev 21:9)

Thus the last two chapters of the Apocalypse, and indeed, of the entire scriptural canon, are steeped in spousal imagery. The very last words in the entire canon of Scripture end in the register of the Song of Songs. They express a profound spousal longing that opens out to the Bridegroom at the end of time:

> *And the Spirit and the Bride say: "Come!" And let him who hears say, "Come." And let him who is thirsty come, let him who desires take the water of life without price . . . And he who testifies to these things says, "Surely I am coming soon." Amen. Come, Lord Jesus!* (Rev 22:17, 20)

Chapter Eight

THE GENTILE WORLD THAT CHRISTIANITY ENCOUNTERED

8.1 The Church's long pilgrimage of history

WE NOW SET OUT on the church's long pilgrimage through history toward that longed-for consummation in the age that is to come. The church on earth, aptly called by the medievals the Church *Militant*, is indeed the Church *in via*; the contest with the Enemy is very much engaged.

> In those days a decree went out from Caesar Augustus that all the world should be enrolled. This was the first enrollment, when Quirinius was governor of Syria. (Luke 2:1)

Christianity, even in its Jewish and Semitic cradle, moved in the milieu of the Graeco-Roman world. In the dispensation of God, which makes no mistakes, God the Word took flesh in the days of the Roman Commonwealth, early in that period of its history called the Principate, i.e. Octavius Caesar's new settlement, after the civil wars of the first century BC. The language of Christianity's first cultural transposition was Greek, the common tongue of the Mediterranean basin.[1] The way had long been prepared by the Judaism of the diaspora, with all its Scriptures

---

1. *Graeca leguntur in omnibus fere gentibus; Latina suis finibus, exiguis sane, continentur* ("Greek works are read in nearly all the nations; Latin works are confined to their rather small territory," Cicero, *Pro Archia Poeta* 23.) How things change! It is intriguing that the eventual spread of Latin across Western (and in one case Eastern, i.e. Romanian) Europe gave rise to a family of neo-Latin vulgar languages, whereas Greek, so widespread from the time of Alexander, did not give rise to a family of neo-Greek vulgar languages (except modern demotic Greek). The Slavonic derived languages occupied that niche in Eastern Europe from the eighth century AD.

and discourse in Greek. Gentile Christianity is the heir of hellenized Judaism. It is true that a strong Semitic presence continued in the church among Aramaic/Syriac speakers. Even so, they too were largely part of the imperial *oikoumené*, and in constant interaction with the church's Greek-speaking cultural base.[2] All the ancient churches can be found chanting in their liturgy, verbatim, *Kyrie eleison!*

Jesus yearned for the advance of the Gospel among the Gentiles.

> *Now among those who went up to worship at the feast were some Greeks. So these came to Philip, who was from Bethsaida in Galilee, and said to him, "Sir, we wish to see Jesus." Philip went and told Andrew; Andrew went with Philip and they told Jesus. And Jesus answered them, "The hour has come for the Son of Man to be glorified. Amen, amen I say to you, unless a grain of wheat dies, it remains alone, but if it dies it bears much fruit."* (John 12:20–24)

One might sketch the Graeco-Roman world as an international Roman military, administrative and juridical polity built on a substrate of Greek culture, that generalized Hellenistic culture that took shape after the conquests of Alexander the Great in the late fourth century BC.[3] We need to consider certain aspects of that culture, if we are to understand the problematic of the early church in the area of marriage and family.

8.2 The pan-sexualism of society

St Paul's graphic exposé of the chaotic sexualism in pagan society (Rom 1:24–32), shows the daunting moral landscape in which early Christianity had to make its way.

---

2. The great Aramaic/Syriac-speaking Christian civilization flourished in the Near East over the centuries, its metropolis the illustrious city of Edessa. In this culture, educated monks, ecclesiastics, and scholars were bilingual in Syriac and Greek. It was from these Syriac Christian scholars that Muslim Arabs first came into contact with the ancient Greek philosophers.

3. "From the point of view of the preaching of the Gospel message, the first-century Mediterranean basin may be imagined as three concentric circles. The outer circle (the governmental and social context) was created by the Roman world; the next inner circle (that of culture, education and philosophy) was the product of the Greek world; and the most immediate circle (that of religion, namely monotheism and a history of divine activity and promises and the ethical thought related to that religion) was provided by the Jewish matrix. These were not hermetically sealed compartments; they interacted with and mutually affected one another. This is the world that the early Christians encountered, changed, and healed." (Francis Martin, "Marriage in the New Testament Period," in Olsen, ed., *Christian Marriage*, 69–70.)

Prostitution was widespread throughout the Graeco-Roman world, as normal a social institution as marriage, concubinage, or slavery. The terms used for "prostitute," πόρνη in Greek, and *meretrix* in Latin, come from commerce. They are about selling "sex" as a commodity. "In the ancient world, the flesh trade was a dominant institution, flourishing in the light of day. The sex industry was integral to the moral economy of the classical world."[4] Apart from an elite class of educated courtesans, prostitutes, male and female, were of very low status, usually slaves. Exposed infants were often taken and brought up by pimps to be put to work in this industry. One can only think with pity of the wretched lives to which these poor children were condemned.[5]

Homosexuality in its various forms was very well known, the most common form of it pederasty. The Greek term παιδεραστία[6] denoted a sexual relationship between an adult male and a παῖς, genitive παῖδος. The Latin equivalent is *puer*—meaning, in terms of physical descent, a child, and in terms of social status, a slave or servant. In this context, it meant "boy," but boys between puberty and full physical manhood, in short, youths or young adults.[7]

Except for a brief florescence of romantic love poetry with Catullus and the elegists—and while we are at it, Christians studying Classical Latin and wincing to deal with this so-called "erotic" poetry should realize what a paradoxical positive such romance represents in the social context—sex in the ancient world was largely regarded as an unequal affair between one of superior status, the one engaged in the active role, and an inferior, the one serving the passive role. The criterion was whether or not the body were invaded or "violated" in the sexual act. Thus sex was mixed in with ideas of social disparity, power, and the competitive ascendancy of the individual.

In this respect one is loath to let Aristotle off the hook. He argued that the female body was inferior by *nature* to the male body. This lent a "scientific" air to ideas of the inequality of the sexes.[8] Plato on the other

---

4. Harper, *From Shame to Sin*, 3.
5. See now McGinn, *Prostitution, Sexuality and the Law*.
6. Plato, *Symposium* 181C. In *Plato: Lysis*, 110–11.

7. In my early days of studying Latin I was intrigued to learn that the Romans considered a male "adolescens" until about the age of forty, at which time he might graduate as "adultus."

8. Aristotle reckoned that women were defective and not to be thought of as fully human: "we should look upon the female state as being, as it were, a deformity"

hand had no such idea. Also commendable, from the Christian point of view, was Plato's wish to curb the indulgence of homosexuality, male or female, as both unnatural and a hindrance to ascesis in virtue.[9]

The so-called "Sexual Revolution" in Western society has led, it has been said, to a "pan-sexualist" ethos. Yet it is clear that the Graeco-Roman world in which the Christian Church had first to make her way was also riven by its own kind of pan-sexualism.[10]

8.3 Controlling fertility

Sex as a commodity of pleasure led, of course, to another concern: how to be free of its obnoxious consequences. That meant the control of fertility. We need to grasp the fact that contraception, procured abortion, and the exposure of infants or infanticide were widespread practices in the ancient world. To a Christian believer who grew up thinking that the morality of our society began to seriously unravel in the 1960s with the invention of the anovulant pill, the triumph of the sexual revolution, and the repudiation of *Humanae Vitae* by many Catholics, it has been an eye-opener to learn how far back humans have been seeking ways and means to sterilize the sexual act. Egyptian papyri as old as 2000 BC record contraceptive recipes and practices.[11]

(*Generation of Animals* VI.6, 460-61). "In regard to the sexes, the male is by nature superior and the female inferior, the male ruler and the female subject" (*Politics* II.12, 20-21). Inheriting this strand of Hellenic science, Galen taught that women are males who fail to develop fully in the womb, describing the female half of the human race as "imperfect, and, as it were, mutilated." (*De usu partium* 14.6, 158-65) Galen's commentaries on Hippocrates continued to be influential for many centuries. See Brown, *The Body and Society*, 10.

9. Plato, *The Laws*. 636B-D, 836C-E, 839E, 840DE. In *Plato: The Laws*, Volume 1, 40-41, Volume 2, 150-53, 158-59, 164-65.

10. From the fourth century BC: "Mistresses we keep for our pleasure, concubines (*pallakas*) for the daily care of our persons, but wives to bear us legitimate children, and to be faithful guardians of our homes." (Pseudo-Demosthenes, *Against Neaera* 1.22, in Murray, trans., *Demosthenes*, 445-46)

11. "The oldest surviving documents are from Egypt. Five different papyri, dating between 1900 B.C. and 1100 B.C., provide for contraceptive preparations to be used in the vulva. The Kahun papyrus has three different formulas: pulverized crocodile dung in fermented mucilage; honey and sodium carbonate to be sprinkled in the vulva; and a substance, whose name is now indecipherable, to be mixed with mucilage and sprinkled into the vulva. In the Ebers papyrus it is said that pregnancy may be prevented 'for one, two or three years' by a recipe of acacia tips, coloquintida, and dates, mixed with

The term that covers the use of contraceptive and abortifacient drugs in the ancient world is φαρμακεία. From this Greek word, of course, we derive our "pharmacy," "pharmacology," and "pharmaceutical." At its root φαρμακεία refers generically to drugs, whether used for healing, i.e. medicines, or for harm, that is, poisons. English Bibles often translate φαρμακεία as "sorceries,"[12] which means that the implicit reference to contraceptive and abortifacient drugs is elided, although it does highlight the fact that the dark arts of the use of poisons commonly called on magical practices as well, such as the use of amulets, incantations, and spells.[13]

The Hippocratic tradition of medicine renounced any involvement with the procuring of abortions or euthanasia. The ancient Hippocratic oath of graduating physicians said:

> *I will neither administer a lethal drug* (φάρμακον θανάσιμον) *to anyone if asked to do so, nor suggest such a course of action; likewise, I will not give an abortifacient pessary* (πεσσὸν φθορίαν) *to a woman ... I will be chaste and religious in my life and practice.*[14]

There have been various attempts in recent decades to "retranslate" the Hippocratic oath in order to edit out its pointedly pro-life tenor. Ethical medicine, therefore, was solely for healing, not for killing—ever.

The distinction was not always clear between drugs intended as contraceptives and those which might act as early stage abortifacients. The Stoics in this respect had a bad influence. To them the baby *in utero* was like a plant, and only became an animal at birth on drawing its first breath. This view weakened ethical opposition to procured abortion. Dioscorides (first century AD) and Galen (second century AD) mention many plant products, taken orally or as vaginal suppositories used to provoke abortions. The physician Soranus of Ephesus (2nd century AD) advised on contraception, distinguished between miscarriage and

---

honey, to be placed in the uterus. The Ramasseum Papyrus IV reports that to prevent pregnancy, crocodile dung should be placed on moistened fibers, in the opening of the uterus. A recipe to prevent pregnancy in the Berlin papyrus is fumigation of the uterus with the seed of a particular grain." (Noonan, *Contraception*, 11)

12. *Pharmakeia* occurs in NT lists of reprehensible sexual behaviors: Galatians 5:19–21 *fornication, impurity, lewdness, idolatry, sorcery* (= *pharmakeia* using drugs to procure murder, sterility, abortion); Revelation 9:21 *nor did they repent of their murders or their sorceries* (= *pharmakeion*) *or their fornications*; Rev 21:8 *as for murderers, fornicators, sorcerers* (*pharmakois*), *idolators* . . .

13. The website advertising the Depo-Provera contraception injection is named "Pharmacia."

14. *Hippocrates*, 298–301 at 298–99.

procured abortion, and between contraception and abortion, justifying the latter if the woman's life is in danger (*Gynaeceia* 1.19.60, 1.20.59-65). Take note: he listed seventeen abortifacient and contraceptive recipes!

If contraception and abortion failed, there was always infanticide, if the baby were deformed, the result of rape or incest, an economic burden, or simply "surplus to requirements." Infanticide was not usually practiced by direct killing but by "exposing" the new-born infant to its fate. Greeks and Romans thought it noteworthy that Egyptians and Jews reared *all* the children born to them.

8.4 Human sacrifice and human blood-sport

Another feature of Roman culture making for the debasement of human life was the institution of *spectacula* or the public shows of murderous human blood-sport. The rationale of this cruelty was that its victims—slaves, vagrants, and criminals—were not "persons" in law. They had no "face," for such is the meaning of *persona*: having a public and legal *face*.[15] Since these unfortunates were destitute of civil dignity or legal protections, they were readily exploited as grist for the mill of public entertainment. The bloody theatre of staged human violence and murder gained traction in the early Principate until it became feature of urban life, a strong marker of coarsening public sensibilities.

The Carthaginians, great enemies of the Romans in the third century BC, were, as descendants of the Phoenicians/Canaanites, devotees of the god Moloch, and practiced human sacrifice.[16] According to Pliny, under the consuls Crassus and Lentulus (97 BC) the Romans proscribed human

---

15. One etymology of the Latin *persona* derives it from the Greek τὸ πρόσωπον, "face." The Hebrew for "face" is *pneh*. A major theme of Scripture is that of "the face" or "countenance," and the "look" or "gaze," above all the "face of God." Cf. Ps 6:6, Matt 17:2, and 2 Cor 4:6.

16. It should be remembered that the ancient Greeks also practiced human sacrifice, in the collective torture and execution of selected victims called *pharmakoi*, singular *pharmakos*. The paroxysm of collective violence that vents itself on an arbitrary victim recurs throughout Greek myths and plays, especially those reflecting the cult of Dionysos (e.g. Euripides' *The Bacchae*). "Before placing too much confidence in Nietzsche, our era should have meditated on one of the sharpest and most brilliant sayings of Heraclitus: 'Dionysos is the same as Hades.' Dionysos, in other words, is the same thing as Hell, the same thing as Satan, the same thing as death, the same thing as the lynch mob. Dionysos is the destructiveness at the heart of violent contagion." Girard, *I See Satan*, 120. Girard studies the "horrible miracle" of Apollonius of Tyana in 2nd century AD Ephesus, when he extemporized a *pharmakos* ritual against a poor blind beggar, in *I See Satan*, 49–61. It was six centuries after Socrates and Plato.

sacrifice. But in the end, the Romans were doing much the same thing, really.[17] Such cinematic epics as *Quo Vadis, Spartacus,* and *Gladiator* showcase this grim aspect of Roman "culture," to which many Christian martyrs fell victim, sharing so deeply and gloriously in the "non-person" status and the ignominy of our Lord before a Roman tribunal, and in his fate, and in his eternity.

8.5 Marriage in Roman Law

In this degraded moral scene, the many expressions in Roman literature that say a man takes a wife for the procreation of children acquire their significance. The institution of Roman marriage was ordered expressly to the establishment or continuance of a *familia* through the bearing of legitimate children—so much so that the very Roman word for marriage, *matrimonium,* derives from *mater,* or "mother." It means, in effect, "the state of making a mother."

There are two famous definitions of marriage in Roman law. Christians found them so impressive that they were later incorporated into both Greek and Latin canon law. The first is by the Roman jurist Ulpian (160–228 AD):

> *Nuptiae autem sive matrimonium est viri et mulieris coniunctio, individuam consuetudinem vitae continens* ("Marriage or matrimony is the union of a man and a woman, embracing a unique community of life."), Ulpianus, *Institutes* 1.9.1.

The second is by Herennius Modestinus (d. 244 AD), a student of Ulpian and the last great jurist of the classical era:

> *Nuptiae sunt coniunctio maris et feminae et consortium omnis vitae, divini et humani iuris communicatio* ("Marriage is the union of a male and a female and a partnership of the whole of life, a sharing of divine and human rights") *Digest* 23.2.1.[18]

---

17. In *de Spectaculis* 12 Tertullian equates the ancient human sacrifices and the grim public entertainments in the arena. To him these venues were infested with demons. "Both in scale and nature, the entertainments favored by the late Romans suggest a sensibility nourished by something more monstrous than just the common human appetite for playful malice. They speak of the very special sadism of the disinterested voyeur, and it is far from unreasonable to think that a culture that accepted such cruelty as a matter of course—and in fact as one of its principal sources of public or private entertainment—suffered from a fair degree of spiritual *ennui* or decadence." (Hart, *Atheist Delusions,* 133–34)

18. Cited in Pius XI, *Casti Connubii* no. 63.

David E. Fellhauer comments on these definitions:

> It was in some ways fortunate for the early Church to find itself situated in a society where the law of marriage was the Roman law. There was much about Roman marriage which the Church could readily accept. It was monogamous, in principle (at least) permanent, in design procreative. Roman marriage was ideally a complete community of man and wife, a *corporum coniunctio totius vitae,* which implied the duty of conjugal love. The Roman wife, unlike the woman in many other cultures, was accorded dignity and respect. The Church added, of course . . . its own notion of indissolubility. The Roman law definitions of marriage were themselves significant. The two celebrated formulations indicated explicitly an understanding of marriage as a unique conjugal community, an *individua consuetudo vitae.* The two definitions evidently describe more than the legal aspects of marriage, but rather marriage as an ethical and social reality. Perhaps it is partly for this reason that the Roman law definitions were destined to have a life of far greater duration than the culture from which they sprang.[19]

Although the ceremonies that grew up around Roman marriage had social and religious weight, it was not they that gave it legal force. A marriage was enacted when a man and a woman came to live together with the mutual intention of regarding each other as husband and wife. This disposition was called *affectio maritalis.* Mutual consent, therefore, and not consummation, made the Roman marriage. Moreover, if one or both parties were under *patria potestas,* the consent of the *paterfamilias* was also essential under law.

Patria potestas was the legal power held by a Roman citizen, the oldest living male, over his *familia,* which extended to all his descendants through the agnatic (male) line. Women held no comparable power. The *paterfamilias* had power of life and death over slaves and even over a newborn child; he chose whether to acknowledge and rear the child or not. The vigor of traditional *patria potestas* was already waning in the first two or three centuries AD. Fully fledged *matrimonium* involved the transfer of a woman from the *manus* (or hand) of her *paterfamilias,* to the *manus* of her husband or his *paterfamilias.* Although the *matrona,* Roman wife and mother, was in a subordinate position, she had considerable dignity as the chaste mother of legitimate children, the keeper of the keys, and the mistress of the domestic economy.

19. Fellhauer, "The *consortium omnis vitae,*" 17–18.

There was a flagrant gap between the moral standards expected of husbands and of wives. For a husband, "adultery" meant sexual relations with a married woman other than his wife. The offense was against the married woman's *husband*, not his own wife. A husband's sexual relations with an unmarried woman were tolerated, if not praised. The extramarital affairs of Julius Caesar on the one hand, and Pompey's renown for marital fidelity on the other, show that Romans were quite capable of noting marital virtue in a man. A wife's virtue, however, consisted in complete marital fidelity. For her, adultery consisted in sexual relations with *any* man, married or not, other than her husband. The offense was against her husband, and was grounds for divorce. The scandal surrounding Augustus' daughter Julia is a case in point. This double standard concerning adultery was not dissimilar to that also found in Jewish tradition.

If *affectio maritalis* ceased in one or both of the parties, the marriage was, in effect, at an end. No legal authority had to grant the divorce. In the case of unilateral divorce, the *repudium* was given orally, or in writing, or by a messenger, followed by separation and perhaps legal action to recover property, e.g. the wife's dowry. Initially only the husband or his *paterfamilias* could initiate a divorce, but under Augustus the right was extended to the wife. Children usually stayed with their father. There was an epidemic of divorces among the upper classes in the late Republic and early Principate, the marital career of Cato Uticensis and his second wife, Marcia,[20] being a case in point.

In order to stem the moral decay of which this rash of divorces was a symptom, and to above all to promote the procreation and rearing of children, Augustus enacted strict marriage laws.[21] His adultery law even gave *patres-familias* power to kill adulterous daughters taken in the act. These controversial laws led however to the development of the *concubinatus* (concubinate), an informal union of a man and a woman without *affectio maritalis* and *honor matrimonii*. A woman in such a union might not be under anyone's *potestas*. She might even be *sui iuris* and retain her own property. Since *matrimonium* between disparate classes, such as

---

20. When his first wife, Antistia, proved unfaithful, he divorced her and married Marcia, whom he divorced in turn so that his friend Hortensius could marry her. After Hortensius's death, Marcia returned to Cato.

21. The *lex Iulia de maritandis ordinibus* (18 BC), and the *lex Papia Poppaea* (9 BC). Together they are known as the *lex Iulia et Papia Poppaea*. I thank my colleague, Bronwyn Hopwood, for advice on Roman marriage legislation. See Hopwood, "The Good Wife," and Treggiari, *Roman Marriage*. On Roman Law, see Buckland and Stein, *A Text-Book of Roman Law*.

nobles and *plebs,* or citizens and slaves, was illegal or socially stigmatized, the concubinate, in such cases, was the resort.

8.6 The family household among the Greeks and the Romans

The pattern of the Graeco-Roman family does not differ too much from that of the Jewish family. The Greek family or household, οἶκος, while it had at its core the marriage and blood relationship of a nuclear family, was often enlarged as a stem family with the inclusion of grandparents, and as an extended family with the inclusion, most commonly, of unmarried female relatives, such as aunts, sisters, nieces and cousins. The household, especially among the aristocracy, might also include non-blood relatives as its members: servants or slaves, guests, even workers on far-flung estates. The aristocratic household could be quite a ramified and complex institution. Some slaves, such as teachers of the children, had a higher status than others. The father, or, in his absence, the senior male of the household, such as the eldest resident son, was *kyrios,* or head of the household, and took charge of official relations with the outside world. Widows sometimes took over that role, and did it very well.

Most of this applies to the Roman family, with the added note of the *patria potestas,* as mentioned above. The coercive power of an upper-class Roman family over any of its members was very great, since the standing of the *familia* was woven into the political fabric of the Roman Empire. It was a serious moral, social, and economic enterprise, a complex stem and extended family, laden with symbolic status and governed by protocol and duty. King George VI's private "joke" of calling the British royal family "the firm," is instructive. Not a few Christian saints in the early centuries had sometimes to show great tenacity to pursue the claims of God when opposed to the interests of their family. On the other hand, the nature of the Roman family could also work in favor of evangelization, especially when the mother of the household turned to faith in Christ. The importance of these influential *matrones,* or *matres-familias,* for the spread of Christianity in the first centuries can hardly be overstated.

8.7 The philosophers

We have seen how Roman law built a bulwark around *matrimonium.* Other cultural salvages are also to be found in the Graeco-Roman traditions. Genesis showed us how in the midst of man's degradation after the

Fall the Spirit of God still found those who would respond to him; so in the world of Greece and Rome, there were those who thought deeply on ultimate questions and sought a better way. They might be quite ordinary, private people, who acquitted themselves of devoted marriages and an honorable family life according to their lights, as we see attested in surviving epitaphs and inscriptions.[22] Then there were the philosophers.[23] Some of their ideas and terms we have to be aware of, because their seminal influence.

Important philosophic schools of classical Antiquity were Pythagoreanism, Platonism, Aristotelianism, Cynicism, Epicureanism, Stoicism, and Neoplatonism. As for their impact on Christian discourse, we can rule out Cynicism and Epicureanism from the start, except that Cynicism did supply some useful diatribes against the pagan gods. Although Aristotle was known and used by the Church Fathers, especially for his contributions to formal logic, the "Stagirite" as he was known, had limited appeal in the early church, except to heretics.

> O wretched Aristotle, who invented for these [Valentinus and other Gnostic intellectuals] dialectic: a pretended art (*artificem*) of building up and pulling down, subtle in its proposals (*verisipellem in sententiis*), strained in its conjectures (*coactam in conjecturis*), relentless in its arguments (*duram in argumentiis*), laborious in its disputes (*operarium contentionum*)—a vexation even to itself, reexamining everything, lest it actually settle on anything (*omnia retractantem ne quid omnino tractaverit*)![24]

---

22. Two examples: in the time of Trajan, an otherwise unknown Marcus Cocchius inscribed a monument to his wife "cum qua vixit annos xxxv diebus xi sine querela" ("with whom he lived for thirty-five years and eleven days without a harsh word"). It is preserved in the porch of Santa Maria in Trastevere, Rome, in the lower right-hand corner of the right-hand wall. See Huntley, "The Earliest Church," 9. At the upper end of Roman society, there is the impressive testimony of a husband's enduring love for his wife, even in the case of childlessness, in the so-called *Laudatio Turiae*, epigraphic fragments of a husband's funeral tribute to his wife, from the early Augustan Age. See Hemelrijk, "Masculinity and Femininity."

23. In a philosophical dialogue, the Romanized Greek, Plutarch, extolled faithful monogamous marriage, and the erotic love of husband and wife. See Rist, "Plutarch's *Amatorius*."

24. Tertullian, *Liber de Praescriptionibus* 20A. In this famous chapter, Tertullian goes on to identify dialectic with *the unprofitable questions* of Titus 3:9 and *the words which metastasize like a cancer* of 2 Tim 2:17, and cites Paul's warnings against *philosophy and vain deceit* in Col 2:8.

Aspects of Pythagoreanism were subsumed early into Platonism, while Platonism itself informed the last of the philosophical schools: Neoplatonism. That leaves us essentially with two philosophies which helped form the discourse of early Church thinkers: Platonism and Stoicism.

How can I encapsulate Plato in one or two paragraphs? Plato, who notably elected a life of continence for the sake of philosophy, rejected the relativism, opportunism, and amorality of the contemporary Sophists, insisting on the objectivity and high transcendence of truth, and the necessity of practicing virtue as part of the intellectual quest of the truth. The approach has been called transcendental realism, for to Plato, the realm of absolute truth is more real than this phenomenal, sensible world, which has only a kind of limited, partial reality. He invoked a theory of "forms," the transcendent absolute source of such qualities as "beauty" or the various virtues, which are refracted partially and unevenly in this lower realm. He would say, for example, that a flower "can only be beautiful insofar as it partakes of absolute beauty."[25] As time went by, he thought in terms of a Form subsuming all forms: the Good, or the One, which was considered to be ἀκίνητος, unmoved; ἀμετάστατος, unchangeable, ἀπάθης, impassible or not subject to passion or suffering; ἀγενής, not subject to "becoming," all of which terms became commonly accepted in Christian theology as divine attributes.

The true human good lay in the purification and freeing of the soul that enabled it to participate in this noetic realm. Plato's famous parable of the soul's progress is the analogy of the cave in the *Republic*,[26] in which he shows how the trapped finite soul is impelled by the dynamism of *eros* to regain its ultimate home, facilitated by moral purification and *ascesis*. This *eros* he investigates in *the Symposium*. In a soul that knows its poverty, *eros* arises as a powerful attraction to the good, the true, the beautiful. While *eros* may be initially involved in sexual desire, it would be a sorry thing to leave it there. Its immense potential is unlocked by training (ascesis) in virtue, and realized in assimilation even to "the divine beauty."[27]

> Plato points out admirably in his *Phaedrus*—being in love constitutes the only truly awakened state, in which we break the fetters of indolence and cease dragging ourselves dully through life.[28]

25. *Phaedo* 100C. In *Plato: Euthyphro*, 344–345.
26. Plato, *The Republic* Book VII, 514A–518C. In *The Republic*, volume 2, 106–21.
27. τὸ θεῖον κάλον. Plato, *The Symposium* 211E. In *Plato: Lysis*, 172–209 at 206.
28. von Hildebrand, *Marriage*, 16. Cf. Plato *Phaedrus* 245AB, 249D, 251CD. In

Platonic thinking is marked by a sharp dualism between the "noetic" realm on the one hand (amenable only to contemplative intuition) and the realm of the senses and matter on the other, between the immortal higher soul and the mortal body. The *ascent* of the soul to the divine in Plato, had yet to meet the *descent* of God's *philanthropia* in Christ. All the aspirational élan of humans had yet to meet the scandal of the humility of God. Where Platonism *was* corrected by the Christian mystery of the Incarnation and its sense of sacramentality—indeed by the cross of our Lord Jesus Christ—it helped articulate the dynamic, and, indeed, to use my old term, anagogical qualities of Christian faith. Uncorrected, its hyper-spiritualizing had harmful effects. The Arianism that racked the church in the fourth century was largely an attempt to reframe the Holy Trinity along the sophisticated lines of Neoplatonist "emanationism."

To conclude with Plato, I cannot forbear telling one of my favorite stories from the desert fathers. There was once a monk who, in his cell, indulged himself in berating the pagan philosophers. He used to curse Plato in particular, until one day Plato appeared to him, and said: "Stop cursing me, man! You are only doing yourself harm. For you must know that when the Lord descended into Hades I was among the first to go forward to meet him."[29]

Stoicism was founded about 300 BC by Zeno and named after the *Stoa Poikile*, the painted portico in Athens. Late in the second century BC two of its exponents, another Zeno—*of Tarsus*—and Panaetius, brought this philosophy to the Roman elite, especially Scipio Aemilianus and his circle. Roman Stoicism was particularly focused on moral questions. Later wisdom writers, e.g., the book of Wisdom, and St Paul are sometimes said to have been influenced by Stoic discourse. It is a curious thing that at least three major Stoic philosophers are all surnamed "of Tarsus."

The god of the Portico is identified with *logos* or reason, with *physis* or nature, and with the material element of fire; this god generates the world from itself through λόγοι σπερμάτικοι, seminal or generative "reasons" and is itself the soul of the world. For the Stoics, the entire universe is animate, rational, and divine. Thus, it is pantheist and materialist in tenor, although what one might paradoxically call it a "spiritualizing materialism." The Stoic philosopher aims to live in harmony with "nature" (ὁμολογουμένως φύσει ζῆν, Chryssipus) or "the natural law." The guiding

---

Plato: *Euthyphro*, 468–69, 482–83, 488–89.

29. The story is told by St. Anastasius of Sinai, a seventh-century abbot of St. Catherine's, Sinai, in *Interrogationes et responsiones*, Question 111, PG 89, 764 B–D.

principle of nature is *logos* or the divine reason, which manifests itself as εἱμαρμένη, fate or necessity, and πρόνοια, divine providence. Yet human action is free and responsible. Some ingenuity is spent on reconciling these apparent opposites: fate and individual moral responsibility. To be wise and to be virtuous, that is, to live in accord with reason, is the only essential good, *not* to be virtuous the only evil—no other considerations affect our happiness, but must be treated as ἀδιάφορον, indifferent. So interconnected are the virtues that to truly possess one is to possess all. The wise man is known for his ἐγκράτεια, his self-control—because he knows that pleasure is not a good or an end in itself—and for his ἀπάθεια, freedom from passions, and for his αὐτάρκεια, self-sufficiency, all terms of moral philosophy with a future in Christian discourse.

Platonism and Stoicism were melding together even as Christianity began:

> Middle Platonism is the Stoicized form Platonism had taken from the beginning of the first century BC, which provides the intellectual background of many of the Fathers and is the form in which the idea of the soul's ascent to God is understood.[30]

8.8 Pagan civilization: darkness and half-lights

We have had to dwell on certain aspects of the Gentile civilization in which Christianity first made its way, so that we might see where the light of the Gospel most needed to shine. This was a society which offered plenty of scope for "base practices." In the public sphere, there was slavery and human blood-sport, prostitution, the tolerance of "fornication" for married men, homosexuality in all the array of its manifestations, an industry of contraceptive and abortifacient drugs, magic, infanticide. In the face of this moral darkness, we noted three monuments to the capacity of man to approach some standard of the good—in scriptural terms, to live the covenant of Noah.

Firstly: in the midst of the pan-sexual swamp, Roman law unsentimentally demarcated and strictly protected the institution of *matrimonium*. Without any Judaeo-Christian input, pagans were quite capable of figuring out the primordial and self-evident truth: marriage is a stable bond of common life between one man and one woman, ordered to

---

30. Louth, *The Origins*, 17.

bringing forth children from that union, protecting them, and rearing them in a family.

Secondly: the Hippocratic tradition of medicine. It is as if Hippocrates, who was no more than a child of the covenant of Noah, by the light of a healthy natural reason, somehow intuited the stern choice put to Israel: *I have set before you life and death, blessing and curse; choose life therefore, that you and your descendants may live* . . . (Deut 30:19). Hippocrates chose *life* for the medical art, because "the *medical*, by definition, *remediates*,"[31] and hence must never use its skills to destroy a human life. Nevertheless, it was deemed needful to make this commitment to life explicit in a religious vow administered to graduating physicians, for the ancient culture of death and negotiable expediency was after the souls of physicians in his day.

Thirdly: the thinkers of antiquity, the philosophers, worked out a moral and spiritual critique of human behavior and an account of the higher end of human life. Though they had yet had to discover the Creator and the creature, the divine *philanthropia* and the light of Christ to fallen man, the best of them encouraged man to aspire *upwards*, to reach for something surpassingly lofty: a transcendent Good, True, and Beautiful, whose name, and the measure of whose love and grace, they did not yet know.

---

31. Esolen, "Belial's Witness."

Chapter Nine

THE APOSTOLIC FATHERS AND THE APOLOGISTS

9.1 Asking the Fathers

WE NOW TURN TO the earliest sources of the Christian tradition after the apostles, the Fathers of the Church, in order to discover the witness borne by the early church to the Gentile world. The early centuries of the church are sometimes called the *Patristic* era, after the *Patres*, or *Fathers* of the Church, the great teachers and theologians of the church. They were called *Fathers*, because most of them—though not all—were bishops, bearers of apostolic office.[1]

St Vincent of Lerins, in his *Commonitorium* (434) says that the Church Fathers are *those alone, who, though in diverse times and places, yet persevering in the communion and faith of the one Catholic Church, have been approved as teachers.*[2] They are known, therefore, for orthodoxy of doctrine. The church was saved from shipwreck in severe doctrinal crises thanks to the great Fathers raised up at the time, such as the proverbial St Athanasius.

They were also known for holiness of life. After all, the first duty of the apostle was *prayer*, even before *the ministry of the word* (Acts 6:4),

---

1. In the early church, *Father* was the proper address of bishops, not of presbyters; similarly in the early Latin west *sacerdos* was more used for the bishop than the presbyter.

2. Quasten, *Patrology* vol. 1, 9–12, draws on Vincent of Lerins, Jerome, and Pope Gelasius for the notes of a genuine Father: orthodox doctrine, holiness of life, church approval, and antiquity.

following the pattern set by Jesus himself in the days of his flesh. As familiars of the Holy Spirit breathed by the Lord Jesus upon his church as he expired on the cross, and again on the first day of the resurrection, and at Pentecost, they participated in the *paradosis* ("handing on," "passing on") of the Mystery of God in Christ, from Christ to the apostles, and from the apostles to all believers.

They are also known for their approval by the church, especially in the general councils, and by the use of their doctrinal testimony in the *magisterium* of the church both East and West. Sometimes it happens that a Church Father is a little "off-center" in one or other aspect of his teaching, by some overemphasis here, or some shortfall there, or an unfortunate expression somewhere else. The same is true of the doctors of the church who succeeded the Fathers at a later period. And is this not true of most of us, including the present author? So it is important always to see the Fathers as inserted into and complemented by the whole *ecclesia* and her tradition. They, as teachers in the Church, are, first and foremost, children *of* the Church.

The Fathers have a further significance for the distressed, weakened situation of the church in the West today. We need to recover the *spirit* of the Church Fathers. It is not just a question of *what* they taught, but *how* they thought and prayed towards the Lord, their *phronesis*. *The theologian,* said Evagrius of Pontus, *is one who truly prays.*[3] Their thinking and teaching is born at best of a prayerful and ecclesial disposition. Scriptural exegesis, dogmatic and moral teaching, and even political life flows from and leads back to participation in the Mystery of Christ, above all in the Liturgy. This is very much the sapiential quality of the Gospel of John we noted in an earlier chapter. Finally, a word of exhortation from Pope John Paul II, given at Rome on October 30, 1993:

> The development of patristic studies is close to my heart, for there can be no true formation of Christian understanding without constantly drawing on the tradition of our Fathers in the faith. As I said at the beginning of my pontificate in the Apostolic Letter, *Patres Ecclesiae*, "the Church never tires of returning to their writings, full of wisdom and incapable of ageing—and of renewing their memory continually . . ."[4]

---

3. Evagrius, *Chapters On Prayer*, 61: "If you are a theologian, you will pray truly; and if you truly pray, you will be a theologian."

4. Quoted by Claire Russell, *Glimpses*, xix. See also John Paul II, Apostolic Letter *Patres Ecclesiae* on the sixteenth centenary of the death of Saint Basil the Great, January 2, 1980.

9.2 The Apostolic Fathers: St Ignatius of Antioch

We begin with the Apostolic Fathers, who were contemporaneous with the later writings of the New Testament or with the generation or two after the apostles. They had either known the apostles themselves or were nurtured in churches that preserved their recent living memory. Such was St Ignatius of Antioch, third bishop of Antioch after Evodius and St Peter himself. Coming from the city where we were first called "Christians," he is the first to speak of "the Catholic Church."[5] Ignatius had known the Apostle John himself, who lived to about 100 AD, and himself died in the arena in Rome a mere ten or twelve years later. This is *very* early in the church's tradition. In his *Letter to Polycarp*, bishop of Smyrna and martyr, also a familiar of the Apostle John, Ignatius appeals:

> Flee from base practices (κακοτεχνίας), and preach more strongly against them. Speak to my sisters that they love the Lord, and be content with their life partners (συμβίους) in flesh and spirit. In like manner, exhort my brothers in the name of our Lord Jesus Christ to *love their wives as the Lord loved the Church* (Eph 5:25). If anyone is able to remain in continence (ἐν ἁγνείᾳ μένειν) to the honor of the flesh of the Lord, let him remain so without boasting. If he boasts, he is lost; and if he is more recognized than the bishop, he is ruined. It is proper for men and women who wish to marry to be united with the approval of the bishop (μετὰ γνώμης τοῦ ἐπισκόπου), so that their marriage may be *according to the Lord* (1 Cor 7:39), and not according to lust (ἐπιθυμίαν). Let all things be done to the honor of God.[6]

Notable here is the centrality of the episcopacy, of which Ignatius is eloquent elsewhere. He uses the family language of the early Church: "my sisters" and "my brothers." Since he is speaking of marriage, the κακοτεχνίας, "base practices," or "evil arts" refer to magic practices and "sorceries," i.e. the malevolent use of drugs. He exhorts husbands and wives to exclusive fidelity, citing St Paul on marriage as the image of Christ's love for his church.

---

5. St Ignatius of Antioch, *Letter to the Smyrnaeans* 8.2, Lake, trans., *Apostolic Fathers* vol 1, 250–67 at 260–61.

6. St Ignatius of Antioch, *Letter to Polycarp* 5, Lake, trans., *Apostolic Fathers* vol. 1, 266–77 at 272–73; ANF I, 100; cf. the Syriac version of the *Letter to the Philadelphians* 4, ANF I, 81.

Marriage at this stage was transacted according to civil custom. What gave it its Christian character was that the partners were baptized believers of the church. We see Ignatius asserting its ecclesial character by requiring the Christian bride and groom to seek their bishop's approval.[7]

Ignatius attests the practice of life-long virginity for the Lord in the earliest Christian communities, and the honor that attaches to it. He admonishes those unmarried for the Lord to humility in relation to their married brethren. He warns that, just as Christian marriages properly take place with the bishop's approval, so also, virgins and celibates must keep to their right order in the church through communion with their bishop.

Finally, a perennially timely word on those who would undermine the Christian family with alien practices:

> Make no mistake, my brethren: corrupters of families (οἱ οἰκοφθόροι, cf. Prov 6:19) will not inherit the kingdom of God. If those who have practiced such things according to the flesh have died (εἰ οὖν οἱ κατὰ σάρκα ταῦτα πράσσοντες ἀπέθανον), how much worse will it be if someone corrupts through evil teaching the faith of God for which Jesus Christ was crucified. Such a one will go in his foulness *into the unquenchable fire* (Mark 9:43), as also anyone who listens to him.[8]

9.3 The Didache and the Letter of Barnabas

Another very ancient document is the *Didache*. Either the document itself or the sources embedded in it may go back to the first century. Its latest date of redaction is c. AD 140. Such is the value of this testimony: it expresses the moral mind and practice of the church at a very early stage, outside the scriptural record:

> The second commandment of the teaching: You shall not murder. You shall not commit adultery, you shall not seduce boys (παιδοφθορήσεις), you shall not commit fornication, you shall not steal, you shall not practice magic (μαγεύσεις), you shall not use poisons (φαρμακεύσεις), you shall not murder the child

---

7. It was not till the ninth century in the East, and the eleventh century in the West, that the church took over from civil society complete jurisdiction over the celebration of marriage for Christians.

8. St Ignatius of Antioch, *Letter to the Ephesians* 16, in Lake, trans., *Apostolic Fathers* I, 190–91.

by abortion or kill it when it is born (οὐ φονεύσεις τέκνον ἐν φθορᾷ οὐδὲ γε[ν]νηθὲν ἀποκτενεῖς) . . .

But the way of death is this: First of all it is evil and full of cursing: murders, adulteries, lusts, fornications, thefts, idolatries, magic arts (μαγεῖαι), poisonings (φαρμακίαι) . . . murderers of children, aborters of God's handiwork (φθορεῖς πλάσματος θεοῦ).[9]

Here then is a direct confrontation of that spectrum of vices described in the last chapter. And how strangely modern it sounds! In this ancient text, the church reveals herself as unapologetically pro-life from the outset; she repudiates the use of contraceptive drugs, procured abortion and infanticide, and the sexual abuse of children; she defends the sanctity of human life in the womb. How did Christians define themselves in relation to the corrupt morals of surrounding society? By *refusing* to "adapt" culturally at all.

This text demonstrates that the church opposed contraception from her very beginning. Contraceptive practices are covered by the term φαρμακεία and its cognates, itself but one of a raft of immoral practices touching life and sexuality. In taking this position the Apostolic Fathers are in direct continuity with the New Testament. There, the term φαρμακεία is used three times: Gal 5:19–21, Rev 9:21, and Rev 21:8. The very list in which it occurs in Galatians is instructive: *fornication, impurity, lewdness, idolatry, sorcery (pharmakeia)*.

On abortion, the language could hardly be clearer. The unborn is expressly called a "child," and "God's handiwork," i.e., that which is "being fashioned" by God in the womb. Procured abortion is bluntly named murder. Note too, that the corrupting of boys for sexual purposes is condemned. That is the primary meaning of παιδοφθορήσεις though it would also include the selling of boys or girls into the prostitution industry. A passage from St Justin Martyr, *First Apology* 27 suggests as much. Justin was what is called an *apologist*, and also the first philosopher in Christianity. He describes the Christian attitude to the common practice of exposing new-born infants:

But as for us, we have been taught that to expose newly-born children is the part of the wicked. This we have been taught lest we do anyone an injury, and lest we should sin against God, firstly, because we see that almost all so exposed—not only the

---

9. The *Didache* 2.1, 5.1, 2; Jurgens, ed., *The Faith* I, 2, *ANF* VII, 377; Lake, trans., *Apostolic Fathers* vol 1, 310–13, 316–19.

girls, but also the boys, are brought up to prostitution . . . and again we fear to do so, lest some of them not be picked up, but die, and we become murderers.[10]

Further evidence of the early Church's stance on pro-life issues is found in the so-called *Letter of Barnabas,* dating from the late first or early second century.[11] We find much the same list of abominations as in the *Didache.* Evidently such lists were a catechetical *vademecum* of the time. The author adds a few notes. After mentioning the seducing of boys, he adds: "you shall not let the word of God issue from your mouth in any kind of impurity." So much was required of any Christian: not to combine any kind of depraved behavior while maintaining some kind of a Christian show, least of all in the liturgy. The author bids parents not to withdraw their hand—that is, their acknowledgment and protection—from a newborn child, but to rear it in the fear of the Lord. That ruled out for Christians the use of the *patria potestas* over the life or death of the newborn. It also points to the role of Christian parenthood in rearing their children, not for this world only, but for God.

One cannot omit the following short but electric statement from the beautiful *Letter to Diognetus,* dating from the mid-second century:

> [Christians] marry, like everyone else, and beget children, but they do not cast away that which is begotten (οὐ ῥιπτοῦσι τὰ γεννώμενα). They have a common table, but not a common bed. Their lot is "in the flesh," but they do not *live according to the flesh* (Rom 8:5). They pass their days upon earth, yet their *citizenship is in heaven* (Phil 3:20).[12]

Christians "do not cast away that which is begotten!" We see how the apostolic fathers and apologists speak of the baby in the womb as "child," "that which is begotten," and "God's handiwork," or "God's fashioning."

9.4 Hermas

Now for the oldest post-scriptural exposition of the Matthaean exception clauses, found in *The Shepherd,* by Hermas. According to the Muratorian

---

10. St Justin Martyr (c. AD 100–155), *First Apology* 27, 29. In ANF I, 172.

11. *Epistle of Barnabas* 19, 20, Lake, trans., *Apostolic Fathers* vol 1, 404–7; ANF I, 148, 149.

12. *Epistle to Diognetus* 5, Lake, trans., *Apostolic Fathers* vol 2, 350–79 at 360–61; ANF I, 26.

Fragment, Hermas was a brother of Pope St Pius I, which would place his work approximately in the 140s. A devout married man, he was grieving over his children's loss of the faith and their degenerate behavior. Is there anything new? His subjects are practical and moral issues, but he writes in a visionary and apocalyptic genre, like the book of Revelation. The authority of *The Shepherd* was so high that it was regarded in some quarters as scriptural—it is appended to the Scriptures in the Codex Sinaiticus— until the church began to define the canon of Scripture more closely from the late second century.

In the following passage Hermas asks whether Christians can divorce and remarry. The "Shepherd" here, is the Angel of Repentance.

> I said to the Shepherd, "Sir, permit me to ask you a few questions." "Speak," he said. "Sir," said I, "if someone has a wife who is a believer in the Lord, and he discovers her in some adultery (ἐν μοιχείᾳ), does the husband sin if he cohabits with her?" "As long as he is ignorant', said he, "he does not sin, but if the husband knows her sin, and the wife does not repent, but continues in her fornication (τῇ πορνείᾳ), and the husband cohabits with her, he makes himself a partner to her sin and an accomplice in her adultery."
>
> "In that case, sir," said I, "what shall the husband do, if his wife persists in this passion (ἐπιμείνῃ τῷ πάθει τούτῳ)?" "Let him dismiss her (ἀπολυσάτω αὐτὴν)," he said, "and let the husband remain by himself (ἐφ' ἑαυτῷ μενέτω). *But if having dismissed his wife he marries another, he himself also commits adultery* (καὶ αὐτὸς μοιχᾶται, Mark 10:11)."
>
> "If then, sir," said I, "after the wife is dismissed, she repents and wishes to return to her own husband, is she not to be taken back?" "Indeed! (καὶ μὴν)," he said, "if the husband does not take her back, he sins and brings great sin upon himself. It is necessary, in fact, to take back the sinner who repents, but not repeatedly, for the servants of God have only one repentance. It is in view of repentance, then, that the husband is obliged not to marry another. And this is the practice enjoined on both husband and wife alike."
>
> "Not only," he continued, "is it adultery if someone defiles his own flesh, but whoever does the same things that the heathens do, also commits adultery. If anyone continues in such practices and does not repent, depart from him and do not cohabit with him; for otherwise you will be a partaker in his sin. It was enjoined on you, however, to remain by yourselves (ἐφ' ἑαυτοῖς), whether husband or wife, because in such cases

repentance is possible. I, therefore," he said, "am giving no occasion for this practice be terminated; rather, it is in order that the one who has sinned, may cease to sin. And for the former sin there is One who can give healing, for it is He who has power over all."[13]

This is the case: a Christian husband who divorces his wife may not remarry, even in the worst case, when his wife persists in adultery.[14] He is not to be indulged with a bit of fornication—because after all he has his sexual needs, and we can't have him condemned to chaste singlehood, for which he may not be "suited." No, with the Angel of Repentance we must look for another discourse. And why? Because the model of spouses is Christ; their marriage is enfolded in him. If the worst happens between husband and wife, the Image, the Pivot, the Source still holds steady. The Shepherd actually thinks Christ is going to mean that much to a Christian. Thus he allows only "separation from bed and board." Christian spouses therefore may separate, for dire reasons, but must remain single. The Gospel of Mark is quoted in support of this strictness. In fact, marital intercourse with a spouse who is *known* to be continuing in adultery or other unspecified "base practices," is itself sinful. Confirming our earlier discussion of terms, Hermas interchanges the use of μοιχεία (adultery) and πορνεία (licentiousness or unchastity).

What is asked of the wronged party is, above all, a tenaciously Christian spirit. Is such steadfast marital forgiveness *possible*? Need one remind oneself of the breathtaking example of the prophet Hosea? Charity for his or her spouse and a desire for the spiritual good of the sinning spouse governs his or her choices. He or she must take back a repentant spouse—indeed not to do so is a great sin. Hermas offers a profound thought that as marriage reflects the mystery of the church in relation to Christ, so the readiness of a wronged spouse to forgive even the grave offense of the other, if it is repented, reflects Christ's own healing power and the church's administration of the keys.[15]

13. Hermas, *The Shepherd* 4.1. Cf. Lake, trans., *The Apostolic Fathers*, II, 1–305 at 78–81.

14. See also Justin Martyr, *First Apology* ch. 15, entitled "What Christ himself taught." Referring to Christians who remarry according to the civil law he says: "So that all who by human law are married, are in the eyes of our Master, sinners, and those who look upon a woman to lust after her."

15. See Arendzen, "Ante-Nicene Interpretations." This study highlights the widespread early Christian aversion to *digamy,* a second marriage even after the death of a spouse.

9.5 The Apologists

We find a remarkable confirmation of the practice attested by Hermas in the *Second Apology* of St Justin Martyr (100–165). Chapter Two outlines the case of a pagan husband and wife, both of loose moral habits. She however comes to the faith of Christ, turns her conduct to "sobriety," and, naming Christ, valiantly strives to persuade her husband to the same. She holds out for a while hoping for his reform. He brazenly continues his whoring. She eventually resorts to a *repudium* (civil divorce), lest by sharing his table and bed she become complicit with his vices. He "gets back" at her by delating her to the authorities as a Christian; legal reprisals follow, and martyrdoms. Three points: she deemed it her duty to separate from a persistently adulterous husband, without her own remarrying; the Christian wife as well as a husband rightly so acts; and that truly faithful Christian discipleship might cost us the ultimate in witness.

That her resort to a *repudium* did not mean that a Christian might remarry, Justin's *First Apology* chapter 15 makes clear. He distinguishes between what is allowed in Roman law, and what Christians do. Following several scriptural citations, Justin affirms that they who divorce and marry a second time "according to human law," are, in the eyes of our Master, sinners.

Finally, in *First Apology* 29, Justin asks why do Christians marry?

> We Christians either marry, with but one thought, to bring up children, or if we decide not to marry, we are completely continent.... that you may understand that promiscuous intercourse is not one of our mysteries.

Athenagoras of Athens (c.130–c.190), in his *Embassy* or *Plea for the Christians*, written 176–180, sets out the beliefs and practices of Christians before the Emperor Marcus Aurelius and his son Commodus. He rebuts the popular slanders against Christians with a series of *a fortiori* arguments: we certainly do not do *that*, because we will not even allow *this*.[16] Thus Christians certainly do not use the divorce and remarriage

---

16. E.g., he defends Christians from the charge of murder by explaining their horror at abortion: "When we say that those women who use drugs to bring on abortion commit murder and will have to give an account to God for the abortion, on what principle should we commit murder? For the same person would not regard that which is begotten in the womb as a created being, and therefore an object of God's care, and then, when it has passed into life, kill it. Nor would the same person avoid exposing an infant, because those who expose them are liable for child-murder, then,

available in Roman law[17] because they will not marry a second time even after the death of a spouse:

> With us, one either abides as one was born, or in a single marriage (ἢ ἐφ' ἑνὶ γάμῳ), for a second is decorated adultery (εὐπρεπής ἐστι μοιχεία). *He who dismisses his wife,* He says, *and marries another commits adultery* (Mark 10:11, Luke 16:18), allowing a man neither to dismiss her whose virginity he ended, nor to marry again afterward (οὔτε ἐπιγαμεῖν). For whoever, divesting himself of his first wife (ὁ ἀποστερῶν ἑαυτὸν τῆς προτέρας γυναῖκος), even if she has died (καὶ εἰ τήθνηκε), is a cloaked adulterer (παρακεκαλυμμένος ἐστι μοίχος), who on the one hand side-steps (παραβαίνων) the hand of God—since *in the beginning* God fashioned one man and one woman—and on the other, dissolves that union of the flesh with flesh that is for [marital] intercourse leading to the fellowship/communion of family (λύων δὲ τὴν σάρκα πρὸς σάρκα κατὰ τὴν ἕνωσιν πρὸς μίξιν εἰς τοῦ γένους κοινωνίαν).[18]

This passage attests the strong early Christian aversion to the practice of διγαμία or *digamy,* i.e. a second marriage even after the death of one's spouse—serial bigamy as it were—because marriage *in the Lord* (1 Cor 7:39) was held to imitate the strict monogamy (= marrying once only) of the first creation. *A fortiori,* such Christians will scarcely "marry" a second time while a first spouse is still alive.[19]

---

on the other hand, when it has been reared, destroy it." *Embassy for the Christians* 35, ANF II, 147. Translation is adapted.

17. That the ante-Nicene and post-Nicene Fathers maintained the gospel and apostolic teaching on Christian marriage against the provisions for divorce and remarriage in Roman law, see Crouzel, "Divorce and Remarriage," 476–77. "This Christian conception is already clear at the end of the second century in Tertullian's *Ad Uxorem* II, VIII, 6, and revolutionizes the idea of marriage: indissolubility is the consequence explicitly drawn from it. After this, how does one maintain that Christians could not have a notion of repudiation different from that of Roman law?" (477)

18. Athenagoras, *Embassy for the Christians,* 33. PG 6, 965–68. ANF II, 146–47 renders the difficult last clause: "and dissolving the strictest union of flesh with flesh, formed for the intercourse of the race." Arendzen, "Ante-Nicene Interpretations," 232, translates: "He transgresses the precept of God, for in the beginning he created *one* man and *one* woman, and he breaks the union and bond of the flesh for sexual intercourse."

19. There is a striking example of the same thinking two centuries later, in St Gregory of Nyssa's *Life of Macrina* (written 381). When Macrina was twelve, her father arranged for her future betrothal to a young man, who died before the betrothal could take place. She exploited her father's prior decision, in order to prosecute her resolve

Like Justin, Athenagoras expands on why Christians do marry:

> Possessing therefore the hope of eternal life, we despise the things of this life, even to the pleasures of the soul, each of us reckoning her as his wife whom he has married according to the laws laid down by us, and that only for the purpose of having children. For as the husbandman who has cast seed into the ground awaits the harvest, not sowing more upon it, so to us the procreation of children is the measure of our indulgence in appetite. Indeed, you would find many among us, both men and women, growing old unmarried, in the hope of living in closer communion with God.[20]

Athenagoras and Justin speak here for the perennial tradition: Christian marriage is ordered *definitively* to the procreation and nurture of children. One has to report a common mind of the Fathers of the Church on this point, be they eastern or western, Greek, Latin, or Syriac speaking, long before St Augustine ever had to answer the Manicheans' contempt for procreation: all concur that Christians enter the married state in order to bring children into the world and rear them.

Where there is scope for differing nuances is whether they treat the "unitive end" of marriage (following Pope Paul VI's *Humanae Vitae*), the good-in-itself of the union of the two spouses—and when they do address it, what value they place on it. For urgent reasons in our time, the church is having to discover anew and stress the importance of this unitive good of marriage—always, of course, inseparably from its procreative end. This, however, is not something new. Some wonderful testimonies to the unitive good of marriage are to be discovered among the Fathers, which we shall canvass shortly.

---

for virginity. She did so by citing the traditional Christian aversion to digamy, almost giving a theology of it: "when her parents brought her proposals of marriage—which often happened, due to the many who aspired to her hand because of the fame of her beauty—she would say that it was out of order and unlawful not to be loyal to the marriage that had been authorized for her once and for all by her father, and be put under pressure to consider another; since by nature marriage is but once only, as there is one birth and one death. She insisted that he who had been joined to her by her parents' decision had not died, but that in her judgment he was *alive to God* (Luke 20:38; Rom 6:11) through *the hope of the resurrection* (Acts 23:6), and was only away on a journey, not dead, and that it was out of order not to keep faith with one's bridegroom who had gone abroad." Silvas, *Macrina the Younger*, 114–16.

20. Athenagoras, *Embassy for the Christians*, 22, 23, 25, ANF II, 146–47. PG 6, 889–972.

9.6 Knowing herself to be in the world but not of it

We began by stressing the importance of Fathers of the Church as the witnesses to the church's tradition of the faith after the apostles. They are known for orthodoxy of doctrine, holiness of life, and subsequent approval by the church. We began to "ask the Fathers" about marriage and the family by turning first to the Apostolic Fathers who had personally known the apostles or lived in the generation immediately after them.

We found that these witnesses are *unashamedly* and confidently countercultural in matters of sexual morality. They document the early church's clear, determined, and specific response to the amoral practices of the Graeco-Roman society in which she found herself.

> "Christian norms simply ate through the fabric of late classical morality like an acid, without the least consideration for the well-worn contours of the old ways."[21]

In short, the church knew herself to be in the world but not of it. From the very beginning to live *in Christ* meant refusing the anti-life practices and the sexual licentiousness widely tolerated. Under the recurring terms —κακοτεχνίας, base practices, and φαρμακεία, drugs, including poisons used for murder, contraception, and abortion—St Ignatius, the Didache and the Letter of Barnabas flatly reject the use of devices for procuring sterility. Looking further to the Letter to Diognetus and the apologists Sts Justin and Athenagoras, we found that "that which is begotten" in the womb is called both "child" and "God's fashioning"; abortion is bluntly named murder—we "do not cast away that which is begotten," exclaims Athenagoras. Infanticide is repudiated; parents are exhorted to cover the newborn with their protection and to bring up their children in the fear of God. Horror is expressed at the sexual predation of children. Although weddings continue according to the civil rites, already in Ignatius' time it was normative that Christian bride and groom seek their bishop's approval.

We found that Hermas strongly upheld the indissolubility of marriage for Christian believers; the doctrine is tested in the hardest case: adultery by one of the spouses. Marriage, according to Hermas, is meant to convey the disposition of Christ's mercy, even towards grave sin, if it is repented. We then continued with the great apologists, Sts Justin and Athenagoras, who voice the universal tradition: Christians enter into

---

21. Harper, *From Shame to Sin*, 12.

marriage for the purpose of procreation and family, and so far from contemplating divorce and remarriage, they do not marry again even after bereavement ("digamy").

Our survey of the Apostolic Fathers reveals that in moral terms the world Christianity first met was not so dissimilar to what our liberal Western society has re-become in recent times. What we once thought "normal" was *never*, historically, to be presumed at all; it had to be fought for, and even died for. It was the outcome of centuries of the gradual Christianization of society. And what an immense historical and cultural achievement that was! We are now seeing a drastic unravelling of the moral economy of Western society, not less than its re-paganization, only this time the paganism will be worse than the old paganism. One thinks of the passage in the prophet Isaiah describing the "uncreation" of the land (24:1–13), the quickening dissolution into anomie and violence. Something like this looks to be happening to Western and indeed planetary society.

Chapter Ten

THE EARLY THEOLOGIANS

10.1 Encratism

BEFORE WE TAKE UP the great thinkers of the third century, we must consider a false teaching about marriage that vexed the early church: Encratism. The word comes from ἐγκράτεια, the very *self-control* or *self-mastery* listed by St Paul as one of the fruits of the Spirit (Gal 5:23). Applied to the sexual sphere, it can also imply continence or abstinence. The Stoics, as noted above, stressed this virtue. While Christians from the beginning esteemed virginity for the Lord, when this esteem became entangled with contempt for creation and matter, and indeed for the body, it could become an *ideological* rejection of marriage and procreation. Encratism might be thought of more as a wrong-headed hyper-ascetic enthusiasm than a distinct sect. It showed itself in some of the early heresies, the intellectualist ones, like Gnosticism, and the more emotivist ones like Marcionism and Montanism.

Tatian, a late second-century Syrian apologist active in Rome, was an encratist. He formulated a doctrine based on Adam's fall and damnation which was said to be passed on to the whole human race through procreation. As a consequence, procreation was to be regarded as a more than suspect activity for a Christian to be involved in. Tatian bequeathed to the early Syrian church an encratist tendency—in some quarters the conferral of Holy Baptism was considered tantamount to a vow of lifelong virginity or continence.

Encratism was also a mark of Manichaeism, a Persian gnostic religion which began to spread in the West in the third century AD.

"Manichaeism" is St John Paul II's code-word for Encratism. He means by it an attitude of contempt for the body and for the bodily union of husband and wife. Later enthusiasts like the Eustathians in mid-fourth-century Asia Minor, and their successors the Messalians in late fourth-century Syria, also had strong tendencies to encratism.

10.2 The Church Fathers' response to Encratism

St Irenaeus of Lyons (c. 140–202), Father of heresiology, stigmatised Encratism. He too is an example of the living *paradosis* of apostolic tradition: in his childhood he had listened to St Polycarp in Smyrna, who in his childhood had listened to St John. Taking his cue from the First Letter of St John, Irenaeus consistently brought heretical teachings to the bar of the Incarnation. He says:

> Those who are called Encratites preach against marriage, thus setting aside God's original creation and reproaching Him indirectly for making male and female for the propagation of the human race. Some of them have also introduced abstinence from animal food, thus proving themselves ungrateful to God who fashioned all things. They also deny that Adam, who was first created, was saved.[1]

It is admirable that the *Symposium* of St Methodius (260–312), written to commend virginity for the Lord, takes great care in its Discourse II, titled "Theophila," to lay a groundwork of respect for the godly work of marriage and childbearing.

The Canons of the Council of Gangra are found in all the major canonical collections, both East and West. In 340/341 a meeting of bishops in the capital of Paphlagonia discussed unsettling aspects of an enthusiast movement led by Eustathius of Sebasteia. They were concerned about its disparagement of married and family life. These are some of their conclusions:

> Canon I. If anyone finds fault with marriage, reviling and finding fault with her who sleeps with her husband, though she is a believer and devout, as if she were not able to enter the Kingdom, let him be anathema.

---

1. Irenaeus of Lyons, *Adversus Heraeses* 1.28.1.

> Canon 9. If anyone practising virginity or continence has withdrawn himself because he reviles the married state, and not on account of the beauty and holiness of virginity, let him be anathema.
>
> Canon 10. If anyone practising virginity for the Lord's sake exalts himself over those who are married, let him be anathema.
>
> Canon 14. If any woman forsakes her husband and would withdraw herself, because she reviles the married state, let her be anathema.
>
> Canon 15. If anyone forsakes his own children and does not nurture them and, as far as in him lies, brings them up in fitting habits of piety, but, on a pretext of asceticism, neglects them, let such a one be anathema.
>
> Canon 16. If any child, specially of the faithful, withdraws from his parents on a pretext of piety and will not pay the honor due to his parents, as if, indeed, piety had a higher claim on him, let him be anathema.
>
> Conclusion: We write these things not in order to cut out those in the Church of God who desire to practise asceticism according to the Scriptures, but rather those who make asceticism a pretext for pride, who exalt themselves against those who lead simpler lives and who introduce innovations contrary to the Scriptures and the Canons of the Church. For indeed, we, too, highly esteem virginity when joined with humility, and approve continence when practised with reverence and piety. We both approve withdrawal from worldly affairs, when practised with humility and at the same time honor the reverent cohabitation of marriage. . . . To sum up all in a word, we pray that there be observed in the Church all that is handed down by the divine Scriptures and the apostolic traditions.[2]

The great Fathers worked hard to tame an unruly ascetic enthusiasm. Most confronted Encratism by combining a defense of the goodness of marriage with an affirmation of the higher good of virginity for the Lord. The right balance was not always preserved. The soundest realized that the right way to commend virginity for the Lord was to affirm and expound the goodness of what virginity renounced. They often warn virgins and celibates against pride, a theme we saw appearing as early as

---

2. Translated from Mansi, *Sacrorum Conciliorum*, II, 1097–1106.

St Ignatius. In this connection Hebrews 13:4 was a constant reminder of the honor due to Christian marriage. It was received as an apostolic rule.

St Cyril, Bishop of Jerusalem in the mid-fourth century, and the great "mystagogue," or expounder of the sacred Liturgy, speaks to both states of life, beginning with a traditional warning to the virgins and celibates:

> As you maintain perfect chastity, do not be puffed up in vain conceit against those who walk a humbler path in marriage. As the Apostle says: *Let marriage be held in honor, and let the marriage bed be undefiled* (Heb 13:4). Besides, you who keep your chastity: were you not born of those who had married? Because you are in possession of gold, do not on that account hold the silver in contempt.

> So let those also be of good cheer who are married and use their marriage properly, who have entered marriage lawfully, and not from wantonness and unbounded licence, who recognize periods of continence so that they may give themselves to prayer (cf. 1 Cor 7:5), who in the assemblies bring clean bodies as well as clean garments into church, who have embarked upon the married state for the procreation of children, and not for the sake of indulgence.[3]

Down in Egypt, the great St Athanasius had to deal with Hieracas, leader of an influential community in Leontopolis in the delta region of the Nile. Slanderous of Christian marriage, he had a fierce virgins-and-ascetics-take-all idea of Christianity. Athanasius, a champion of monks if ever there was one—author of the *Life of Antony*—rebuked this outbreak of Encratism:

> Especially take courage and condemn Hieracas, who says that marriage is evil inasmuch as virginity is good. Thus it would have to be said that the sun is evil because the angel is more excellent, and that the human being is evil because the sun is more excellent . . . For the number sixty is not evil because the number one hundred is greater; rather it is good, but the other is better. For both are from the same seed: the one is great, the other greater.[4]

---

3. *Catechetical Lectures* 4.25; Jurgens, ed., *The Faith* I, 351.

4. On Hieracas, see Brakke, *Athanasius*, 44–47, and Goehring, "Hieracas of Leontopolis," in Goehring, *Ascetics, Society, and the Desert*, 110–33.

"Both are from the same seed." Now *that* is a thought to conjure with!

A later Greek Father, St John Damascene (AD 645–749), perfectly sums up the orthodox attitude of the church, both East and West:

> Virginity is the regime of the angels (τὸ τῶν ἀγγέλων πολίτευμα), the property of all bodiless nature. We say this without disparaging marriage, far be it! For we know that the Lord blessed marriage by His presence [at Cana], and him who said: *Marriage is honorable and its bed undefiled* (Heb 13.4), but we acknowledge that however good marriage may be, virginity is better (ἀλλὰ καλοῦ κρείττονα τὴν παρθενίαν γινώσκοντες).[5]

As a last example, let us have the great St Gregory the Theologian (329–389) who is of all the Fathers especially surefooted on marriage and family:

> *Marriage is honorable* (Heb 13:4); but I cannot say that is loftier than virginity; for virginity were no great thing if it were not better than something good. Now do not be irate at this you women who are subject to the yoke [of marriage]. We must obey God rather than man. But be bound together, both virgins and wives, and *be one in the Lord* (cf. Gal 3:28), and let each be the adornment of the other. There would be no unmarried (ἄγαμος) if there were no marriage. For how otherwise would the virgin have passed into this life? Marriage would not have been venerable unless it had born virgin fruit to God and for life.[6]

10.3 Tertullian (c. 155–240)

We now turn to the great Christian writers of the third century, the luminaries of the Ante-Nicene period, that is, Fathers and other prominent writers who flourished before the Council of Nicaea in 325.

Tertullian (155/60–240) was a prominent lawyer of Carthage in North Africa. On his conversion in the year 193 he brought his considerable gifts into the service of the faith. The Christian Latin tradition begins

---

5. *The Fountain of Knowledge* (c. AD 743) 3.4.24. The third part of the *Fountain* came down in the West as *De Orthodoxa Fide*. Translated from PG 94, col. 1209BC; see NPNF second ser. IX, 97.

6. *Oration* 37.10, *On Matthew* 19.1–12. Translation is adapted from NPNF second ser. VIII, 341.

with him. Jerome supposed him a priest, but that is uncertain. He was married, as the famous *Letter to his Wife,* from which we are about to hear, attests. Over the years Tertullian gave much thought to women, marriage, and the family, writing three treatises on marriage,[7] one on the dress of women, and one on the veiling of virgins.[8] His *Letter to his Wife,* was written as a spiritual testament in the event of his death. In this work is a passage called by Pope John Paul II in *Familiaris Consortio* a "deservedly famous page." Here is the passage, in full:

> How can we ever express the happiness of the marriage which the Church joins together, the Offering strengthens, the blessing seals, angels announce and the Father ratifies [*Unde sufficiamus ad enarrandam felicitatem eius matrimonii, quod Ecclesia conciliat, et confirmat oblatio, et obsignat benedictio, angeli renuntiant, Pater rato habet*]—for even on earth children do not rightly and lawfully wed without the consent of fathers? How wonderful the bond between two believers [*quale iugum fidelium duorum*], who are of one hope, of one discipline, of the same religious service! [*unius spei, unius disciplinae, eiusdem servitutis*] They are both brethren [*ambo fratres*] and both fellow-servants; there is no separation between them in spirit or flesh; in fact they are truly *two in one flesh* (Gen 2:24, Matt 19:5, Eph 5:31), and where there is but one flesh, there is but one spirit. Together they pray [*simul orant*], together they prostrate themselves [*simul volutantur*], together they undertake their fasts [*simul ieiunia transigunt*] (Matt 6.5,16), mutually teaching [*alterutro docentes*], mutually exhorting [*alterutro hortantes*] (Eph 5:19, Col 3:16), mutually supporting [*alterutro sustinentes*]. Side by side they are in the Church of God [*In ecclesia Dei pariter utrique*], side by side at the Banquet of God [*pariter in convivio Dei*], side by side they bear hardships, persecutions and consolations [*pariter in angustiis in persecutionibus, in refrigeriis*]. Neither conceals anything from the other, neither shuns the other, neither is troublesome to the other. The sick person is visited, the indigent relieved, in freedom (Matt 25:31). Alms are given without torment [*eleemosynae sine tormento*] (Matt 6:2), sacrifices made without scruple [*sacrificia sine scrupulo*]; daily diligence suffers no hindrance—no stealthy signings, no trembling greetings, no mute blessings. Psalms and hymns re-echo from one to the other [*sonant inter duos psalmi et hymni*] (Eph 5.19)—indeed

---

7. Tertullian, *To his Wife* (AD 200/206), *Exhortation to Chastity* (c. 212), *Monogamy* (217).

8. Tertullian, *On the Veiling of Virgins* (AD 200/206).

they challenge each other to see who shall sing to God more worthily [*et mutuo provocant, quis melius Deo suo cantet*]. When Christ sees and hears these things he rejoices. On such a couple he bestows his peace (cf. John 14:27), for where there are two together, He himself is there (Matt 18:20), and where He is, the Evil One is not.[9]

It would be difficult to find anything to surpass this in praise of the unitive good of marriage between two believers in the Lord. Note that by comparison with the Letter of St Ignatius, the Christian wedding is now firmly situated in a liturgical setting. Secondly, note the domestic liturgical life: Husband and wife chant the psalms and Scriptures from side to side in their own home.

Tertullian also notably bears witness to the Christian rejection of abortion. He is the heir of the apologists in a work which itself is called *Apology*:

> To us murder is forbidden once and for all; thus it is not lawful for us to destroy even that which is conceived in the womb (*etiam conceptum utero*), while as yet the blood is still being drawn on to form the human being. To hinder a birth is to hurry a murder (*homicidii festinatio prohibere nasci*). It makes no difference whether one takes away the life once it is born or destroys it in coming to birth. He is a human being who is becoming one; certainly the whole fruit is already in the seed.[10]

10.4 St Clement of Alexandria (c. 150–216)

A few hundred kilometers east of Libya, on the same southern coast of the Mediterranean lived a contemporary of Tertullian who went by a very Roman name: Titus Flavius Clemens. We know him as St Clement of Alexandria. Born in Athens, resident in the greatest Greek-speaking metropolis in the world, Clement wrote in Greek. In the early third century he was head of the catechetical school in Alexandria. He brought to

---

9. Tertullian, *To his Wife* 2.8.6–8. CCSL 1.393, ANF IV, 48. Partly cited in John Paul II, *Familiaris consortio*, no. 13.

10. *Apologeticum* 9. Translated from PL I, 257–536 at 319–20. Increasingly upset at the poor quality of the contemporary church, Tertullian in later life was sympathetic to the stricter discipline and spiritual fervor of the Montanists. In a work from this later period he excoriates Pope Callistus for what to him is a series of laxities and misuse of the power of the keys.

his work as an expositor of Christian doctrine a mastery of philosophy, poetry, mythology and literature, the Scriptures and the Christian and heretical writers. His willing use of the culture of the day in service of the gospel, we know, was not the line taken by Irenaeus, Theophilus or Tertullian. According to Quasten, "he proved that faith and philosophy, Gospel and secular learning, are not enemies but belong together." Quasten even calls him "the founder of speculative theology."[11]

Clement is an outstanding theologian in the field of sexuality, marriage, and family—indeed it is difficult to select what to quote from him, so much of it is worth hearing. So positive is his attitude to marriage and so attentive even to the bodily realities of marital union, pregnancy, and childbirth, that either he was married himself, or experienced in medical practice, or in pastoral work with the married.[12] He is not in the least prurient in discussing such matters.

His three major works follow a progressive pattern. The first, Προτρεπτικὸς πρὸς Ἕλληνας, *Exhortation to the Greeks*, aims to persuade the non-Christian to accept the revelation of the *Logos*, the divine Word; the second, Παιδαγωγός the *Tutor, Trainer,* or *Educator*, exhorts those who have embraced the Christian life to make progress; the third, Στρωματεῖς, *Stromateis* or *Stomata*, i.e. *Miscellanies*, points to the perfection of the life in Christ. The *Stromateis* is very long, somewhat haphazard work, almost like a journal in which Clement records the deep thoughts of his mind and heart.

There is a fair measure of both Stoic and Platonic elements in Clement. As noted earlier, it was the Stoics who gave great importance to the concept of natural law. Clement is committed, therefore, to elucidating the truth from a contemplation of nature. When he applies this to the consideration of human sexuality, he presents something reminiscent of Pope John Paul II's "theology of the body":

> There are others who approve of marriage. "Nature has made us," they say, "well fitted for marriage, as is clear from the fashioning of our bodies, which are male and female."[13]

---

11. Quasten, *Patrology* II, 7 and 20.

12. Possible evidence for Clement as a celibate is in *Stromateis* 3.7.59: "So we embrace self-control out of the love we bear the Lord, and out of its honorable status, consecrating the temple of the Lord." However, in this very context he holds "self-control" to be proper to the married as well: "If a man marries in order to have children he ought to practice self-control," 3.7.58.

13. *Stromateis* 2.23, PG 8, 1098A. Cf. "*On Marriage*," ANF II, 377–78.

From the natural provision and purpose of sexual intercourse he argues at length against the unnatural sexual act:

> Now not every field is primed for the reception of seed, and even if it were, not at the hands of the same husbandman. Seed should not be sown on rocky ground or outrageously scattered whereever (cf. Matt 13:3–24, Plato, *Laws* 8), for it is the primary substance of generation and possesses in itself the reasonings of nature. It is undeniably godless, then, to dishonor the reasonings of nature by wasting the seed irrationally on resting places contrary to nature . . .
>
> Hence it is manifestly and professedly clear to us that we must condemn the couplings of males (τὰς ἀρρενομιξίας), all fruitless sowing of seed (καὶ τὰς ἀκάρπους σπορὰς), inverse roles in bed, and unnatural androgynous couplings (καὶ τὰς κατόπιν εὐνὰς, καὶ τας ἀσυμφυεῖς ἀνδρογύνους κοινωνίας). We must follow rather nature itself, which obviously disapproves of such from her fashioning of bodily parts, having masculinized the male member, not for receiving seed, but for ejecting it (ἑπομένους τῇ φύσει αὐτῇ, ἀπαγορευούσῃ διὰ τῆς τῶν μορίων κατασκευῆς, οὐκ εἰς παραδοχὴν σπέρματος, εἰς δὲ τὴν πρόεσιν αὐτοῦ, τὸ ἄρρεν ἀνδρώσασα) . . .[14]

Clement goes on to link unnatural sexual couplings to contraception and abortion:

> Yet marriage itself merits esteem and the highest approval, for the Lord wished humanity to *be fruitful and multiply* (Gen 1:28). But he did not bid them "be licentious," or intend that they abandon themselves to pleasures, as though born only for sexual relations . . . To come together not for the generation of children is to outrage nature, which we should enroll as our teacher . . . The yearning to procreate children is marriage (γάμος δὲ ἡ παιδοποιΐα ὄρεξις), but the promiscuous scattering of seed contrary to law and to reason definitely is not. If we were to master our desires from above and not kill off the human race sprung into being from the divine providence, by means of vicious practices (μὴ κτείνουσί τε τὸ ἐκ προνοίας θεϊκῆς φυόμενον τῶν ἀνθρώπων γένος κακοτέχνοις μηχαναῖς), then our whole lives would unfold in accordance with nature. But those who resort to abortifacient drugs (φθορίοις συγχρώμεναι

---

14. *The Teacher* 2.10 (93), PG 8, 497B, 501C. Cf. Clement, *Christ the Educator*, 167.

φαρμάκοις) kill not only the embryo, but along with it, all human kindness (φιλανθρωπίαν).[15]

Clement here relays the Christian teaching that marriage exists most certainly for the sake of bringing children into the world, which he sees as so privileged a collaboration with God the Creator that it even makes spouses, in a way, god-like:

> It is time for us to consider why sexual intercourse is reserved only to those who have married. The goal of those who wed is the begetting of children, and its fulfilment is generous childbearing, just as the hope of a crop moves the farmer to plant his seed, while the fulfilment of that hope is in the harvesting of the crop. But he who sows in a living soil is far superior, for the one tills the land to provide food only for a season, the other to secure the preservation of the human race; the one tends his crop for himself, the other for God. We have received the command: *Be fruitful* (Gen 1:28) and we must obey it. In this role man becomes an ikon of God (εἰκὼν ὁ ἄνθρωπος τοῦ Θεοῦ γίνεται), when he cooperates with the bringing to birth of another human being.[16]

In another beautiful sample of the same teaching, Clement portrays the glory of this participation of spouses in God's creative power:

> The crown of the wife must be considered the husband (cf. Prov 12:4), while the crown of the husband is his marriage; and for them both the flowers of their marriage are their children, which are indeed the flowers that the divine Husbandman culls from the meadow of the flesh. *The crown of the old is their children's children and the glory to the children are their parents* (Prov 17:6), it is said. Our glory is the Father of all, and the crown of the Church is Christ.[17]

"The flowers of the marriage are the children born to them both." This brings us to Clement's loftiest utterance. The whole of *Stromateis* Book Three is devoted to the topic of marriage. In chapter ten Clement discusses various applications of our Lord's saying, *where two or three are gathered together in my name there am I in their midst* (Matt 18:20). As Tertullian did before him, Clement applies this to the family:

---

15. *The Teacher* 2.10 (95–96), PG 8, 512A,B. Cf. Clement, *Christ the Educator*, 173–4.
16. *The Teacher* 2.10 (83), PG 8, 497AB; Clement, *Christ the Educator*, 164.
17. *The Teacher* 2.8, PG 8, 480B; Clement, *Christ the Educator*, 154.

> Who are the *two or three who are gathered together in the name of Christ*, with whom the Lord himself is their center (Matt 18.20)? Are the three not husband and wife and child, since a wife is joined to her husband by God?[18]

On the recompense of those who nurture and bring up children for the Lord he says:

> For one who brings forth children in obedience to the Word, nurtures them, and educates them in the Lord, since he has parented children in the catechesis in the truth, a reward is laid up, as there is also for the elect seed.[19]

To Clement, the family household of husband, wife, and children is a fellowship of wayfarers upon the earth who are bound for eternity:

> We must indeed walk in harmony with reason. Even if we have a wife and children at hand, a household is no burden if it has but learned to follow in the company of the wayfarer who practices self-mastery. Invariably the wife who loves her husband will stay by his side, keeping to the journey. Both of them will be wayfarers carrying provisions best suited for the journey to heaven: moderation, as of footwear (cf. Matt 10:10), so also of the possession of the body.[20]

This passage brings out a major theme of Clement's teaching that should already be clear: the importance of the virtue of ἐγκράτεια, i.e. temperance, self-mastery. This virtue is not the particular province of the virgin, but very much part of the discipline of Christian marriage, not the least of the sexual relations of spouses.[21]

Flatly refuting Encratism, Clement affirms Christian marriage as a holy way of life:

> But if marriage that is according to the Law, is sinful—really I do not see how anyone shall say that he knows God, if he alleges

---

18. *Stromateis* 3.10, PG 8, 1169B. Cf. Jurgens, ed., *The Faith* I, 182; Clement (trans. Ferguson), *Stromateis*, 298.

19. *Stromateis* 3.15, PG 8, 1197BC. Cf. Clement (trans. Ferguson), *Stromateis*, 317–88.

20. *The Teacher* 3.7, PG 8, 609B. Cf. Clement, *Christ the Educator*, 231.

21. This the theme of *Stromateis* 3.7, *PG* 8, 1161–4. Cf. Clement (trans. Ferguson), *Stromateis*, 292.

that the commandment of God is sin. If *the Law is holy* (Rom 7:12), then marriage is holy (ἅγιος ὁ γάμος).²²

He elucidates how this personal sanctification is brought about in marriage:

> A marriage, therefore, that is consummated in obedience to the Word, is sanctified, if the union is subject to God, and conducted *with a true heart, in full assurance of faith, having hearts sprinkled from an evil conscience, and the body washed with pure water, for He is faithful who promised* (Heb 10:22). The happiness of a marriage ought never to be estimated by wealth or beauty, but by virtue.²³

He synthesizes several of the above themes in the following passage:

> It is unmanly and weak to avoid a life with wife and children. For the possession of something whose loss is an evil, is by all means a good, and this is so in general. But if, as they say, the loss of children is among the chiefest evils, then the possession of children is a good; and if this be so, so also is marriage. It is said "Without a father there never could be a child, and without a mother conception of a child could not be. Marriage makes a father, as a husband a mother" . . . Therefore every foul and polluting practice must be purged from marriage, so that we do not have the coupling of irrational animals cast in our teeth as more in accord with nature than human conjunction in procreation . . . Marriage therefore is pure, a kind of sacred image, which must be guarded from all that would defile it (καθαρὸν οὖν τὸν γάμον, ὥσπερ τι ἱερὸν ἄγαλμα, τῶν μιαινόντων φυλακτέον). We must rise with the Lord from our slumbers, and retire to sleep with thanksgiving and prayer, "both when you sleep and when the holy light comes," confessing the Lord by our whole life, possessing piety in the soul, and extending self-control to the body.²⁴

"It is unmanly and weak to avoid a life with wife and children." Clement urges the harnessing of masculine energies to the mature responsibilities of marriage and family. Notwithstanding, he maintains here and abundantly elsewhere, that the higher vocation is virginity for

---

22. *Stromateis* 3.12, PG 8, 1135A. Cf. Jurgens, ed., *The Faith* I, 182; Clement (trans. Ferguson), *Stromateis*, 309.

23. *Stromateis* 4.20, PG 8.1337A. Cf. Jurgens, ed., *The Faith* I, 185; ANF II, 543.

24. *Stromateis* 2.23, "On Marriage," PG 8, 1093A, C, 1096A. Cf. ANF II, 377–8.

the Lord. But then, virginity for the Lord is not the same thing as remaining fecklessly unmarried to escape responsibility:

> And one is not really shown to be a man in the choice of a single life; but he surpasses men who, without pleasure or pain, has disciplined himself by marriage, by the begetting of children, and by care for a household; who, in his solicitude for his household abides inseparable from God's love, and withstands all temptations arising through children and wife or through domestics and possessions. He, however, who is without a family (τῷ δὲ ἀοίκῳ), for the most part escapes temptation. Caring, then, for himself alone, he is surpassed by one who is inferior to him in what pertains to his own salvation, but superior to him in the conduct of life . . .[25]

10.5 The perils and gains of the second and third centuries

We began this chapter with Encratism, the wrong-headed tendency of ascetic enthusiasts, who thought that zeal for self-control and continence necessitated a contempt for Christian marriage and the created order. We saw how the best of the Fathers tried to steer a steady course between maintaining the honor due to Christian marriage, and according to eschatological virginity a higher honor, even as they warn virgins and celibates against pride.

We then moved on to the great writers of the third century, beginning with Tertullian, the first Church writer in Latin. We heard the "justly famous page" lauding the unitive good of marriage that is found in his *Letter to his wife*. We ended with St Clement of Alexandria, who is one of the most interesting and important of the early Fathers on marriage and the family. He penned one of the most famous statements concerning the family as domestic church:

> Who are the *two or three who are gathered together in the name* of Christ, with whom the Lord himself is their center (Matt 18.20)? Are the three not husband and wife and child, since a wife is joined to her husband by God?

---

25. *Stromateis* 7.12, PG 9.497C–500A. Cf. Jurgens, ed., *The Faith* I, 185, ANF II, 543.

Chapter Eleven

THE CAPPADOCIAN FATHERS

11.1 The story of a family

WE NOW PASS INTO the post-Nicene era. Our focus in this chapter will be on the Cappadocian Fathers. We may introduce ourselves to them through one of the most illustrious family households in Christian history. The family of which we speak lived in Asia Minor, in the province of Pontus, south of the Black Sea. Early in the fourth century the family featured Saint Macrina the Elder and her husband. This Macrina had been guardian of the traditions of the church of Neocaesarea, preserving the sayings and memory of its great apostle in the third century, St Gregory the Wonderworker. She and her husband were confessors of the faith, suffering confiscation of property and years as fugitives in the wild mountain gorges of Pontus during the last savage persecution of Christians in the Roman Empire under the Emperor Maximian. Their son, Basil (the elder), became a lawyer and teacher of rhetoric in Neocaesarea. He in turn married Emmelia from Cappadocia, also a scion of fervent Christian forebears; her own grandfather had died as a martyr in the Decian persecutions.

Basil the Elder and Emmelia had ten children, of whom one died as an infant. And what children they had! Their first-born was Saint Macrina the Younger, who led the rest of her family in ascetic zeal. Among the sons, three were bishops, two of them Fathers of the Church: Saint Basil the Great, called "the shining light of the whole world,"[1] and Saint

---

1. Βασίλειος ὁ μέγας, ὁ τῆς οἰκουμένης φωστήρ, Theodoret, *Ecclesiastical History,*

Gregory of Nyssa, called "the founder of Mystical Theology." The caliber of the youngest was such that his brother Gregory called him "the great Peter." This is St Peter II, metropolitan of Sebasteia. The second born son, Naucratius, was the first of the sons to choose the ascetic life, but tragically drowned at the age of twenty-six. Another daughter, Theosebia, is the subject of a glowing encomium by St Gregory the Theologian. Here is an extraordinary unfolding of generational holiness: from great-grandparents and grandparents prepared to suffer and to die rather than forfeit their allegiance to Christ, Christianity was passed on in the children till in the third or fourth generation it bore these fruits.

Since Basil the elder died just as their last child was born, clearly he and Emmelia never gave up marital relations, despite a certain trend to marital continence among the devout married at that time. In this regard, one is reminded of the teaching of a twelfth-century saint, Hugh of Lincoln, "who taught that married people who never went beyond the requirements of their state should not be considered without the honor of chastity, but would be admitted side by side (*pariter*) with virgins and celibates to the glory of heavenly beatitude."[2]

St John Paul II was much concerned to promote models of married holiness. In my opinion, there are few examples more worth retrieving from the ancient church and celebrating than that of Saints Basil the Elder and Emmelia. Their feast days in the Greek Church are May 8 and 30. They are so outstanding a Christian couple, I submit, that they merit being placed in the universal calendar.

On Emmelia, let us hear the glowing testimony from the great St Gregory Nazianzen, friend of St Basil the Great:

> I marvelled when I looked on Emmelia's family so great and so good—all the wealth of her mighty womb; but when I considered how she was Christ's cherished possession of pious blood, this is what I said: "No wonder! The root itself is so great!" This is the holy recompense of your piety, you best of women: the honor of your children, for whom you had but one desire.[3]

St Basil himself bears witness to the advantage he had of being brought up in a thoroughly Christian family environment:

4.16; ὁ τῶν Καππαδοκῶν, μᾶλλον δὲ τῆς οἰκουμένης φωστήρ ("the shining light of the Cappadocians, or better, of the whole world"), Theodoret Letter 146.

2. From Douie and Farmer, eds., *The Life*, vol. 2, 45–48.

3. *Epigram* 162, *The Greek Anthology*.

> I was delivered from the deceitfulness of the tradition of those outside [the faith], having been brought up from the very beginning by Christian parents. With them I learned from infancy the Holy Scriptures.[4]

Indeed, the great Basil cites the education in the faith he received from his mother and grandmother as the guarantee of the orthodoxy of his doctrine:

> Nay, the conception of God which I received in childhood from my blessed mother [Emmelia] and my grandmother Macrina, this, developed, I have held within me; for I did not change from one opinion to another with the maturity of reason—rather, I perfected in myself the principles that they handed down to me.[5]

11.2 The domestic ascetic movement

St Basil is well known as the Father of Greek monasticism. But the monastic life associated with his name was in some way an organic outgrowth of the domestic ascetic movement. This does not refer so much to individuals, typically women, living an ascetic life within their natural family, but the commitment of an *entire family* to a life of Christian faith and piety.

It began when spouses—typically with the wife in the lead—took their conversion to Christianity and their baptism seriously. These devout married converts gradually exchanged the values of the pagan civic culture for more explicitly Christian virtues. They fostered the Scriptures and church traditions and psalmody in their homes, practiced hospitality, personal frugality, and gospel charity, in which the idea is no longer philanthropy with a view to civic kudos, but the self-effacing succor of the poor in the love of Christ. In these ways they redefined themselves as Christian in relation to civil society. It is not surprising that in times of crisis martyrs and confessors came from their ranks, and in times of peace, virgins. These devout families were nurseries of Christian radicalism. While they themselves did not normally cross the line into an ostentatious break with society's demands, yet when really put to the test they were willing to do so and they left to their posterity memories of actually

---

4. Translated from *de Iudicio Dei* (*On the Judgement of God*), PG 31, 653–76.
5. *Letter 223*, *St Basil: The Letters* III, 282–313 at 299.

having done so. It was their children or perhaps more pertinently, their grandchildren who tapped this potential for gospel radicalism as a life option, precisely in the mid- to late fourth century when many in the church were becoming increasingly accommodated to the prevailing imperial and social mores.

Palladius's married friends in Ancyra, Verus and Bosporia, are another example of devout Christian spouses. Everything he tells of their way of life—the abandonment of class distinctions in their household, their withdrawal to the country, and their practical sharing with the poor—is equally compatible with their adopting marital celibacy or not. Like Macrina the Elder and her husband, this couple show that the very way baptized Christian spouses remade their household along expressly Christian lines took on what one might call "proto-monastic" features.

The next stage in the domestic ascetic movement was marked by the commitment to perpetual continence. This is seen especially clearly in the households of devout widows. In the late 340s and 350s there was Emmelia herself, who exemplifies the tradition of widow ascetic, almost as a forerunner. The widow Magna of Ancyra, like Emmelia, reorganized her household as a devout Christian community. Down in Antioch the devout Anthousa, widowed at twenty years of age, refused to remarry, to the admiration of the pagan intellectual, Libanius. She had borne just one child, the illustrious St John Chrysostom. In Constantinople, the very wealthy and very ascetic St Olympias, widowed at twenty-two years of age, also would not marry a second time. She became the patroness and friend of bishops such as Sts Gregory Nazianzen, Gregory of Nyssa, and, especially, John Chrysostom. Many devout widows and virgins flocked to her community. At Rome there was a whole class of noble widow ascetics, such as St Jerome's friend St Marcella, whose house on the Aventine became a center for the Roman ascetic circle, notably St Paula and her two virgin daughters.

Another stage was reached when continence was embraced while both spouses were still living. This had marked social consequences when they were of the aristocracy and presiding over the complex household typical of their class. In such cases the whole household gradually, almost organically took on the aspects of a celibate Christian community, a kind of "pre-monastery."

In St Gregory Nazianzen's wonderful funeral oration for his sister Gorgonia, he tells us that once she had borne children and wished to consecrate herself wholly to God, she persuaded her husband to join her in a life of perpetual continence. Of particular interest: he was a priest. And we don't even know his name. Their two surviving sons—they had had five children—became monks.

In Italy at the end of the fourth century St Therasia inspired her husband, St Paulinus to seek baptism. They lived together in continence for some years before he became a bishop. Their continuing household at Nola became a monastic-like establishment.

As can be seen from the above account, women were overwhelmingly the movers of the domestic ascetic movement, in all stages of its manifestation.[6] It is also clear that the ascetic community shaped by the transformation of a family household, was not something entirely different or alien to the domestic realities which preceded it, but rather a result of the gradual penetration of the radical understanding of the gospel and baptism in a domestic setting. Between the households of devout and committed Christian spouses—especially but not exclusively when electing marital continence—and of ascetic "brothers" and "sisters" in community, there was not so sharp a distinction to be drawn.

Emmelia's household at Annisa under her daughter Macrina's guidance, exemplifies the evolution of devout Christian household to monastic community. Thanks to the wonderful *Life of Macrina* written by her brother Gregory, we see the process nowhere else in such detail. The roots of the Annisa phenomenon ran all the deeper for its slow maturation, as its influence in the life of the Church was destined to be far reaching. The steps were as follows:

- Beginning with St Macrina the Elder and her husband, the zealous converts and confessors early in the century, it continued with

- the devout married urban household of Sts Basil senior and Emmelia in the 330s in the city of Neocaesarea of Pontus. In this household, Macrina the Younger dedicates herself to virginity about the year 340. Then, after Basil senior's death in about 345,

- Emmelia the widow transferred the household to a country estate called Annisa in the late 340s and early 350s, being assisted in every way by her daughter, Macrina.

---

6. The feminine "predilection for chastity" did not escape contemporary notice. Elliott, *Spiritual Marriage*, 57, cites Augustine, "Placuit continentia mulieri, viro non placet" ("sexual abstinence is more pleasing to women than to men") *De adulterinis coniugiis* I.4.4, J. Zycha, CSEL 41.351. Cf. Gregory the Theologian later in this chapter, and Chrysostom on marital continence in Chapter 13.

- Macrina persuades her mother, Emmelia, to abandon class distinctions, and to adopt the common life and a common simple dress with the women of the household in the mid-350s.
- Eventually, with Peter's coming of age in about 362/3, a way was found to incorporate a house for male celibates or monks at Peter's profession.
- Thus, by the 360s and 370s Annisa was a fully fledged monastic community, comprising separate houses for men and women ascetics, children and guests presided over by Macrina, with Peter as head of the men's section. Peter was ordained a priest in c. 371 by Basil and served the whole community as priest.

"From her retreat in Pontus, ten days' journey from Caesarea, Macrina presided over the disintegration of a civic dynasty," says Peter Brown. That is one modern judgment—"from below" so to speak. From her own intensely spiritual perspective, however, Macrina presided over the patient but thoroughgoing transposition of the natural order, the earthly family, into an "angelic" order, one whose *citizenship was in heaven* (Phil 3:20).

Before we leave the great Macrina, let us note Basil's spiritual debt to his elder sister. On his return from his years of study in Athens in 356, he "was excessively puffed up" says Gregory, and about to launch a secular career. His sister "quickly took him in hand"—i.e., she challenged him to rekindle his earlier intentions, and induced him to seek Holy Baptism and with it the life of Christian virginity and asceticism. She was a splendid example of a holy sister and a spiritual mother in the church.

St Basil's teaching on the cenobitic ("common life") community in his *Asketikon*, borrows not a little from this domestic background. His insistence on the importance of community life for ascetics, conceived of as a well-ordered "body-corporate" of men, women, children, and guests who profess a kinship based on evangelical love, who seek a common goal of Christian piety, practice voluntary poverty, give themselves to productive work ordered to service, carefully educate the young to piety and maintain this in adulthood by a system of mutual witness and correction, collaborate with the wider church in communion with the bishop, and use a "family language" (brother, sister, father, mother, household, family, kinship, communion): all this shows the lineaments of the devout Christian family household in St Basil's cenobitic monasticism, embodied in an exemplary fashion at his sister's community at Annisa. We see a collaboration of devout family life, blood relationship, and spiritual purpose, such that marriage, the begetting and rearing of children, widowhood and virginity, asceticism, and consecration to the Lord were not at odds with each other, but conspired towards a common heavenly goal.

11.3 St Basil on marriage

St Basil the Great, father of Greek monasticism, is not the first Church Father one might think of when it comes to marriage and family, and yet there are passages that invite our attention. Basil has no notion of a distinction between evangelical "precepts" and "counsels," or between "secular" and "religious" life for Christians. The only choice he sees put before the baptized, according to Scripture, is between virginity for the Lord and *marriage ... in the Lord* (1 Cor 7:39). Even then he seems to think that if you are really earnest about the goal of piety, there is no contest. In our era there has been talk of "spiritualities" for this and "spiritualities" for that, "theologies" for this and "theologies" for that, "charisms" for this religious order or movement and "charisms" for that. Such a discourse is unknown to Basil. In his teaching, the idea of having to anxiously "discern" whether one had a "vocation" to marriage, or to this Order or that movement scarcely enters the picture. For him, there is one paramount Christian vocation: to embrace Holy Baptism and the gospel life in all seriousness. This means that there is only *one* Christian "spirituality": the life in Christ. "The life of the Christian is of only one kind," he says, "having but one goal—the glory of God," and elsewhere: "There is only one way leading to the Lord and all who travel toward him are companions of one another and travel according to one agreement as to life."[7] As far as he is concerned, *all* who have dared to go down into the waters of baptism to die with Christ have, *ipso facto*, elected the one *narrow way* of the Gospel. What Paul says about *putting on Christ* (Gal 3:27) applies equally

---

7. Μονότροπός ἐστιν ὁ Χριστιανοῦ βιός, ἕνα σκοπὸν, τὴν δόξαν τοῦ θεοῦ LR 20.2. To Basil the basis of the Christian ascetic life is the same "narrow way" of the gospel undertaken by *all* Christians in baptism, chrismation, and Eucharist. A similar statement occurs in Letter 150 (*The Letters* II, 365): "There is only one way leading (μίαν εἶναι ὁδόν) to the Lord, and all who travel toward him are companions of one another and travel according to one agreement as to life (Κατὰ μίαν συνθήκην τοῦ βίου)." Cf. also *Homily on Ps 114*, PG 29, 484–493 at 492D: "There is, therefore, no male and female in the Resurrection but there is a single life and it is of one kind" (ἀλλὰ μία τίς ἐστι ζωὴ καὶ μονότροπος). Cf. his discussion of the married life in relation to the ascetic brotherhoods in LR 12.

to all the baptized. So how does that sound when Basil turns to speak to the married? Here is his clarion call to married believers: you have no permission to slacken off in a "worldly" type of Christianity; if you are baptized, your vocation too is to total gospel obedience:

> Then do you think the Gospels apply to those with a wife? Look, it has been made clear to you that we shall all have to give an account of our obedience to the Gospel, both monks and those who are married. The only concession (συγγνώμη) to one who has entered into marriage will be the lack of self-control (ἀκρασία) in his desire for and congress with the female (τῆς πρὸς τὸ θῆλυ ἐπιθυμίας τε καὶ συνουσίας). But the other commands have been laid down for all alike and are fraught with peril for any who transgress them. For when Christ proclaimed the Gospel of the Father's commands, He was addressing those in the world. He clearly testified to this by his answer when he was privately questioned by His disciples: *And what I say to you, I say to all* (Mark 13:27).
>
> Do not slacken then, you who have chosen communion with a wife (κοινωνίαν γυναικός), as if you had some kind of right to embrace the world. Rather, you have need of greater labors and vigilance in gaining your salvation, inasmuch as you have chosen to dwell in the midst of the toils and in the very stronghold of the rebellious powers, and night and day all your senses are impelled toward desire of the allurements to sin that are before your eyes.
>
> Be sure of this that you will not escape doing battle with the Evil One or gain the victory over him without a great struggle to observe the Gospel teachings. How shall you, stationed in the very thick of the battle, be able to win the contest against the Enemy, *who wanders over all the earth* under heaven, and rages about like a mad dog, *seeking whom he may devour* (cf. 1 Pet 5:8), as we learn from the history of Job. If you refuse battle with your antagonist, then take to yourself another world where he is not; there you shall be able to avoid conflict with him and take your ease without peril to Gospel teachings.[8]

It seems in Basil's thinking a certain stigma attaches to marital relations due to ἀκρασία, lack of self-control, requiring some concession (συγγνώμη). He replays both these Greek terms, of course, from 1 Corinthians 7:5–6. It would be well to remember this Greek Father when

---

8. Translated from *On Renunciation*, PG 31.625C–648B at 629A. See also Clarke, *The Ascetic Works*, 60–71 at 61–62.

we come later to consider St Augustine on concupiscence in marital intercourse. On a more positive note, St Basil offers a thought-provoking term for the theology of marriage today, *koinonia,* when he speaks of "communion with a wife" (κοινωνίαν γυναικός).

Three of St Basil's letters on the administration of penance, written to the young Bishop Amphilochius, were later incorporated into Eastern Canon Law. It will surely be sobering to learn what it meant when a baptized Christian committed a truly grave sin like adultery in those days. Basil reports:

> He who has committed adultery shall not partake of the sacraments for fifteen years, mourning for four years, hearing for five, in prostration for four years, standing without Communion for two.[9]

Thus to undertake penance for mortal sins after Baptism in the fourth-century church, was like being returned to the catechumenate all over again, to pray and be prayed for, and to be retrained at length in the imperatives of baptism and the life in Christ, before being readmitted at last to the Eucharist, the sacrament of ecclesial communion.

One important canon has everything to say to the issue of abortion. Listen to this bold statement of bioethics, fourth-century style, entirely of the same mind as Tertullian's statement quoted above. Basil excludes the Stoic account of prenatal human life:

> A woman who has deliberately committed abortion incurs the penalty for murder (ἡ φθείρασα κατ' ἐπιτήδευσιν, φόνου δίκην ὑπέχει). And any fine distinction about its being formed or unformed is not admissible among us (ἀκριβολογία δὲ ἐκμεμορφωμένου καὶ ἀνεξεικονίστου παρ' ἡμῖν οὐκ ἔστιν). For in this case not only the child which was to be born is vindicated, but she who plotted against her own self, since women very often die in such attempts. In addition to this there is the abortion of the embryo, another murder (ἡ φθορὰ τοῦ ἐμβρύου, ἕτερος φόνος)—at least that is the intention of those who dare such deeds.[10]

---

9. *Letter* 217. In *St Basil: The Letters* III, 240–267 at 249, otherwise Canon 58, *3rd Canonical Letter to Amphilochius, Bishop of Iconium.*

10. *Letter* 188. In *St Basil: the Letters* III, 4–47 at 20–21, otherwise Canon 2, *1st Canonical Letter to Amphilochius, Bishop of Iconium.*

Basil's Canons 9 and 21 uneasily report a customary accommodation of penance to the pagan double moral standard for the sexes. We reserve discussion of this till later.

11.4 St Gregory the Theologian

The custom dubiously reported by Basil is brusquely repudiated by St Gregory the Theologian.[11] In his *Oration* 37, on Matthew 19:1–12, he takes Christian marriage for his theme. In the following passage, he rebuts the idea that Christians can possibly entertain the double standard of Roman law and social custom:

> With regard to chastity, I observe that most men are ill disposed, and that their laws are unequal and irregular. For what reason do they restrain the woman but indulge the man? A woman who commits evil against her husband's bed is guilty of adultery, and for this the penalties of the law are very severe; but a husband committing fornication against his wife, has he no account to give? I do not accept this legislation. I do not approve this custom. Those who made the laws were men, and their legislation is harder on women....
>
> How can you demand chastity while you yourself do not observe it? How can you require that which you yourself do not pay? How can you, who are equally a body, legislate unequally? If you enquire into the worse: yes, the woman sinned—but so did Adam. The serpent deceived them both: one was not found stronger and the other weaker in this. Do you want to reckon who is the better? Christ saves both by his passion. Was he made flesh for the man? So also was he for the woman. Did he die for the man? The woman also is saved by his death. He is called *of the seed of David* (Rom 1:3) and so perhaps you think the man is honored; but he is born of a Virgin, and this is on the woman's side. *The two*, it says, *shall become one flesh* (Eph 5:31); so then, let the *one flesh* have equal honor ...[12]

A passage closely following the above citation is used by the Eastern Orthodox in support of their later *oikonomia* of divorce and remarriage. Gregory has just been expounding Ephesians 5:32 and reminding his

---

11. See the assessment of Gregory on divorce and remarriage in Crouzel, *L'Eglise primitive*, 151–60.

12. Gregory the Theologian, *Oration* 37.6, 7. Translation adapted from Jurgens, ed., *The Faith* II, 34, and NPNF second ser. VII, at 339–41.

hearers of the incorporation of Christian marriage into the Mystery of Christ and his church. He then says:

> I think that the Word here is deprecating digamy (δοκεῖ μοι γὰρ παραιτεῖσθαι τὴν διγαμίαν ἐνταῦθα ὁ λόγος). For if there were two Christs, there may also be two husbands or two wives; but if Christ is one, and one Head of the Church, then let there be also *one flesh* (Gen 2:24), and a second be spurned (ἀποπτύεσθω). And if He prevents a second, what shall be said of a third? The first is law, the second is indulgence (συγχώρησις), the third is transgression (παρανομία), and anything beyond that is swinish, of which kind of wickedness there are not many examples. Now the [Roman] Law grants divorce for any cause (ὁ μὲν νόμος κατὰ πᾶσαν αἰτίαν τὸ ἀποστάσιον δίδωσι), but Christ not for any cause (Χρίστος δὲ οὐ κατὰ πᾶσαν αἰτίαν). He concedes instead only separation from the fornicatress (ἀλλὰ συγχωρεῖ μὲν μόνον χωρίζεσθαι τῆς πόρνης), while in all other matters he commands patience—separation from the fornicatress because she corrupts the offspring (ὅτι νοθεύει τὸ γένος), whereas in all other matters let us be patient and endure (καρτερῶμεν καὶ φιλοσοφῶμεν), or rather, endure and be patient all you who have accepted the yoke of marriage.[13]

The question in *Oration* 37:8 in no way concerns whether it is good for a Christian to marry again *while a lawful spouse is still alive*. Gregory rather addresses the *digamy*[14] of which we heard Athenagoras speak in the second century, i.e. the idea, widely distasteful to many early Christians, of a second marriage after the death of one's spouse, because death itself is but a passing moment in an eternal trajectory. Here he interprets the Matthaean infinitive ἀπόλυειν to endorse "separation from," not divorce proper with a right to remarry. For this he uses the term τὸ ἀποστάσιον. Gregory's attitude here scarcely differs from that of Hermas in the early second century.

He reveals the same approach in his Letter 144, written to a father who finds his son-in-law objectionable, to deter him from persuading his

---

13. Gregory the Theologian, *Oration* 37.8. Translation adapted from NPNF second ser. VII, 338–44 at 340, consulting PG 36, 291–94.

14. See Percival, "Excursus on second marriages, called Digamy," NPNF, second ser. XIV, 72–73. Gillian Clark points out that even pagan Roman society admired the *univira*, the woman of only one husband, but this was an ideal: "there was no point in censuring a woman who remarried unless she behaved badly to her children." Clark, *Women in Late Antiquity*, 29–30.

daughter to divorce her husband. He reminds him that the standards of Roman civil law are not those of the law of Christ. This most eminent of Greek Church Fathers declares:

> Divorce is wholly repugnant to our laws, even if the laws of the Romans determine otherwise (Τὸ ἀποστάσιον ὃ τοῖς ἡμετέροις ἀπαρέσκει πάντως νόμοις, κἂν οἱ Ρωμαίων ἑτέρως κρίνωσι.).[15]

There is much else one could explore of St Gregory's attitude to marriage, family, and the dignity of woman. We heard his praise of St Emmelia above. On his own parents and his sister and their families he has not a little to say, and all of it in praise of the high virtue of their marriages and family life in Christ.

In taking leave of Gregory we could hardly do better than have his magnificent hymn to the unitive good of marriage. Unsurprisingly it occurs in a poem-song *In Praise of Virginity*, for, as is the way of all sound thinking on these matters, Gregory means to commend virginity for the Lord by generous and warm-hearted praise of the great good which virginity renounces. Here the great Father adopts the voice of Christian spouses:

> We whose concerns are the bonds of the married life follow the law of human generation and of our blood, which the Child of the Eternal Father (Πάϊς ἀθανάτοιο Πατρὸς) established when he joined the first Adam to the woman from his side, that man might be born as the fruit of man, and, through generation abide in his offspring as in an ear of grain. In carrying out this law and this mutual yolk of love (ὁμοζυγέην τ᾽ ἐρατεινὴν), we come to the help of each other, since we are born of the earth, and we follow the most ancient law of the earth, which is also of God ...
>
> See what prudent marriage offers the human race. What has taught dear wisdom, sought out the depths, the things that are at work on the earth, in the sea, and under the heavens? What has given laws to the cities and, even before these laws, built the cities and discovered the arts? What has filled the public squares, the houses and arenas? What has supplied the army in times of war and the table in times of feasting? What has set up the choirs chanting in the temples suffused with incense? What has assuaged the primitive life, tilled the soil, taught agriculture, set the black ship upon the seas in the face of the winds? What has bound together the earth and the moist paths of the ocean into one, and brought together what was afar off, except marriage?

---

15. Letter 144. Translated from *Saint Grégoire de Nazianze: Correspondence* II, 35.

As if this were enough, I will sing of things far loftier yet. Through our mutual yolk we are hands, ears, and feet to each other. Marriage redoubles our strength, brings great joy to our friends, and grief to our enemies. A sharing of cares lightens our trials. A sharing of joys sweetens us both. Our thinking as one makes riches more cheerful, while such concord is still more cheering for those without wealth. Marriage is the key of moderation for both, and the harmonization of desires, the seal of a necessary friendship ... the unique drink *from a fountain enclosed*, not to be tasted by strangers and inaccessible to those without. United in the flesh, of a common mind, and both of devout faith, the spouses urge each other on by the goad of their mutual desire. For marriage does not distance one from God, but brings all the closer to him, for it is God himself who draws us to it.[16]

11.5 St Gregory of Nyssa, Father of Mystical Theology

After Basil died in 378, sadly too young, his younger brother[17] stepped to the fore as his successor in the theological defense of the faith. Gregory of Nyssa (c. 335–394) was a key player in the 381 Council of Constantinople, which finally put paid to the Arian heresy that had ravaged the church for sixty years. By the late 380s he was being sought out by the communities formed in Basil's ascetic discipline, eager for his exegesis of Scripture, his spiritual instruction and inspiration. It is in this context that his ascetic and mystical theology matured, for which he became known as a Father of Christian Mystical Theology.[18] Two well-known works in this genre are *The Life of Moses,* and his much longer *Homilies on the Song of Songs,* in which nuptial imagery is brought to bear in his account of the Christian spiritual life.

---

16. *Poem in Praise of Virginity,* lines 223–277, PG 37, 539A–40A, 541A–42A, 543A. Translation revised from the Greek with grateful acknowledgments to Ramsey, *Beginning to Read*, 138–39.

17. For a survey of Gregory of Nyssa's life, see "Biography" in Silvas, *Saint Gregory of Nyssa*, 1–57, and on Gregory's marriage, 15–25.

18. Pope Benedict XVI called him "a great Father of Christian Mysticism," *The Fathers,* "St Gregory of Nyssa," 91–100 at 93. This chapter comprises two addresses given on August 29 and September 9, 2007. J. Daniélou had called Gregory "the Founder of Mystical Theology" in *Platonisme et théologie mystique,* 6. He was called "the Father of the Fathers" by Epiphanius the Deacon at the seventh ecumenical council, Nicaea II (787), 6th session, and "the shining light of Nyssa" by Nicephorus Callistus *H. E.* 11.19.

Gregory himself had married. When Emperor Julian the Apostate died in 363, the rhetorical profession was again open to Christians. Gregory pursued this option in the metropolis of Caesarea in Cappadocia. Rhetoric required a mastery of the whole field of traditional Hellenic *paideia*, including philosophy. He married in about 364, and may even have had a son, if the Strategius whose education he is arranging in his Letter 20 to Libanius is his own. It seems, however, that his wife died early, possibly in childbirth. It is possible to read between the lines in his *On Virginity* that this loss caused him much anguish, understandably. He belonged to a family that very much held that marriage was a once only affair in this life. He faced a long widowerhood. However, in September 370 his own brother, the great Basil, became metropolitan bishop of Caesarea; it was not too long before Gregory found his considerable gifts drawn into another channel, that of service of the church as a bishop.

We could call on Gregory for a range of contribution to the themes in this book: Christian anthropology, heterosexuality and homosexuality, his notable use of the *eros* of Platonic discourse. We press on, however, to the summit of this thinking in Mystical Theology. But first let us pause to hear him comment on the act of marital union:

> We, for our part, know this about marriage, that while the zeal and the desire for divine things come first, one should not scorn the moderate and measured use of the duty of marriage (τοῦ γάμου λειτουργίας).[19]

What makes this so interesting is the Greek of the phrase here translated as "the duty of marriage." From λειτουργία, meaning in ancient times a 'public service', comes our word *liturgy*. This is perhaps only a linguistic wisp, yet Gregory's use of this term for the marital embrace does give one pause.[20] In fact, St John Paul II will bring this pregnant word into the heart of the discourse of Christian marriage when he says:

> In this way, the "language of the body" becomes the language of the liturgy: it is anchored in the deepest way possible, namely, by being set into the mystery of *the beginning*.[21]

---

19. *On Virginity* 19. In *Ascetical Works*, 31–35.

20. See Hart, "Reconciliation of Body," especially 468. After his phenomenology of the disappointments of marriage undertaken for lower motives, Gregory turns to the high worth of Christian marriage undertaken as a *leitourgia*.

21. John Paul II, *Man and Woman*, Catechesis 116:2. St John Paul II is speaking in the context of Tobias's and Sarah's "Prayer before Consummation."

> *The liturgy*, liturgical language, *elevates the conjugal covenant* of man and woman, based on the "language of the body," reread in truth, *to the dimensions of the "mystery,"* and at the same time enables that covenant to be fulfilled in these dimensions through the "language of the body"... In this sense we affirm that liturgical language becomes the "language of the body." This signifies a series of acts and duties that form the *"spirituality"* of marriage, its *ethos*. In the daily life of the spouses these acts become duties, and the duties become acts. These acts—likewise also the obligations—are of a spiritual nature, but they are still expressed at the same time with the "language of the body."[22]

11.6 Epektasis and the elusive Bridegroom

Towards the end of his life, sought out by the brothers and sisters of Basil's ascetic communities, Gregory turns wholly to the themes of ascetic and mystical theology, the attempt to give an account of the vicissitudes and necessities the believer experiences in the upward ascent to God. Trinitarian theology has a direct bearing on the understanding of this progress. Arian, and especially Eunomian, theologians had an overweening confidence in the power of rational argument to define what God is, and so to "grasp" his essence. No, said Basil and the two Gregorys, the nature and essence of God cannot be "grasped" by any human being, or indeed by any creature, even the angels. God can only be humbly known and participated through his *energeia*, or activities, operations. Gregory of Nyssa himself enlarged this doctrine of the incomprehensibility of the Divine *ousia* or substance/essence, with his note of the Divine infinitude. It was a break with the Platonic and Origenist tradition, which held that the "perfect" was something defined, complete, and whole. No, this is not the nature of the God revealed to us in Christ, said Gregory. That nature is limitless and boundless.

Pondering the "ungraspability" and the infinity of the Divine nature led Gregory to expound a major theme of mystical theology, that of *epektasis*, or "stretching forth." He takes the idea from Philippians 3:13: *Brothers, I do not reckon I have attained, but there is only one thing, forgetting what lies behind I stretch forward* (ἐπεκτεινόμενος) *for what lies ahead*. The participle here is a compound of the Greek word for *tonos*,

---

22. John Paul II, *Man and Woman*, Catechesis 117b:2–3.

or tension, being stretched or taut, like a bow-string or stringed musical instrument.

Gregory uses this theologically formed idea of *epektasis* to interpret the distress of the Bride in the Song of Songs 3:1–2. He teaches that the Bride's experience of the Bridegroom's absence, her bewildered sense of *aporia* (lit. "resourcelessness," impasse, impossibility), her experience of "the sting of intolerable yearning" for an elusive Divine beauty that is not able to be "grasped," is a paradoxical disclosure of the very consummation of all her strivings, even in eternity. In her experience of the Bridegroom's seeming absence, her *eros* is crucified, and yet mysteriously renewed in a never-ending progress in intimacy with this infinite Divine beauty. Paradoxically she apprehends something of the *truth* of her Lover. Let us conclude our study of Gregory with our thoughts turned towards heaven and eternity with the following passage in which he interprets the Bride's experience of absence in the Song of Songs:

> The soul, having gone out at the word of her Beloved, looks for Him but does not find Him . . . In this way, she is in a sense, wounded and beaten because of the frustration of what she had been longing for, now that she thinks that her yearning for the Other cannot be fulfilled or satisfied. But the veil of her grief is removed when she learns that the true satisfaction of her desire consists in continuing to go on with her quest and never ceasing in her ascent, seeing that every fulfillment of her desire continually generates a further desire for the Transcendent. Thus the veil of her despair is torn away and the bride realizes that she will always discover more and more of the incomprehensible and unhoped for beauty of her Spouse, throughout all eternity. Thereupon she is torn by an even more urgent longing, and she . . . communicates to her Beloved the affections of her heart. For she has received within her God's special dart, she has been wounded to the heart by the shaft of faith, she has been mortally wounded by the arrow of love. For *God is love*. (1 John 4:8, 16)[23]

This is what the Nuptial Mystery, obediently received in all its Divine endowment and calling, opens us up to radically: infinite Being, infinite love, the infinite communion of the Divine persons.

---

23. *On the Song of Songs*, Oratio XII, PG 44.1037C, *Gregorii Nysseni Opera* vol. VI, 369–370. The text here is slightly adapted from *From Glory to Glory*, 45.

Chapter Twelve

ST AUGUSTINE AND THE CHURCH IN THE WEST

12.1 St Ambrose of Milan (c. 333-397)

WE NOW TURN TO our heritage from the Latin Church Fathers. We shall look first at the bishop who baptized St Augustine in the year 387, the great St Ambrose of Milan. None have jumped ecclesiastical rank quicker than he, who shot from unbaptized catechumen to metropolitan bishop in a week. Bilingual in Greek and Latin in the way of the old fashioned Roman elite, Ambrose drew much on his Greek preceptors in his doctrinal and exegetical works. He came into his own in his moral and ascetical writings, a major resource for pastoral theology in later times.

In an exhortation to virginity preached for the veiling of a virgin, Ambrose presented Mary the Mother of God as the model of virgins. All the same, he strongly defended the genuineness of her marriage to St Joseph. In so doing made a very important point about marriage:

> Neither does it make any difference that the Scripture says: *Joseph took his wife and went into Egypt* (cf. Matt 1:24; 2:14); for any woman espoused to a man is given the name of wife. It is from the time that a marriage begins that the marital terminology is employed. It is not the deflowering of virginity (*defloratio virginitatis*) that makes a marriage, but the marital pact [or covenant] (*pactio coniugalis*). It is when the girl accepts the yoke that the marriage begins, not when she is known by her husband

in intercourse (*denique cum iungitur puella, coniugum est, non cum virili admixtione cognoscitur*).[1]

This is a patristic *locus classicus,* later incorporated into Western canon law in support of the teaching that the marital bond is established in the act of mutual consent, not of consummation. Ambrose bases this teaching not only on the Roman legal tradition, but also on the marriage of Mary and Joseph.

Ambrose is quoted in the *Catechism of the Catholic Church,* no. 2349 on marriage as an integral part of the church's way of life. Here is a slightly fuller version:

> And so we are taught that there are three forms of the virtue of chastity: the first is that of spouses, the second that of widows, and the third that of virgins.[2] We do not set forth any one of these to the exclusion of the others ... This is what makes for the richness of the discipline of the Church, that she has those whom she may set before others, but has none whom she rejects—and would that she never could have any! We have so spoken of virginity as not to reject widowhood, we so reverence widows as to reserve for marriage the honor that is its due.[3]

In *Familiaris Consortio* no. 25, St John Paul II quotes a passage from Ambrose's commentary on the creation accounts of Genesis, in which he reminds the husband that the wife given to him as a helpmate, is co-equal with him in dignity:

> You are not her master, but her husband; she was not given to you as your handmaid, but as your wife ... Reciprocate her attentiveness to you, and be grateful to her for her love (*Non es dominus, sed maritus: non ancillam sortitus es, sed uxorem ... Redde studio vicem, redde amori gratiam*).[4]

Ambrose is so mindful that the marriage of believers is *in Christ*, he deems it a sacrilege if believers do not choose a spouse who shares the same faith in Christ. He reflects the common tradition of the church that if the baptized marry, it must be to fellow believers. This reflects

---

1. *On the consecration of a virgin and the perpetual virginity of Mary* (c. 391/392) 6.41, Jurgens, ed., *The Faith* II, 172.

2. That is to say: marriage, perpetual continence, and dedicated virginity.

3. *On Widows* 4.23 (c. AD 378) PL 16, 225A, NPNF second ser. X, 395; cited in CCC no. 2349.

4. St Ambrose, *Hexaemeron*, V, 7.19, CSEL 32/1 (1897), 154.

1 Corinthians 7:39 where St Paul says that if a widow does remarry, it should be *in the Lord*. This is how Ambrose puts it:

> But there is scarcely a more serious matter than being joined in marriage to an outsider [i.e. an unbeliever]. This is where the instigations of lustful appetite and the provocations of disharmony and the shameful crimes of sacrilege all lead. For if marriage itself needs to be sanctified by the priestly veil and blessing, how is it possible to speak of a marriage when there is no agreement in faith?[5]

The text also shows that, just as we saw in Tertullian, the marriage of Christians is a public liturgical act, completed by the priestly blessing.

In upholding the indissolubility of Christian marriage against the misuse of the exception clauses in the Gospel of Matthew, it took centuries for the church to work out the criteria of valid and invalid marriages. An early stage of that process can be seen in the following passage of St Ambrose:

> If every marriage is from God it is not licit to dissolve any marriage. How, then, does the Apostle say, *If the unbeliever departs, let him depart* (1 Cor 7:15)? What is remarkable in this saying is that, far from intending Christians to find in it an excuse for divorce, he shows that not every marriage is in fact from God; for Christians, in God's tribunal (*Dei iudicio*), cannot be joined to pagans, when the law forbids it. . . .
>
> You dismiss your wife, therefore, as if by right and without being charged with wrongdoing; and you suppose it proper for you to do so because no human law forbids it—but the divine law forbids it. Anyone who obeys men ought to stand in fear of God. Hear, then, the law of the Lord, which even they who propose our laws must obey: *Whatsoever God has joined together let not man put asunder* (Matt 19:6).[6]

---

5. St Ambrose, *Letter to Bishop Vigilius* (c. 385), Jurgens, ed., *The Faith* II, 147.

6. *Commentary on the Gospel of Luke* (c. 389) 8.2,5, Jurgens, ed., *The Faith* II 163, 164.

12.2 St Augustine (354–430)[7]

And now for the great St Augustine. The historian of medieval philosophy Étienne Gilson found Augustine's manner of thinking and writing something of a conundrum:

> One never really knows whether St Augustine is talking as a theologian or as a philosopher, whether he is proving the existence of God or developing a theory of cognition, whether the eternal verities of which he speaks are those of understanding or of morality, whether he is expounding a doctrine of sensation or the consequences of Original Sin; everything holds together so well that Augustine cannot seize one link of the chain without drawing the entire chain to himself.[8]

Much the same could be said of many Greek Fathers, especially the Cappadocians. So it might be worth "reframing" Augustine somewhat, seeing him as a great Latin Father who is still operating with the common patristic sensibility and theological method of the church, both East and West.

12.3 St Augustine: the early years

When approaching St Augustine's writings, it is always important to situate them in their specific historical milieu and in the overall unfolding of his thought. He recounts in his *Confessions* that after a licentious adolescence he lived for years in a relationship with a mistress, by whom he had a son. During most of those years, from c. 374 to 383, he had been a Manichean of sorts—not the class of "the perfect," committed to continence, but among the "hearers" who still dallied in sexual relations, but were warned off procreation, and indeed practiced contraception to avoid the horror.

For Augustine, the long process of conversion to faith in Christ and the church was at the same time a moral journey to chastity. There is little doubt that the sheer internal struggle Augustine sustained—*Domine, da mihi castitatem et continentiam, sed noli modo* ("O Lord, give me chastity and continence, but not yet")—informs his discussion of concupiscence

---

7. The following reflections are indebted to Fitzgerald, ed., *Augustine through the Ages*, especially the articles "Marriage" (535–37), "Concupiscence" (224–27), and "Sexual Ethics" (327–28).

8. Gilson, *Introduction à l'étude*, 311–12.

in the spiritual contest of the life in Christ. Early in his conversion, the late 380s and early 390s, his teaching on marriage is patterned against the Manichaean disparagement of marriage and sexual intercourse in general, and of procreation in particular. In his *On the Morality of the Catholic Church* and *Against Adimantus, a Manichaean disciple*, he cites Matthew 19:3–9, 1 Corinthians 7, and Ephesians 5 to demonstrate that marriage was established by the Creator, and confirmed and elevated in the New Testament.

12.4 St Augustine On the Good of Marriage

After he became a bishop in 396, Augustine worked on a major statement on marriage, his famous *De Bono Conjugali*, "On the Good of Marriage," finishing it in the year 401. The context was a current of hostility against virginity and asceticism in Rome and the West, from Helvidius in the early 370s through Jovinian in the 390s to Julian of Eclanum in the 410s and 420s. Helvidius, in his polemic against monasticism denied the ever-virginity of the Mother of God. This was shot down in flames by the brilliant invective of St Jerome. Then came Jovinian, a renegade Roman monk who denied that consecrated virginity was any better than marriage, or that there were any distinctions of gravity in sins or of reward and punishment in the life to come. Alas, this time Jerome, in defending the higher good of virginity for the Lord, did a hatchet job on marriage. It would be hard to defend him from a charge of encratism. As a result, Augustine felt that the need of the hour was to confirm the good of Christian marriage. Thus he wrote his *On the Good of Marriage*, in which he famously articulated the "three goods" of marriage, which became a staple of the Latin theology of marriage ever after:

> The good of marriage (*bonum nuptiarum*) throughout all nations and all men consists in its being the occasion of procreation (*in causa generandi*), and in the fidelity of chastity (*in fide castitatis*). But in the case of the people of God, there is also the sanctity of the bond (*in sanctitate sacramenti*), on which account a woman is not permitted, even if she leaves with a repudiation (*etiam repudio discedentem*),[9] to be married to another while

---

9. That is, if she receives a civil divorce. "Some conclude from such passages as the present one that only the wife was forbidden to remarry, and not the husband. But it is false to conclude from this frequent silence that the husband was permitted to remarry.... Augustine makes it clear that the man too, who dismisses his wife for any

her husband still lives, not even for the sake of bearing children. Although this is the only reason why marriage takes place, yet even if this for which it takes place does not follow, the marriage bond is loosed only by the death of the husband or wife. . . .

The Apostle himself is a witness that marriage is for the sake of begetting of children when he says: *I wish the younger women to marry.* And as if someone said to him, "Why?," he immediately adds: *to bear children, to be mothers of families (filios procreare, matres familias esse*—cf. 1 Tim 5:14).[10]

As to the fidelity of chastity, there is that saying: *The wife does not have power over her own body, but the husband has; likewise the husband does not have power over his own body, but the wife has* (1 Cor 7:4). As to the sanctity of the bond (*ad sacramenti sanctitatem*), there is that saying: *the wife is not to depart from her husband, but if she does depart, she is to remain single, or be reconciled to her husband; and do not let the husband put away his wife* (1 Cor 7:10–11).

All these are the goods on account of which marriage itself is a good (*Haec omnia bona sunt, propter quae nuptiae bonum sunt*): offspring, fidelity, and the bond (*proles, fides, sacramentum*).[11]

At the beginning of his discourse Augustine describes the union of husband and wife, as "the first natural bond of human society," leading, through the connexion of fellowship in children, to *societas amicalis* (9), the "friendly association" of the human race, i.e. human community. In 3 he uses attractive expression "the natural companionship of the two sexes" (*sed propter ipsam etiam naturalem in diverso sexu societatem*) for the unitive good of marriage in itself. He describes *Fides* or conjugal fidelity, as the commitment to sexual relations solely with one's spouse, and to the mutual support of each other's weakness in the ordering of sexual desire.

> For this is why such spouses were married, that concupiscence itself might be directed toward a legitimate bond and not flow in a disordered or haphazard way. Concupiscence bears a weakness

---

reason, adultery or not, cannot remarry. He does, however recognize a difference in the degree of guilt of the man who remarries after divorcing a wife for adultery, and the man who remarries after divorcing a wife for cause other than adultery." Jurgens, ed., *The Faith* III, 71.

10. Cited by Pius XI in *Casti Connubii*, note 14.

11. *De bono coniugali*, 24/32, PL 40, 394. Translation adapted from *On the Good of Marriage* 32, NPNF first ser. III, 412. Cited by Pius XI in *Casti Connubii*, note 10.

of the flesh that cannot be restrained, but from marriage it receives a bond that cannot be dissolved (5).

Because the spouses are in Christ, a third good of marriage, a *sacramentum* is bestowed on their union. This word, *sacramentum*, we saw, was used to translate the *mysterion* of Ephesians 5:32. As Augustine uses it, it means that bond between spouses which, in its signifying the union of Christ and his church, cannot be broken.

12.5 The Pelagian controversy

A new phase in Augustine's considerations of marriage began with his embroilment in the Pelagian controversy, and "embroilment" is the word. The Pelagians had an overweeningly optimistic view of human nature, and of what anyone could achieve with a bit of robust effort. It was a sort of blithe perfectionism. "The conflict centered around Augustine's idea of original sin, and specifically, on how the sin of Adam and Eve affected the character of human sexual desire."[12] The Pelagians held that Augustine's exposition of original sin implied a condemnation of marriage.

In his *Literal Commentary on Genesis* Augustine pondered the shame experienced by Adam and Eve in Genesis 3:7. Once they had disobeyed God's command, he says, "they cast their eyes on their bodies and, in a movement which they had not known before, they lusted (*concupeverunt*)."[13] Their bodies became subject not only to disease and mortality, but also "to that same movement which gives animals the desire to copulate."[14] Their progeny, the human race born of them, bears this same "bestial motion" in their members, which operates independently of human reason or will.

The Pelagians' views on original sin incurred censures in a series of North African synods from 411, and a censure by Pope Zosimus early in 418, after which Pelagius himself dropped from view.[15] The very able

---

12. Hunter, in Fitzgerald, ed., *Augustine through the Ages*, 536.
13. Augustine, *De Genesi ad Litteram*, XI.31/41, PL 34, 416D.
14. Augustine, *De Genesi ad Litteram*, XI.32/42, PL 34, 417A.

15. After Pelagius appeared before a synod of Greek-speaking bishops held at Diospolis-Lydda in Palestine in the year 415, the bishops ruled: "now since we have received satisfaction on the points which have come before us touching the monk Pelagius, who has been present; since too he gives his consent to the pious doctrines, and even anathematizes everything that is contrary to the church's faith, we confess him to belong to the communion of the Catholic Church." (Augustine *de gestis Pelagii*

Bishop Julian of Eclanum took his place. Augustine's book *On Marriage and Concupiscence*, written in 419/420, is the fruit of his engagement with this tenacious opponent. In the following he endeavors to explain how parents who are baptized yet pass on the effects of the Fall to their children:

> Concupiscence, which is atoned for only by the Sacrament of regeneration [Baptism], does most certainly, by means of generation, pass on the bond of sin to the progeny, if they are not loosed from it by the same regeneration. For concupiscence itself is certainly no longer a sin in the regenerate, if they do not consent to illicit deeds and their members are not applied by the ruling mind (*a regina mente*) to the performance of such deeds . . . But because the guilt (*reatus*) of concupiscence is prevalent in a man who is born, that is called 'sin' in a certain manner of speaking which was effected by sin and which, if it conquers, produces sin. This guilt, however, through the remission of all sins, is not allowed to prevail in the man who is reborn, if he does not obey it when in some way it commands him to perform evil works.[16]

Augustine goes on to say that even when the use of marriage is directed to its best end, concupiscence can scarcely be absent.

> Licit and honorable cohabitation itself cannot be effected without the ardour of lust in order to accomplish that which belongs to reason and not to lust . . . This concupiscence of the flesh is the daughter of sin, as it were, and, as often as it consents to shameful deeds, it is the mother of more sins. Whatever offspring is born of the concupiscence of the flesh is bound by original sin (*originali est obligata peccato*), unless it be reborn in Him whom the Virgin conceived without that concupiscence;

XX.44). Pelagius had argued that Augustine's position as defined in opposition to himself contained a doctrine contrary to the Catholic faith, specifically as it had been interpreted in the East. (*de gestis Pelagii* XI.25) Augustine strove to refute that charge and to vindicate the Catholic orthodoxy of his doctrine of grace. The Eastern Christian understanding of the relation between grace and free will avoided the Western dichotomy between Augustinianism and Pelagianism by stressing both, as in the oft-quoted formula of Maximus the Confessor (from his *Quaestiones ad Thalassium*) that salvation is "a reward as a gift to those who have believed Him, namely eternal deification" (Notes from Pelikan, *Confessor*, 32–33).

16. *De nuptiis et concupiscentia in duobus libris* I.23/25, PL 44, 423. Translation adapted from Jurgens, ed., *The Faith* III, 136. See also NPNF first ser. V, Book One: 260–80, Book Two: 283–308.

for which reason, when He deigned to be born in the flesh, He alone was born without sin.[17]

Here is an important soteriological argument: that the virginal conception of Jesus in the womb of Mary stayed the descent of sin by generation of the flesh from Adam and Eve, so that it is only through our being *reborn* through baptism in Him, the Virgin-born, that we are freed from original sin.

Julian had argued that concupiscence was a natural bodily impulse created by God for procreation. In the following Augustine counters Julian's claim that his explanation that human sexual desire is corrupted by the Fall renders marriage itself evil:

> Marriage is not the cause of the sin that comes with being born and is expiated in being reborn; rather, the willful sin of the first man is the cause of original sin (*voluntarium peccatum hominis primi originalis est causa peccati*) ...
>
> Why then does he [Julian of Eclanum] ask us: "Whence is it that sin is found in an infant: through will, or through marriage, or through his parents?" ...
>
> For all this the Apostle has an answer. He accuses neither the will of the infant, which is not yet matured in him for sinning; nor marriage as such, which has not only its institution from God but also a blessing as well; nor parents as such, who are licitly and legitimately joined together for the procreation of children. Rather, he says *Through one man sin came into this world, and through sin death; and thus it passed through into all men, for in him*[18] *all have sinned* (*in quo omnes peccaverunt*—Rom 5:12).[19]

Augustine did take one point from Julian's critique even as he maintained a strong doctrine of original sin, when, a little later (c. 421), in a letter to Bishop Atticus of Constantinople he conceded the possibility of a sinless desire in this life, that is a *concupiscentia nuptiarum,* "concupiscence of marriage," which is the desire for children. It is to be distinguished

---

17. *De nuptiis et concupiscentia* I.24/27, PL 44, 429. Translation adapted from Jurgens, ed., *The Faith* III, 136.

18. St Augustine is often taken as the originator of the *in quo* interpretation of what in the Greek is ἐφ' ᾧ. But since he did not use the Vulgate, it was already in the *Vetus Itala* translation, which he did use.

19. *De nuptiis et concupiscentia* II.26/42, PL 44, 460–461. Translation adapted from Jurgens, ed., *The Faith* III, 137.

from *concupiscentia carnis,* the "concupiscence of the flesh."[20] He even allowed that in Paradise there might have been an innocent "concupiscence of the flesh" entirely subject to the will, if only Adam and Even had not sinned. That, alas, is not how humans experience it after the Fall.

Augustine excoriated the deliberate procuring of sterility in the marital act, and with it, the procuring of abortion. How, in view of such a patrimony of teaching in the church, could Pope Paul VI have come up with any other response in *Humanae Vitae* than he did? This is Augustine's fiery denunciation:

> Sometimes this lustful cruelty or, if you please, cruel lust goes so far as to use poisonous drugs (*venena*) to procure sterility, or, if this fails, seeks to destroy what is conceived in the womb in some way before birth, in the desire to destroy the offspring before it has life, or if it already lives in the womb, to kill it before it is born. If both man and woman are party to such practices they are not spouses at all; and if from the first they have come together not for wedlock, but for mere licentiousness, if both are not party to these deeds, I make bold to say that either the woman makes herself her husband's harlot (*meretrix*), or the man his own wife's paramour (*adulter*).[21]

Here is a stimulating thought: that even husband and wife can commit adultery with each other in a sense, and that sense is that every sin is an act of idolatry and every sexual sin of whatever kind, a shadow of archetypal adultery.[22]

12.6 Concupiscence and marital intercourse

One aspect of Augustine's thinking invites further attention: the idea that marital intercourse, undertaken other than primarily for the sake

---

20. *Epistulae* 6.5, and 7, CSEL 88, 34–35, 35–36.

21. *De nuptiis et concupiscentia* I.15/17, PL 44, 423–424. NPNF first ser. V, 271. Cited in *Casti Connubii* no. 51.

22. This is similar to the thought of St Gregory of Nyssa in his *Canonical Letter to Letoius,* where he has to discuss the penances for various kinds and grades of sexual sins. After acknowledging a distinction between adultery proper and fornication, he says that to those who think more accurately the offences of fornication are also adultery. He goes on to argue that any union which is "unjust," which is alien to the integrity of one's bodily nature, bears the mark of adultery. See "Letter 31" in Silvas, *Saint Gregory of Nyssa,* 211–25 at 218–19.

of procreation, is in some sense "venial" sin. His discussion centers on 1 Corinthians 7:1-6.

> To escape this evil [of fornications and adulteries], even such embraces of husband and wife that do not have procreation for their object, but serve an overbearing concupiscence, are permitted as being within the range of forgiveness (*tamen secundum veniam concedentur*), though not prescribed by way of a commandment (cf. 1 Cor 7:6). Furthermore, the married couple are enjoined not to deprive each other, lest Satan should tempt them through their lack of self-control (1 Cor 7:5). For this is what Scripture says: *Let the husband render to the wife her due, and likewise the wife to the husband. The wife does not have the power over her own body, but the husband has, and likewise, the husband does not have power over his own body, but the wife has. Do not deprive one another, unless it be with consent for a time, that you may have leisure for prayer; and then come together again, that Satan not tempt you for your lack of self-control. But I speak this by way of permission* (*secundum veniam*), *and not of command* (1 Cor 7:3-6).
>
> Now in a case where concession must be given (*venia danda est*), it cannot by any means be maintained that there is not some measure of sin. But if cohabitation for the purpose of procreating children—which must be admitted as the proper end of marriage—is not sinful, what is it that the Apostle allows as permissible, except that married persons, when they do not have the gift of continence, may require, one from the other, the due of the flesh—and require it, not from a desire for procreation, but for the pleasure of concupiscence? ... This, therefore, must be reckoned among the praises of matrimony, that on its own account, it renders pardonable (*ignosci faciunt propter se*) that which does not essentially belong to it. For the nuptial embrace which serves the demands of concupiscence is so effected that it does not hinder child-bearing, which is the end and aim of marriage.[23]

The argument turns on the word *venia*, used in Augustine's *Vetus Itala* text to translate the Greek συγγνώμη or "concession" of the 1 Corinthians passage. The Vulgate translates the same word as *indulgentia*. *Venia* meant indulgence, kindness, consent, with connotations of forbearance, tolerance, and forgiveness. Thus sins that are more readily forgiven are called *venial*, i.e. pardonable, even if unworthy.

23. *De nuptiis et concupiscentia* I.14/16, PL 44, 423. NPNF first ser. V, 270.

Involved here is an exegetical question: to what precisely does St Paul's "concession" refer? Most if not all of the Fathers, East and West, understood it as referring to all Paul had said about marriage from the beginning of the chapter, and in this case to the "not refusing each other," which would mean that occasional abstinence for the sake of prayer was regarded as an obligation. A more recent interpretation refers the concession simply to the abstinence for prayer, but that is not how the Fathers read it. You will recall we cited St Basil in the last chapter, who certainly understood "concession" to refer to the whole project of marital relations, and the rendering of the "marital debt."

But with the use of the Latin word *venia* in Augustine's writings, marital intercourse undertaken primarily for desire and pleasure, and only secondarily for procreation was regarded in the Western tradition not only as a concession for weakness, as in the East, but also in some sense as venial sin.

12.7 The lasting legacy of St Augustine

After considering texts from St Ambrose of Milan that would prove very important in the later tradition, we turned to the convert whom he baptized, the great St Augustine of Hippo. We noted the importance of situating his writings in their controversial context and in the chronological development of his own thinking. His teaching on the three goods of marriage, developed in his treatise *On the Good of Marriage* entered permanently into the Latin church's theology of marriage. His exposition of the *sacramentum*, the sacred bond bestowed on marriage in, by, and from Christ, was a major contribution to elucidating the indissolubility of Christian marriage.

His later analyses of the effects of original sin in relation to concupiscence in marriage, however, worked out in the atmosphere of anti-Pelagian controversy, what of that? I am grateful to a student, a married man and father, who volunteered in class that *of course* the married have to face the issue of concupiscence—as indeed do all we strugglers *in via* to eternity. [24] Or to put it in another way: prayer, grace and ascesis are as necessarily a part of a truthful Christian marriage, as they are of all

---

24. For a short discussion of concupiscence in marriage, see Jonathon Coe, "Some Marriage Advice for Engaged Couples," at http://www.crisismagazine.com/2016/musings-marriage-good-beginning.

Christian life. When discussing this with a colleague, also a married man and father, he opined that Augustine was a both a "good phenomenologist" and a "good psychologist."

After Augustine, *concupiscence* became a code-word in the Western tradition for that default inclination to sin and to lie to ourselves about it, which is the effect of the Fall in all of us, with which all believers, all who are baptized, must contend, married or not. It was well that he did highlight it, and, like a true spiritual physician, put a diagnostic finger on that wound in our fallen nature that so begs our cooperation with the grace of Christ, if our bodies are to be redeemed and we are to be made whole again.

For the present, we give the last word to St Augustine:

> In marriage, however, let the blessings of marriage be esteemed (*bona nuptialia diligantur*): offspring, fidelity, and the bond (*proles, fides, sacramentum*).[25]

---

25. *De nuptiis et concupiscentia* I.19, PL 44, 424. NPNF first ser. V, 271.

Chapter Thirteen

ST JOHN CHRYSOSTOM AND THE CHRISTIAN EAST

13.1 Beginnings of the estrangement of East and West

AND NOW WE TURN to the Greek Fathers. First, let us pause to consider the beginnings of the estrangement between Greek-speaking and Latin-speaking Christianity. The church in Rome, in fact, had been largely Greek speaking till about the fourth century. The Latin tradition began, not in Rome or Italy, but, as we saw when discussing Tertullian, in third-century North Africa. During the late fourth century the traditional language of the Roman liturgy, Greek, was replaced with Latin, in order to accommodate the prevailing vernacular. St Ambrose had apprenticed himself to the Greek Fathers and had personally corresponded with St Basil; St Augustine however was not fluent in Greek. That he could advance so far the profession of rhetoric without Greek was symptomatic of the times.

The Barbarian invasions of Italy in the fifth century imposed a further cultural divide. There was also the ambition of the see of Constantinople, imperial city of the *oikoumené*. The See of Rome flinched at the idea of altering the status of patriarchal sees to reflect changing civil status; her own ecclesial status was not predicated on secular dignity, but upon the fisherman and the tentmaker. So "the two great branches of the ancient world began to live in different intellectual climates with different theological preoccupations which gradually estranged them from one another."[1]

---

1. Quasten, *Patrology* IV, 7.

Since the fifteenth century patristic studies have steady advanced, resulting in the recovery in the West of a fuller access to the writings of the Eastern Fathers. In the present crisis of the church in the West a fresh irrigation from the Fathers, both East and West, is surely part of the remedy. This was a cause promoted by Pope John Paul II, who from the beginning of his pontificate insisted that the church needs to learn to "breathe again with two lungs, Eastern and the Western."[2]

13.2 St John Chrysostom (347–407)

To that end, we turn our attention to one of the greatest theologians of marriage among the Greek Fathers, St John Chrysostom. Few Church Fathers are held in such high regard by the church, both East and West. In the East, he is arguably the most popular Church Father of all.

John was a native of Antioch, born about 347, son of a Roman father, Secundus, a high-ranking military officer, and a Greek mother, St Anthousa, whom we have already met. Widowed at only twenty years of age, she refused remarriage and devoted herself to rearing her son. John extols her qualities as a Christian mother in the introduction to his *On the Priesthood*. On his heritage Harkens makes an interesting comparison: "His parentage and classical training combined to produce in him the strong will and firmness of the Roman tempered by the versatile and vivacious spirit of the Greek."[3]

John put himself through a severe novitiate in the spiritual life as a monk in a mountain cave outside Antioch. Overdoing the asceticism and permanently impairing his health, he washed up again in the haven of the church in the city. Ordained a deacon in 381 and a priest in 386, he was appointed to the task of preaching, at that time the prerogative of bishops. Most of his theologizing, therefore, was done in the very practical forum of pastoral preaching. Not for nothing is he the patron saint of preachers. Considering the appalling end of his life, as a true prophet

---

2. John Paul II repeated his "the Church must breathe with two lungs, one Eastern and the other Western" to a French Ecumenical Pilgrimage on November 21, 1981, when he noted that he had first used it in Paris. In the interim he employed a variant in an address to the Roman Curia on June 28, 1980, when he said that "it will be necessary to learn to breathe fully with two lungs, the Western and the Eastern." He used it again in an address to the Curia in June 1985. It has appeared elsewhere since. With thanks to Russian Catholic priest, Lawrence Cross, for this information.

3. Harkins, "John Chrysostom, St," 1041.

hounded to an early death by a faction of the leadership of church and Christian Empire, he could very well be named the patron saint of all victims of church politics.

A loftier praise of virginity for the Lord is hardly be found than in John.[4] To him, the sign of the church as the Bride of Christ is instantiated not only in the person of the dedicated female virgin, but also in male monks. Monks too are "espoused to Christ." The basis of male monastic life, too, is nuptial. Nevertheless, John enunciated the principle which is revisited in both the *Catechism* and in *Familiaris Consortio*:

> Whoever denigrates marriage also diminishes the glory of virginity. Whoever praises it makes virginity more admirable and resplendent. What appears good only in comparison with evil would not be especially good. It is something better than what is admitted to be good that is the excellent good.[5]

John lavished many sermons on the good of marriage and family. His sure touch with marriage and the family came from the depth of his own spiritual life, in which he assimilated the Bride in his life as a monk, and the Bridegroom in his life as a priest, his saturation in the Scriptures, his acute intelligence and lively character, and his passionate involvement with his flock. In some ways his temperament reminds us of Paul the apostle himself, whom John greatly loved and ardently emulated.

13.3 The purpose of marriage

Key ideas in John's theology of marriage are: first that the act of marital union is in no way tainted by impurity, but is its remedy. This is the idea of a *remedy for concupiscence* based on 1 Corinthians 7:5. The second is that the two purposes in marriage are chastity and procreation, *in that order*. He states these principles again and again, as in the following passage from one of several homilies on 1 Corinthians 7:1–6:

---

4. "That virginity is good I do agree. But that it is also better than marriage, this I do confess. And if you wish, I will add that it is much better than marriage as heaven is better than earth, as much better as the angels are than human beings. And if there were any other way in which I could say it even more emphatically, I would do so." *On Virginity* 10; translation from Jurgens, ed., *The Faith* II, 88.

5. St John Chrysostom *On Virginity* 10.1, PG 48, 540. Cited in John Paul II, *Familiaris Consortio* no. 16, and CCC no. 1620.

> For Marriage is not a wicked thing! But wicked is adultery and wicked is fornication. Marriage is a medicine for the elimination of fornication (γάμος δὲ πορνείας ἀναιρετικὸν φάρμακον). ...
>
> Marriage was instituted not that we should practice wantonness or fornication, but that we should be chaste. Listen to what Paul says: *On account of fornication, let each man have his own wife and each woman her own husband* (1 Cor 7:2). These are the two reasons why marriage was instituted: that we live chastely, and that we become parents (πάτερες γινώμεθα). Of these two, the reason of chastity leads the way (τῶν δὲ δύω τούτων προηγουμένη ἡ τῆς σωφροσύνης ἐστὶ πρόφασις).[6] When desire entered in, then marriage also began, cutting off immoderation by teaching us to keep to one wife. Though the word of God says: *Be fruitful and multiply and fill the earth* (Gen 1:28), marriage does not always lead to child-bearing. We have as witnesses all those who marry but do not become parents. So chastity is the leading element.[7]

This accords with Augustine's exposition that the bond of marriage is in no way impaired even if the "first good" of children never eventuates, i.e. the couple is unable to have children. As to John's teaching that the purpose of chastity "leads the way," "takes precedence," or "is antecedent," perhaps the key to is to take marital chastity in its highest register, embracing the union of the spouses, their love and fidelity. Even so the twentieth-century theologian of marriage, von Hildebrand, would argue that *love* (*amor*) is the primary *meaning* of marriage.[8] The coming of children into the world as the fruit of the unitive embrace of spousal love—*that* is what God intended for our human coming into being. So John elucidates this truth:

> Behold the mystery of love (ἰδοὺ πάλιν ἀγάπης μυστήριον)! If the two do not become one, they cannot increase to many, while they continue as two. What do we learn from this? How great is the power of their union! The economy of God divided the one into two at the beginning; but, wishing to show that it still remained one even after its division, it did not allow that one

---

6. Cf. γυναῖκα ἄγῃ ἐπὶ σωφροσύνῃ καὶ παιδιοποιίᾳ. "You are marrying a wife for chastity and for the procreation of children," Chrysostom, *Homily 12*, on Col 4:18, PG 62, 386B, NPNF first ser. 13, 317.

7. Chrysostom, *On the Apostle's words*, PG 51, 210BC, 212D–13A. In addition to his long series of homilies on 1 and 2 Corinthians, Chrysostom wrote two other homilies on 1 Corinthians 7, at PG 51, 207–42. The second is on divorce and remarriage.

8. von Hildebrand, *Marriage*, xxvi.

alone should be sufficient for generation. For he is not yet one, but only the half of one ... Do you see now the mystery of marriage? From one man he made the one woman, and again, he made these two into one, and so makes one that a human being is brought forth from a single source, for husband and wife are not two human beings, but one Man (cf. Gen 1:27) ... for if he is the head and she is the body, how are they two? ... She was made from his side, and they are, as it were two halves. God calls her a "helpmate" to show that they are one, and for this reason He honors beforehand the union of husband and wife (cf. Gen 2:24), that he might show that they are one. ...

How then do they become *one flesh*? Just as one separates the purest of gold and mingles it with other gold, so indeed the wife receives the richest part fused with pleasure, nourishes it, cherishes it, and contributing what is hers, she then returns it as a man! The child is a kind of bridge connecting mother to father, so that the three become one flesh, the child connecting each to the other on either side. Just as two cities divided by a river become one if they are joined by a bridge, so it is even more so in this case, for the very bridge is formed of the substance of each! Just as the head and the rest of the body are one, since the neck connects them more than it divides them, so the child, lying between them, brings each together with the other ... That is why Scripture does not say, "They shall be one flesh," but: *they shall be joined together into one flesh,* namely that of the child.

But what if there is no child—do they remain two? No, their coming together has the effect of diffusing and commingling the bodies of each, and they are made one as when perfume is infused into oil.[9]

Here John notably interprets the *two in one flesh* of Genesis 2:24 and Matthew 19:5 as the *one flesh* of the child born of their union. He repeats this exegesis in other homilies.

13.4 Marriage, the incarnation, and the Eucharist

John sees in a profoundly synoptic view the "one flesh" union of marriage, the incarnation, the church, and the Eucharist. This is highly significant, since as the centuries go by the church will source the indissoluble bond of Christian marriage theologically in the hypostatic union of the divine and the human in Christ's "enfleshment," brought to his passion

---

9. *Homily* 12, PG 62, 387D, 388ABC; NPNF first ser. 13, 318–19.

and death by which he espoused himself to his Bride, and in the setting forth of these mysteries in the "wedding feast" of the Eucharist, which *incorporates* and deifies us in Christ. The realities we are dealing with here are far beyond morality and law. They are at core sacramental and liturgical/mystical:

> Let me tell you how marriage is also a mystery of the Church. Christ came to the Church (ἦλθε πρὸς τὴν ἐκκλησίαν), and he came to be from her (ἐξ αὐτῆς γέγονε),[10] and he united with her in a spiritual compact, *for*, he says, *I have espoused you as a pure virgin to one husband* (2 Cor 11:2). But that we are of him, hear how it says that *we are all of his members, and of his flesh* (Eph 5:30 Byz). Thinking then on all these things, let us not disgrace so great a mystery. Marriage is a type of the advent of Christ (τύπος τῆς τοῦ Χριστοῦ παρουσίας) . . .[11]

In the following John perceives that the "Nuptial Mystery" of marital union and its fruitfulness was coded into our human constitution *from the beginning*:

> He shows that a man leaves those who begot him, from whom he was born, and is knit to his wife, and that the *one flesh* is father, mother, and child commingled from the substance of the two. For it is indeed by the commingling of their seeds that the child is brought forth, so that the three are *one flesh* (Gen 2:24). Even so are we in relation to Christ. We become *one flesh* with him by participation—and we much more than the child. And why and how so? Because it was so *from the beginning* (Matt 19:8).[12]

13.5 Marital continence and prayer

John has an important teaching on the prayer life of married Christians and the use of marital continence, or periods of sexual fasting. St Jerome, in his *Against Jovinian* 1.7–8 thought the act of marital union a sin since it impedes prayer. Such was his reading of 1 Corinthians 7:5. Let us hear how John deals with the same passage:

---

10. Here Mary is proleptically assimilated to the ecclesia, whom Christ as God the Word precedes, and from whom as the Word incarnate he proceeds.

11. *Homily 12*. PG 62, 389A, NPNF, first ser. 13, 319.

12. *Homily 20*. PG 62, 140A, NPNF, first ser. 13, 146.

> *Do not deprive one another except by agreement for a season, that you may devote yourselves to prayer* (1 Cor 7:5). Here he is referring to especially earnest prayer. Otherwise, if he forbids those who have marital relations to pray, how could his *pray without ceasing* (cf. 1 Thess 5:17) be accommodated? It is possible both to have relations with your wife and yet give heed to prayer, but prayer is approached more intensely with abstinence. Notice that he does not say *that you may pray,* but, *that you may devote yourselves* (ἵνα σχολάζητε) *to prayer,* since marital relations impose preoccupation (ἀσχολίαν) not impurity.[13]

Moreover, John teaches that each spouse must have a care for the other's chastity. It is far better to forsake continence and safeguard the chastity of one's spouse than to indulge in misguided "spirituality" and a one-sided asceticism. Chrysostom reproved wives who acted this way for setting up their husbands for sin rather than righteousness. Admittedly it looks rather one-sided. We earlier remarked on Augustine as a good phenomenologist in these matters. So too is Chrysostom in this famous passage:

> Consider now a husband and wife, where the wife observes continence without her husband's consent. What then? Perhaps he goes on to commit fornication, or even refrains, but mopes and is rattled, and flares up and picks fights, and provokes a myriad quarrels with his wife. What advantage, then, is all the fasting and continence, when love is fragmented like this (ἀγάπης διερρηγμένης)? None at all! How much abuse and trouble, how great a cause of fighting it is![14]

13.6 A husband's headship, and the equality of husband and wife

Unlike Augustine, who alludes to it sparely, John has a strong doctrine of a husband's headship in marriage, drawn from his reading of Ephesians 5. This has a certain social context. In John's day marriage was often between a man in his mid- to late twenties, who had gone through his education and training and successfully launched his career, and a girl in her mid- to late teens. There might be ten years or more between them,

---

13. *Homily 19*, PG 61, 153C; NPNF, first ser. 12, 106.
14. *Homily 19*, PG 61, 153B; NPNF first ser. 12, 106.

quite unexceptional in a Roman marriage. This will help us to understand it when John describes the role of the husband as leader and teacher of his wife. He also makes passing comments about women's weakness, etc., that would not pass muster today. Yet in one homily he describes Rebecca, Isaac's prospective bride, in glowing terms. He contrasts her presence in the marketplace, yet with modesty, her alacrity in service and her vigor of body, with the closeted and pampered life favored for upper-class young women in his time. He seems to have thought that young women were capable of a more vigorous life than he observed was the case in his day.

In one critical aspect, however, John very loudly insisted on the perfect equality of husband and wife, and that concerns marital chastity. We saw how brusquely St Gregory the Theologian rebuked the double standard of marital chastity in Graeco-Roman society. John also strictly and repeatedly admonishes husbands to the same standard of marital fidelity as that expected of wives. He had his work cut out, for this Christian attitude required quite a revolution if Christian men were to contest the *mores* of the society in which they found themselves.

In an oft-quoted passage John encourages the dispositions with which a man should take a woman as his wife. If we take into account the social context as outlined above, and interpret it for today as equally applicable, *mutatis mutandis,* for a wife's dispositions towards her husband, it presents a glowing conception of the relationship between Christian spouses:

> What I recommend is sobriety, and wisdom and the highest manner of life . . . This will succeed in having its effect on the spirit of your bride. For seeing this she will reason with herself in this way: "Wonderful! How wise this man is! He regards this passing life as nothing; he has taken me into his house to become a mother, to bring up his children and to manage his household." "Yes, but this sort of life will be disagreeable for a young bride!" Perhaps for the first day or two, but not for long. Indeed, she will soon reap from this way of life the greatest delight and free herself from all misgiving . . .
>
> With what language should we address her? First of all, speak to her of your love for her; for nothing will persuade her so well to admit what you say as her assurance that you are speaking to her in sincere affection. How then can you show that affection? By saying: "When I was able to choose among many for a wife—those wealthier or of nobler family—I did not choose any of them, because I was enamored of you and your

beautiful life, your modesty, your gentleness and your sobriety of mind ... Money is no real possession, but most despicable, the common hankering of thieves and harlots and grave-robbers. I passed by all these things till I fell in with the excellence of your soul, which I value above all gold. For a young woman who is discreet and sincere, whose heart is set on piety, is worth the whole world.

"This is why I courted you and why I love you, and prefer you to my life itself. For the present life is nothing, and I pray and beseech and will do all I can that we be found worthy to spend this present life in such a way as to be together in the world to come in perfect security. For our time here is brief and fleeting. But if we are counted worthy of being pleasing to God we shall be able to exchange this life for that one, and be forever both with Christ and each other in far greater delight. I place your love above all things, and nothing would be more bitter or painful to me than to be of a different mind than you."[15]

13.6 The family as domestic church

John Chrysostom is the preeminent follower of St Clement of Alexandria in envisaging the Christian family as domestic church. Let us begin with his homily on Ephesians 6:1–4:

> If we regulate our own households in this way, we shall be fit to preside over the Church, for indeed the household is a little Church (καί ἡ οἰκία γὰρ Ἐκκλησία ἐστὶ μικρά).[16]

In a homily on Genesis John also teaches spouses to make their home a church:

> On returning home [from the liturgy in Church], let us prepare two tables, one for food and one for the Word of God, whereupon the man should repeat the things that were said in Church. Let the wife learn and the children listen; nor should the servants be deprived of this reading. Make of your home a church, because you are accountable for the salvation of your children and servants.[17]

---

15. *Homily 20*, PG 62, 145C, 146B; NPNF first ser. 13, 150. Cited and paraphrased in CCC no. 2365.

16. *Homily 20*, PG 62, 143A; NPNF first ser. 13, 148.

17. *Nine Homilies on Genesis, Homily Six: Epilog*, PG 54, 607BC.

In a homily on the following day he says:

> When yesterday I said, "each one of you must see to it that your home becomes a Church", you responded in loud voices and were pleased at what like words had produced in you.[18]

Then there is John's splendid exhortation in a commentary on the Psalms:

> Do you, presiding over the office of the psalms, rise up from table together with your wife and children and sing holy hymns to God? . . . Make your little home into a church. For where we find psalmody, prayer, and the choral songs of the prophets, there is certainly no mistake in calling such a gathering a "church."[19]

John's depiction of shared psalmody, that is, of psalm-singing in family prayer, reminds us of the domestic prayer life in Nazareth contemplated earlier (p. 52), of Tertullian's testimony to the same practice read above (p. 116), and of the re-proposal of the Prayer of the Hours to families by Popes Paul VI and John Paul II.[20] John has many other teachings on the holy conduct of family life, from which one sample that ends on a splendid note, the high order of married holiness:

> Pray together at home. Let each go to Church; and let the husband talk with his wife at home, and she again with her husband, about what was said and read there. If any poverty should overtake you, cite the case of those holy men, Paul and Peter, who were more honored than any kings or rich men; and yet see how they spent their lives, in hunger and in thirst. Teach her that there is nothing in this life to be feared except for offending God. Whoever marries thus, with these dispositions, will be but little inferior to monks; the married but little below the unmarried.[21]

13.7 Divorce and remarriage

As noted above, John impressed on his people again and again that exactly the same gospel standard of chastity applies to men as to women. He

---

18. *Nine Homilies on Genesis, Homily Seven*:1, 608B, cited in Scola, *The Nuptial Mystery*, 199n35.

19. *Homily on Psalm 41*, PG 54, 157D, 158B.

20. Paul VI, *Marialis Cultus*, nos. 53, 54; John-Paul II, *Familiaris Consortio*, no. 61. They endorse and repeat the invitation of *Institutio Generalis de Liturgia Horarum* (1971), no. 27.

21. *Homily 20*, PG 62, 147C; NPNF first ser. 13, 151.

labored to eradicate from the mind-set of his would-be Christian hearers, but especially the males, the pagan double standard concerning adultery. His "pastoral approach" in this can only be described as *total war*. As part of the same struggle, he insisted that the dominical and apostolic word on divorce and remarriage applies to all Christians, whatever the civil law or prevailing social customs might be. In a passage from a homily on the Gospel of John, he pulls no punches with men who expect leniencies as males for "fornication" while they are married, or concessions for a second marriage after "divorce" from their wives, palliated as "fornication." In view of the traditional aversion for second marriages after the death of a spouse, how much more unthinkable, John says, that a man should "marry" a second time while his wife is still alive, and how much his "fornication" with another woman while his wife is with him, is and should be called "adultery."

> For it is impossible that a fornicator should enter the Kingdom of Heaven (cf. 1 Cor 6:9; Mark 7:21-23). Moreover, this is not fornication, but adultery. For as she who is married to one man, if she has intercourse with another man, has committed adultery, so also if a man who is married to one woman takes another, he too has committed adultery. Such a man, therefore will not be heir to the Kingdom, but will plummet into Hell. . . . If it is not permitted for a man who has divorced his own wife and put her out, to have relations with another woman—for this is adultery (εἰ τὸν ἀπολύσαντα τὴν ἑαυτοῦ καὶ ἐκβαλόντα, ἑτέρᾳ μίγνυσθαι οὐκ ἔνι· μοιχεία γὰρ τοῦτό ἐστιν)—how great a wrong does a man commit who has recourse to another woman while his wife is still in his house? . . . For Scripture says: . . . *If anyone puts away his wife, save on account of immorality, he causes her to commit adultery* (Matt 19:5). . . . Do you not know that those who marry another even after the death of their wife are condemned by many for this, even though the practice does attract punishment? But you, while she is still alive, would marry another? (σὺ δὲ καὶ ζώσης ἑτέραν ἐπεισάγεις) Of what lust is this not a token? Learn what is said of such men as these: *their worm does not die*, Scripture says, *and the fire is not quenched* (Mark 9:44).[22]

Here again is John's pastoral approach: *total war*. In the following, like Gregory the Theologian before him, he makes the sharpest possible

---

22. *Homily 63 on John*, PG 59, 353AB, 354B; NPNF first ser. 14, 234-35.

distinction between what is allowed by Roman civil law, and what is allowed by the law of the gospel:

> What then is the law that Paul established for us? *A wife,* he says, *is bound by the law* (cf. Rom 7:2). Wherefore she ought not be separated from her husband while he lives, or take another bridegroom, or agree to a second marriage. See with what accuracy Paul employs the meaning of his words. For he does not say, let her cohabit with him as long as he lives, but this: she is *bound by the law as long as her husband lives,* so that even though he gives her a writ of repudiation, or leaves the house, or lives with another woman, she would still be an adulteress. . . . And do not read to me the laws laid down by outsiders (μὴ γὰρ μοι τοὺς παρὰ τοῖς ἔξωθεν κείμενους νόμους ἀναγνῶς) which require a writ of repudiation, and so to divorce. Because in that Day, God will not judge you according to these laws, but according to those which He Himself has established.[23]

Such then is the common witness of the sub-apostolic age, the early apologists, and the ante-Nicene and post-Nicene Fathers of the Church, both East and West. The dominical and apostolic doctrine of the indissolubility of Christian marriage was upheld and preached by the great Greek Fathers.

---

23. *Homily on "A wife is bound,"* PG 218D and 219BC.

Chapter Fourteen

CHRISTIAN MARRIAGE IN CONSTANTINOPLE 500-1200

14.1 Canon Law traditions in West and East

OUR CONCERN IN THIS final chapter is to study how and when the Constantinopolitan church lost its purchase on the dominical and apostolic doctrine on divorce and remarriage. This we do by considering how the canon law on marriage in the Christian East and the Christian West began to diverge in the sixth century, until by the twelfth century the gap was very wide indeed. This is the background to the different disciplines of marriage that obtain between the churches in communion with Rome today, and the Eastern Orthodox Churches. We will confine our attention to developments in Constantinople and the Greek Church, whose legacy more or less continued in the distinctive Slavonic Christian traditions that took their rise with Saints Cyril and Methodius in the ninth century. We will not be considering the various non-Chalcedonian churches of the *real* East, i.e. the "Oriental" Churches, except for one extremely interesting look at contemporary events in the Coptic Church.

14.2 A sixth-century watershed: Dionysius Exiguus and John Scholasticus

Clarence Gallagher focuses on three pairs of canonical collections,[1] one Latin and one Greek in each pair, which he thinks exemplify both the

---

1. On the development of canon law in this period, see Gallagher, *Church Law*.

common elements and the divergences of Latin Canon Law and Greek Canon Law. The first pair, in the sixth century, are the canonical collections of Dionysius Exiguus for Rome, and of John Scholasticus for the Greek East. We will largely confine our comments to these two, which set the trends for future.[2]

Dionysius Exiguus was a monk from the Black Sea littoral, the Dobrudgea region of what is modern Romania. Rome and Constantinople were at that time enjoying their first extended schism, the Acacian schism (489–519). Fluent in both Greek and Latin, Dionysius was sent in a monastic delegation to Constantinople, seeking the truth in the midst of fierce christological controversies. It seems he wrote from Constantinople to Rome seeking counsel, and found himself "head-hunted" for the Papal chancery by Pope Gelasius. He arrived in Rome c. 497 only to find that the pope had died. Dionysius nevertheless stayed, and henceforth directed all his efforts to conciliation between the two ecclesiastical centers. His synthesis of church law, called the *Dionysiana*, became an early *Corpus Iuris Canonici* of the Western church for centuries to come. His sources were first of all the conciliar and synodal canons of the third to fifth century, for which he provided fresh and accurate translations from the Greek. But he also incorporated a second source: the formal replies given by the pope of Rome to enquiries about church praxis, which go by the name of papal *decretals*. This was something new. By fixing on these two sources, early church councils and later papal constitutions, Dionysius set something of the tone of the Latin approach to canon law thereafter.

Emperor Justinian (527–65) soon rose to dominate the Eastern Empire for much of the sixth century. His name is forever associated with the codification of Roman law. But let us first consider John Scholasticus. John was a lawyer in Antioch who was inspired by Justinian's legislation and Dionysius's work in Rome, and began, c. 535, a comprehensive collection of Greek canon law, called Συναγωγὴ κανόνων ἐκκλησιαστικῶν εἰς ν΄ τίτλους διῃρεμένη ("collection of ecclesiastical canons divided into fifty titles"), or the *Synagoge* for short. It is the basis of all that followed,

---

2. The second pair, in the ninth century, are the anonymous Pseudo-Isidorean Decretals in the West, and in the East that revision of the *Nomokanon in Fourteen Titles* known as the *Nomokanon of Photios*, published in 882. The third pair, in the twelfth century, are Gratian of Bologna for the West, whose *Decretum*, published in 1141, became the basis of all subsequent study of canon law in the West, and for the East, Theodore Balsamon of Constantinople, the magisterial reviser and commentator of *Nomokanon in fourteen titles*, published in about 1170.

hence John is regarded as the founding father of the canon law of the Greeks. Ordained a priest for Antioch c. 541, he was sent as legate of the Patriarch of Antioch to Constantinople, where he himself became Patriarch from 565 to 577.

As sources of canon law, John first of all used much the same collection of third-to-fifth century conciliar and synodal decisions that Dionysius had used. But the *Synagoge* is distinctive for two innovations. Firstly, it includes St Basil the Great's letters to the new bishop Amphilochius as a source of general church law. He thus initiated the custom of invoking the Church Fathers as juridical authorities for the whole church, which they, as individual bishops, strictly, did not have. The West in turn imitated this trend with Gratian in the twelfth century, a third of whose *Decretum* consists of citations from the Fathers, including Eastern Fathers. Secondly, John Scholasticus also incorporated a selection of Justinian's legislation in church matters as a source of church law. This was a decision fraught with consequences, for it gave imperial and civil legislation a determinative role in the government of the church's internal affairs that, strictly, they did not have. Which brings us back to Justinian.

14.3 Christian Emperors and Roman law: Justinian

If there is a single reason why the Eastern Orthodox churches forsook the ἀκρίβεια ("accuracy") of their observance of the dominical and apostolic prohibition on divorce and remarriage, it is because of the position the Emperor came to assume in the church of the Eastern Roman Empire. The Christian emperors in Constantinople were the continuing, direct heirs of the Eastern Roman emperors. Right up until the catastrophe of 1453 they knew themselves to be, and were styled, emperors, not of the *Greeks*—but of the *Romans*. The sacral character of the Roman emperor in the polity of the *oikoumené* long predated Constantine. It continued, *mutatis mutandis*, in the Christian dispensation, in the marriage of Empire and church, the kind of ideology promoted by Eusebius of Caesarea in his *Panegyric* of Constantine.

Justinian acceded to the throne in 524. In 527 he appointed the jurist Tribonian, who it happens was not a Christian, to the task of reediting the Roman law books. They were all in Latin, although a supplement was later added in Greek, the *Novellae*. Much material, therefore, consisted of pre-Christian Roman Law. Unsurprisingly, the Roman legislation for divorce remained in place in what was, after all, civil law:

One of the more sure-footed recent comparative historians has remarked, "In Justinian's law the Christian concept that marriage was indissoluble is almost completely lacking... However disapproved of and seen as a means of exploring sexual opportunities in remarriage, divorce remained a matter of secular law, into which canonical enactments only slowly and irregularly spilled over."[3]

The long-term result was, as Gallagher points out, that "Justinian's law became a constituent part of Greek Orthodox legal tradition."[4]

The consent that made a marriage in Roman law was a two-edged sword, for the law also provided for divorce in the traditional terms of a withdrawal of consent, and it continued so under the Christian emperors. Nevertheless, it became increasingly difficult for either spouse to remarry. Although Justinian attempted to circumscribe divorce on grounds of mutual consent, he permitted it on other grounds. In 548, he equalized the penalties between the sexes for initiating unjustified divorce actions.[5]

The alienation began when imperial legislation in church affairs, and the emperors' claim to supervise the discipline of the church, came to be accepted into the Eastern canonical collections. In 630 a revision of the *Synagoge in XIV Titles* called the "Nomokanon," endorsed the percolation of the Roman law of divorce into church canons. The very term itself tells the whole tale: the conflation of Roman civil law (*nomos*) and church law (*canon*). Imperial constitutions on ecclesiastical subjects (*nomoi*) and conciliar *canones* were integrated, implying an equal status in the church of the canons issued by church councils and the legislation of the emperors. It established the emperor at the pinnacle of church governance. From then on, the civil lawfulness of divorce and remarriage inherited from pre-Christian Rome gradually filtered through Christian polity, and, as Orthodox theologian John Meyendorff avers,[6] was never formally challenged by the church.[7]

3. Olsen, ed., *Christian Marriage*, 155.
4. Gallagher, "Marriage in Eastern," 8.
5. Olsen, ed., *Christian Marriage*, 175.
6. Meyendorff, *Byzantine Theology*, 82.

7. The common basis for the marriage law of the Orthodox Churches today is to be found in the *sacri canones* listed in the second canon of the Council in Trullo in 692. These "sacred canons" were confirmed by the Second Council of Nicaea in 787, which declared that they had come down from three sources: the apostles, "the six holy and universal synods and the regional councils," and the "Holy Fathers." Cf. Gallagher, *Christian Marriage*, 145.

14.4 St Basil's canons on marriage, adultery, and fornication

It was one thing to allow civil legislation on marriage and divorce to creep into church law. It was another thing to actively defend this novelty in church practice. It would help if you could claim the authority of the Holy Fathers. And Fathers of the Church do not come much holier than St Basil! So it comes as a surprise to learn that the Eastern Orthodox press Basil's "canons" into service of divorce and remarriage.[8]

In his Canon 21, Basil reports the custom as he has found it in the church of his time and place. And he is not happy about it:

> When a husband living with a wife, being dissatisfied with the marriage, falls into fornication, we judge such a person a fornicator and hold him to a longer period under penalty, but we have no canon subjecting him to the charge of adultery if the sin is committed against an unmarried woman . . . He who has committed fornication shall not be excluded from living with his wife. A wife, therefore shall receive back her husband if he returns from fornication, whereas the husband will dismiss the polluted woman from his house. Indeed the reasoning in these matters is not easy, but such is the custom that has prevailed.[9]

Well might the great Father feel uneasy at such "customs"! They have simply absorbed unchallenged the double standard of adultery in Roman law and widespread social custom, rather than that strict moral parity between the sexes that is the law of the gospel.

Canon 9 in particular is the *locus classicus*. It opens with a frank acknowledgment by Basil of the gospel standard:

> The Lord's pronouncement that it is not lawful to depart (ἐξεῖναι) from a marriage save on the ground of fornication, according to its logical sense applies to men and women alike.[10]

Note that the word he uses means "depart from," i.e. "separate from," not "divorce" as in the civil dissolution of a valid marriage. He upholds in principle the parity of the demands applied in the gospel to both men

---

8. For a magisterial reading of Basil's *dicta* on divorce and remarriage, see Crouzel, *L'Eglise primitive*, 133–50; on Basil's "canons," 137–50.

9. Letter 199, in *St Basil: The Letters* III, 102–35 at 112–13, known as Canon 21 in the *Second Canonical Letter to Amphilochius, Bishop of Iconium*.

10. Letter 188, in *St Basil: The Letters*, 4–47 at 34–39, known as Canon 9 in the *First Canonical Letter to Amphilochius, Bishop of Iconium*.

and women alike. Notwithstanding he reports: "Yet custom does not so obtain, but in the case of the woman we find a greater strictness." According to this "custom," the separation of a man from his wife *because of her adultery* is allowable, and if he cohabits with another (unmarried) woman, he is liable *after repentance* to the "longer" penance for fornication, but not for adultery, i.e. seven years exclusion from Holy Communion. The separation of a woman from her husband *because of his adultery*, however, does not receive even this much lenience. If she cohabits with another man she incurs the full penance for adultery, i.e. fifteen years gradated exclusion from Holy Communion. Basil continues in his Canon 9:

> Therefore, she who has abandoned her husband is an adulteress, if she has gone to another man. And he who has been abandoned is pardonable (συγγνωστός), and she who cohabits with such a man is not condemned.

Such a double standard of adultery between the sexes, even if accommodated in local "custom," puzzled Basil, as we noted in his Canon 21. The reason is, of course, its discrepancy from the express teaching of our Lord and the Apostles, which he attests in his own foundational work, the *Moralia*, no. 73:

> That a husband must not separate from (χωρίζεσθαι) a wife, or a wife from a husband, unless one of them is taken in fornication with another, or hindered in piety to God. ...That it is not lawful for him who has dismissed (ἀπολύσαντι) his own wife to marry another, or for her who is dismissed by her husband to marry someone else.[11]

It is exactly as we found it in Hermas! Even so, the differential of penances accorded husband and to wife for the same gravest of sins, adultery, reluctantly reported by Basil in Canon 9, came later to be used as a loophole for allowing divorce and remarriage while one's spouse was still alive.

Compare Basil's Canon 4[12] on digamy, trigamy, and polygamy. Digamy here refers to the second marriage of a widow or widower, not of a divorced, as we saw in earlier centuries, and in contemporary Greek Fathers.[13] Basil reports a penalty of one or two years in the case of digamy, and three or four years in the case of trigamy. That is, such unseemly

---

11. *Moralia*, PG 31.849D, 31.852B.

12. Letter 188, in *St Basil: The Letters* III, 24–27.

13. See Crouzel's exposition of this canon (and canons 24, 41, 50, 53, 80, in *L'Eglise primitive*, 148–50.

remarriages were tolerated, but incurred much shorter penances. Compare "fornication" proper, which incurred a four- to seven-year penance. Basil disapproved serial marriages after the death of one's spouse(s)[14] as much as Gregory the Theologian did.

We saw earlier how vigorously Gregory rebutted the idea that the church could in any way appease the pagan double standard of adultery. As was right! What *should* have happened is never to have allowed any slippage into such disparity at all, as Basil's unease bears witness, still less to have later transposed the "concession" of the penalty for "fornication" to an adulterous husband on the basis of the pagan double standard, to a wife also, so that she too might divorce an adulterous husband and be treated more leniently. Instead, the stricter standard to which the wife was held, which was that of the gospel, should have been assigned also to a husband, and the later surreptitious "reinterpretation" of these unequal customs in favor of the remarriage of the divorced be entirely cut off.

14.5 Fish rotting from the head

After the Nomocanon (630) and the Council in Trullo (692), the conflation of Roman civil law and canon law on divorce began to filter through the Christian *oikoumené* in the eighth century, gathered pace in the ninth and the tenth centuries, and conquered the field in the eleventh. We can only advert briefly to the events in Constantinople that reveal the gradual shift. Like the proverbial rotting fish, the decay began at the head, that is, at the imperial throne, and spread by bad example down the social ranks. At first, monks and clergy responded in the spirit of the fourth-century Greek Fathers: human law does not meet Christian moral standards, and Christians should not think themselves entitled to live by it. Nevertheless, in a slide to the lowest common denominator, whatever was *legal* came to be appropriated as *moral*, as the civil law migrated into the church's

---

14. Basil, in *On the Hexaemeron*, Homily 8.6, 177C, shows the same thinking as the early Christians, and of his own sister Macrina: marriage for Christians is properly a once-only affair. A second marriage *after the death of one's spouse* is unseemly: "They say that the turtledove, once separated from her mate, no longer accepts union with another (μηκέτι τὴν πρὸς ἕτερον καταδέχεσθαι κοινωνίαν), but in memory of her former yokefellow, remains unpaired (μένειν ἀσυνδύαστον), refusing communion with another (τὴν πρὸς ἕτερον κοινωνίαν ἀπαρνουμένην). Let the women hear how the dignity of widowhood (τὸ σεμνὸν τῆς χηρείας), even among the irrational creatures, is preferred to the unseemliness of multiple marriages (τοῦ ἐν ταῖς πολυγαμίαις ἀπρεποῦς προτιμότερον)."

administration of Christian marriage. The emergent loopholes were exploited by the highest echelons of Christian society, beginning with the Iconoclast Emperor Constantine V Copronymus (741–775).

A crisis was reached in the *Moechian* or *Adulterous Affair* in which the higumen Platon and his nephew, the great St Theodore the Studite (759–826), publicly rebuked the second "marriage" of Emperor Constantine VI (780–797) after divorcing his wife Maria the Paphlagonian, who was still alive.[15] Theodore repeatedly denounced the emperor as a "second Herod."[16] Clearly, like Chrysostom, Theodore lacked formation in carefully guarded diplomatic-speak. Not insignificantly, he was one of the last Greek Fathers to insist on collaboration with the Pope of Rome.[17] In a brave last stand, he refuted to the face of Emperor Leo V (813–820) the entire ideology of caesaropapism that had fastened like an incubus on the Constantinopolitan Church:

> Do not, O Emperor, disturb the constitution of the Church! For the apostle said: *and of those God appointed in the church, there were first apostles, second prophets, third pastors and teachers* (1 Cor 12:28). He did not mention "emperors." To you is entrusted the political constitution and the army. Take care of these things, and leave the Church to pastors and teachers, in accordance with the divine word. If you do not wish to pay heed to these for the sake of our faith, then know that even *if an angel* comes *down from heaven* intending to deceive us (Gal 1:8), we will not listen to him, let alone you, O Emperor![18]

This is to be authentically a "prophet" in the church, to bear a flame of apostolic fire in the midst of a tame leadership cowed by mob contagion in whatever form it comes, even from civil rulers. Theodore paid the cost of his witness-bearing with imperial opprobrium, incarceration, public whipping on his bare back, and three periods of exile.

But it was all to no avail, for incidents of emperors remarried in the lifetime of their spouses multiplied through the ninth and tenth centuries, conspicuously in the multiple adulteries and remarriages of Emperor Leo VI (866–912). It reached a crescendo in the eleventh century, with the

---

15. See Theodore's account in his *Eulogy of Platon* at PG 832B–33A, and his Letters 1–3 to Platon in *The Letters*, 903–20.

16. Theodore's letters often name Constantine a "second Herod," e.g. Letters 22, 28, 31, 443. See Garland, *Byzantine Empresses*, 84–87.

17. See his letter 33, to Pope Leo III, in *The Letters*, 1017–22.

18. Translated from de Boor, *Georgii monachi chronicon*, 779–80.

spectacular marital and imperial careers of Empress Zoe (1028–1050)[19] and Empress Maria of Alania (1053–1118).[20] We shall have to elide the sordid tale of divorces, "oikonomias," multiple remarriages, murders, bigamies, and incest that swirled about the Christian imperial throne in this century, all too often with the collusion of a compliant and/or corrupt clergy, right up to and including the patriarch.

Such is the historical matrix out of which the later Eastern Orthodox "theology of *oikonomia*" emerged. It was an apologia *after the fact* of divorce and remarriage, justified initially for high reasons of state, but inevitably filtering into common practice. It was a fair-seeming theology that would overlay the ancient obedience of the church universal, and of the Greek Fathers in particular. Such an accommodation to the secular powers worked by manipulating the semantics of patristic texts, as we have seen, whereby the reluctant concessions made to second and third marriages of widows and widowers, in the fourth century, became the "economic" concessions made in the eleventh century to the second and third marriages of those whose spouses were still alive. And this is what latter-day theologians and prelates in the Western church propose as imitable "pastoral" precedent.

An example is Gallagher himself, who despite clearly tracing the Eastern adoption of divorce and remarriage to its beginnings in the Justinian period, takes a liberal view of the question, suggesting that Eastern "oikonomia" on this point might be a model for the West. He shows little critical awareness of earlier patristic testimonies, or the degree to which later Greek tradition departed from the evangelical witness of the Greek Fathers themselves. In discussing the late Eastern idea that it is the priest's blessing that confers the Christian sacrament upon human marriage, he does not indicate that this liturgical theology too had a history,[21] being settled upon the Constantinopolitan Church by imperial authority between the ninth century with the *Novella* 89 of Leo VI "the Wise"—he of many adulterous remarriages—and the eleventh century with the *Novella* 35 of Alexius I Comnenus—"married" to his adoptive mother, the adulteress Maria of Alania. When Gallagher speaks of "the problem of those

19. See Kalavrezou, "Irregular Marriages in the Eleventh Century," and Garland, *Byzantine Empresses*, Chapter 8, "Zoe Porphyrogenneta" (1028–50), 136–57.

20. See Garland, *Byzantine Empresses*, "The Empresses of Alexios I Komnenos (1081–1118)," 180–98 at 180–86.

21. See Dodaro, ed., *Remaining in the Truth of Christ*, 18–21, especially Vasil, "Separation, Divorce, Dissolution," 93–128.

Christians who would otherwise be condemned to a life of enforced continence through no fault of their own,"[22] we seem to hear the accents of Lutheran pessimism, or of the degraded, deterministic anthropology of late secular modernity.

In a long essay published in 1923 by "S. Troitsky"—possibly Bishop Hilarion Troitsky (1886–1929)—we have a Russian theologian-bishop who was too good a patrologist and too truthful not to see anomalies in the received canonical tradition of his church on divorce and remarriage. Even then he was combatting moves being made in some Eastern Orthodox quarters to allow priests a second marriage after the death of their wives. Troitsky knows his St Theodore and quotes him. He traces the beginning of these "illegitimate" accommodations to the influence of the emperors beginning in the eighth century. In the end he allows that Rome retains the ancient tradition. Note that he uses "digamy" in the later adapted sense of a second "marriage" of the divorced:

> At first the marriage of digamists was a manifestation of illegitimate pressures upon the Church on the part of the State. Theodore Studite thinks that the practice of marrying digamists began during the reign of the dishonorable Constantine Copronymus and iconoclast (741–775) as a result of his trigamy, since "it was not so before that." . . . It was only when a church wedding was mandated by imperial law to make a marriage valid, and as a result of which a refusal of a wedding ceremony was tantamount to the declaration of the union as simple adultery, did the Church permit the marriage of digamists. At first this was allowed only in Constantinople, and this special rite was not found in other [Eastern] churches even in the XIII c., and is not known in Rome to this day.[23]

14.6 The witness of the Coptic Church

Troitsky remarked that the "illegitimate" novelty of divorce and remarriage had not made headway in the other Eastern churches, i.e. the Oriental Churches *not* of the Constantinopolitan communion, as late as the thirteenth century. The Coptic Church, which had perforce made her way outside the imperial *oikoumené* from the seventh century, succumbed as

---

22. Gallagher, *Church Law*, 12.
23. Retrieved from http://www.holy-trinity.org/morality/troitsky.html.

late as the 1930s to the example set by Constantinople, when a liberal policy of divorce and remarriage was introduced. However, beginning in 1971, Pope Shenouda III resolved to return his church to the Coptic heritage, largely that of ancient Christianity, on the indissoluble bond of Christian marriage. A voluble party of dissenters arose, however, who were very clever at using the media. Some of those hankering for a return to a liberal regime of divorce and remarriage have even been willing to convert to Islam to secure a second marriage after divorce. The Copts offer to us an example of an entire *sui juris* church attempting a church-wide repentance, not without painful internal tensions, from an earlier succumbing to laxity. Our Lord warned that the two-edged sword piercing to the division of soul and spirit would pass through one's own "household"—and yes, this can mean even the "household" of the church.

14.7 Long-term trends between Rome and Constantinople

To informed Westerners the later Eastern Orthodox concession of second and third "marriages" in the lifetime of a spouse obviously absorbed easier Roman legal and social regimes. Some echo of the ancient "accuracy" remains. Easterners allow only one crowning, to the first marriage; second and third marriages take place with some tokens of penance. Priests are, or have been, held to the ancient discipline: no remarriage is possible, not only after divorce (which does happen among the clergy), but even after a wife's death. This stricter discipline derives from an apostolic rule that historically governed the marital status of clergy, in both the Eastern and Western churches: *let each man remain in that wherein he was called* (1 Cor 7:20). Thus a married deacon in the West today may not marry again if his wife dies.

To Easterners the Western tradition "lacks pastoral compassion." That is the invariable language. Western "juridicism" is also invoked, or—a favorite canard this one—"Augustinian views of sexuality," to justify a departure from a truth that Westerners maintain is simply the unbroken tradition of the church from the Lord to the apostles to the practice of the early Christian centuries to the Greek Fathers.[24] Thus liberal Easterners often end by marshaling the same types of arguments as secular modernists. Invoking Western "juridicism" is precious, since it was precisely the gradual penetration of "law," i.e. this-worldly civil law,

---

24. Olsen, ed., *Christian Marriage*, 155.

into Eastern church practices that led to the loss of gospel *praxis*. The Western church, in the long run, proved herself more resolute in insisting that for the children of Holy Baptism, that is the children of the church, human sexuality and marriage do indeed belong wholly under the sway of the Mystery of Christ and of his commands, very much so.

The historical expediency of the Orthodox Churches as Catholics see it, reemerged in regard to contraception. When in 1968 Paul VI promulgated *Humanae Vitae*, Patriarch Athenagoras of Constantinople immediately wrote to the pope to congratulate him for having "taken the good step of publishing the encyclical *Humanae Vitae*. We are in total agreement with you."

Nevertheless, many Eastern Orthodox theologians and apologists soon saw otherwise. There was of course the contemporary revolt of many "Catholic" theologians, of which more later. One can sense an unfolding genealogy of ideas in the first half of the 20th century.

Seminal ideas had been coming out of the emigré Russian intelligentsia in Paris, associated especially with the St. Sergius Orthodox Theological Institute. In 1944, Paul Evdokimov published his *Le Sacrement de l'amour*, and in 1962 a revised edition. He came to embrace the practice of marital contraception, or "birth-control" as it was called, a secular idea that had been lapping at the Protestant world in the 1920s, and swiftly conquered the field in the 1930s. It was also affecting the thinking of contemporary Catholic theologians, such as the left wing of the German personalists, and during the 1950s, moral theologian Bernard Häring, who went on to have a huge influence in the post-Vatican II Catholic Church. Another conspicuous feature of *Le Sacrement de l'amour* was its eloquent defense of and advocacy for the liberal Russian Orthodox provision for divorce and remarriage.

The rest of the Eastern Orthodox world, however, had yet to catch up with the sophisticated thinking from the Continent. In 1963 the first edition of new convert Timothy Ware's book, *The Orthodox Church*, laconically concluded its section on the Sacrament of Marriage with: "Artificial methods of birth control are forbidden in the Orthodox Church."[25] This bare statement vanished in later editions, to be replaced by longer, more nuanced passages of 'ifs' and 'buts'. Revisionism among the Eastern Orthodox appears to have quickened after the publication of Philip Sherrard's "*Humanae Vitae*" in 1969. Finally, Evdokimov's influential book

---

25. Ware, *The Orthodox Church*, 302.

was published for the anglophone world in 1985 as *The Sacrament of Love*. The new attractively nuanced "theology," or perhaps rather, *theosophy* of Christian marital contraception appears in full force.[26] Strangely—very strangely—Evdokimov consummates his thoughts on the beauty of Christian marriage with an eloquent, poetic "theology" of the death of marriage, and of divorce and remarriage.[27] It is a bizarre last note.

It seems that today only in the churches in communion with the see of Peter—and perhaps those of the Coptic/Syrian/Armenian/Ethiopian axis—is the dominical and apostolic doctrine defended—if currently under very formidable, subtle, and corrosive pressures—and the unbroken tradition of the early Christian centuries and the Fathers of the Church upheld, that the bond of *marriage . . . in the Lord* (1 Cor 7:39) is unbreakable, because it is Christ who embraces the union of the two, and is himself their bond, and furthermore, that the coherence of the mutual self-gift of husband and wife in the marital embrace, and their shared openness to God's transcendence and creative power, is also unbreakable. This is the truth, it really is the truth.

For what else is this than to ratify in our inmost being *the image of God* (1 Gen 1:27) in which we were first created, now revealed in the fullness of time as the Mystery of Christ (2 Cor 4:4, Col 1:15, 26), and so to resolve to bring God in from the cold where we had expelled him, to place him in the center of our marriages, to take for our inalienable model the living God who is none other than steadfast love and truth, and, in the word that peals constantly through the Greek liturgy, *philanthropos*, "the lover of man."

---

26. Evdokimov, *The Sacrament of Love*, 174–80.
27. Evdokimov, *The Sacrament of Love*, 186–92.

BIBLIOGRAPHY

Anastasius of Sinai, Saint. *Interrogationes et responsiones de diversis capitibus a diversis propositae* ("Questions and answers on various topics, asked by various people"), PG 89, 311A–824C.

Ante-Nicene Fathers. General editors Alexander Roberts and James Robertson, revised by A. Cleveland Coxe; original edition, Buffalo: Christian Literature Publishing Co., 1885. Reprinted Peabody, MA: Hendrickson, 1995.

Arendzen, J. P. "Ante-Nicene Interpretations of the Sayings on Divorce." *The Journal of Theological Studies* 20 (1919) 230–41.

Aristotle. *Generation of Animals.* Translated by A. L. Peck. London: Heinemann, 1963.

———. *Politics.* Translated by H. Rackham. London: Heineman, 1932, rev. 1944.

Augustine. *De nuptiis et concupiscentia* (c. 420). In 2 bks. CSEL 42. Edited by C. F. Urba and J. Zycha. Vienna, 1902, 14–319. PL 44, 413–474. NPNF first ser. 5, 257–308.

———. *De Genesi ad litteram, in twelve books.* PL 34, 245–486. In *The Literal Meaning of Genesis*, 2 vols., translated by J. H. Taylor. Ancient Christian Writers nos. 41–42. New York: Newman, 1982.

———. *De gestis Pelagii* (On the proceedings of Pelagius). PL 44, 191–228.

———. *De bono coniugali* (c. 401). CSEL 41. Edited by J. Zycha. Vienna, 1900, 185–281. PL 40, 373–396. NPNF first ser. III, 395–413.

———. *Epistulae.* In six volumes CSEL 34/1 1895, 34/2 1898, 44 1904, 57 1911, 58 1924, 88; edited by J. Divjak, 1981.

Athenagoras of Athens. *Embassy for the Christians.* PG 6, 889–972. ANF II, 129–48.

Basil the Great, Saint. *St Basil: The Letters.* Translated by Roy J. Deferrari. 4 vols. London: Heinemann, I 1926, II 1928, III 1930, IV 1934.

———. *On the Hexaemeron, Homily 8.* PG 29, 163–188 at 177C. NPNF second ser. 8, 51–107.

———. *The Moralia.* PG 31, 699–870. English translation in Clarke, *The Ascetic Works*, 101–131. *St Basil the Great: On Christian Ethics.* Translated by Jacob N. Van Sickle. Yonkers, NY: SVS Press, 2014.

Benedict XVI, Pope. "Dependence on God makes us free." *L'Osservatore Romano Weekly Edition in English*, August 22, 2012.

———. *The Fathers.* Huntingdon, IN: Our Sunday Visitor, 2008.

Berrouard, M. F. "Saint Augustin et l'indissolubilité du mariage: L'Évolution de sa pensée." In *Studia Patristica* 11 (1972) 291–306.

Bianchi, Ugo. "Augustine on Concupiscence." *Studia Patristica* 22 (1989) 202–12.

Brakke, David. *Athanasius and Asceticism*. Baltimore: Johns Hopkins University Press, 1998.
Brown, Peter. *The Body and Society: Men, Women and Sexual Renunciation in Early Christianity*. New York: Columbia University Press, 1988.
Buckland, W. W., and P. Stein. *A Text-Book of Roman Law from Augustus to Justinian*. Cambridge: Cambridge University Press, 1966.
Caldecott, Stratford. "Male and Female Souls." http://www.theimaginativeconservative.org/2013/09/male-and-female-souls.html.
Cicero. *Pro Archia Poeta Oratio 23*. Perseus under Philologic, 2018 edition, *Latin Texts & Translations*. http://perseus.uchicago.edu/perseus-cgi/citequery3.pl?dbname=LatinAugust2012&getid=1&query=Cic.%20Arch.%202323.
Chrysostom, John. *On Virginity* (before 392). H. Murillo & B. Grillet, *Sources Chrétiennes* vol. 125. Paris: du Cerf, 1966. PG 48, 533–96. English translation in *On Virginity, Against Remarriage*. Translated by Sally Rieger Shore, introduced by Elizabeth Clark, 1–128. Studies in Women and Religion 9. New York: Mellen, 1983.
———. "Address on Vainglory and the Right Way for Parents to Bring Up their Children." In Laistner, *Christianity and Pagan Culture* (Ithaca, NY: Cornell University Press, 1951), 93–122.
———. *Nine Homilies on Genesis, Homily Six (2:17-24)*. PG 54, 604–7.
———. *Nine Homilies on Genesis, Homily Seven (2:9)*. PG 54, 607–16.
———. *Homily on Psalm 41*. PG 55, 155–167.
———. *Homily 63 on John*. PG 59, 349–54. NPNF first ser. 14, 232–35.
———. *On the Apostle's words "on account of fornication"* (1 Cor 7:2). PG 51, 207–18.
———. *Homily 19 on 1 Corinthians 7 (7:1-2)*. PG 61, 151–160. NPNF, first ser. 12, 105–11.
———. *Homily on "A wife is bound"* (1 Cor 7.39-40), otherwise known as *de libello repudii* ("on the bill of divorce"). PG 51, 217–26.
———. *Homily 12 on Colossians (4:12-13)*. PG 62, 299–392. NPNF first ser. 13, 314–21.
———. *Homily 20 on Ephesians (5:22-24)*. PG 62, 135–50. NPNF first ser. 13, 143–52.
Clark, Gillian. *Women in Late Antiquity: Pagan and Christian Life-Styles*. Oxford: Oxford University Press, 1993.
Clark, E. A., ed. *St Augustine on Marriage and Sexuality*. Washington, DC: Catholic University of America Press, 1996.
Clarke, W. K. L. *The Ascetic Works of St Basil*. London: SPCK, 1925.
Clement of Alexandria, Saint. *Stromateis*, in ten books. Books 1–4, PG 8.685–1382, Books 6–10, PG 9.9–602. For English translation see ANF II, 165–604, and *Clement of Alexandria/Stromateis* Books 1–3. Translated by John Ferguson. Fathers of the Church Series vol. 85. Washington, DC: Catholic University of America Press, 1991.
———. *Clement of Alexandria/Christ the Educator*. Translated by Simon P. Wood. Fathers of the Church Series vol. 23. Washington, DC: Catholic University of America Press, 1954.
Comiskey, Andrew. *Pursuing Sexual Wholeness*. Lake Mary, FL: Creation House, 1989.
Crespy, George, Paul Evdokimov, and Christian Duquoc. *Marriage and Christian Tradition*. Translated by Agnes Cunningham. Techny, IL: Divine Word, 1968.
Crouzel, Henri. "Divorce and Remarriage in the Early Church: Some Reflections on Historical Methodology." In *Communio* 41 (2014) 472–503, translated by Michael

Borras from H. Crouzel, "Divorce et remariage dans l'Église primitive," *Nouvelle Revue Théologique* 98 (1976) 891–917.

———. "Le texte patristique de Mt V, 32 et XIX, 9, 19." *New Testament Studies* 19 (1972–1973) 891–917.

———. *L'Eglise primitive face au divorce, du premier au cinquième siècle*. Paris: Beauchesne, 1971.

Daniélou, Jean. *Platonisme et théologie mystique: Essai sur la doctrine spirituelle de saint Grégoire de Nysse*. Paris: Aubier, 1944.

Davies, Philip R., et al., eds. *The Complete World of the Dead Sea Scrolls*. New York: Thames & Hudson, 2011.

de Boor, Carolus. *Georgii monachi chronicon*. Leipzig: Teubner, 1904.

Demosthenes. *Demosthenes: Private Orations, Volume VI: Orations 50–59: Private Cases*. Translated by A. T. Murray. London: Heinemann, 1939.

Dodaro, Robert, ed. *Remaining in the Truth of Christ: Marriage and Communion in the Catholic Church*. San Francisco: Ignatius, 2014.

Douie, Decima L., and Hugh Farmer, eds. *The Life of St Hugh of Lincoln by Adam of Eynsham*, 2 vols. London: Nelson, 1962.

Elliott, Peter. *What God Has Joined . . . : The Sacramentality of Marriage*. Staten Island, NY: Alba, 1990.

Esolen, Anthony. "Belial's Witness." *The Catholic Thing*. https://www.thecatholicthing.org/2018/03/10/belials-witnesses.

Evagrius. *Chapters On Prayer*. Under the works of Nilus, PG 79, 1165–1200. *Evagrius Ponticus: The Praktikos and Chapters on Prayer*, translated by John Eudes Bamberger. Cistercian Studies Series 4. Kalamazoo, MI: Cistercian, 1972.

Evdokimov, Paul. *The Sacrament of Love: The Nuptial Mystery in the Light of the Orthodox Tradition*. Crestwood, NY: St Vladimir's Seminary Press, 1985. A translation by A. P. Gythiel and V. Steadman of *Le Sacrement de l'amour: Le mystère conjugal à la lumière de la tradition orthodoxe*, rev. ed., 1962.

Fellhauer, David E. "The *consortium omnis vitae* as a Juridical Element of Marriage." *Studia Canonica* 13 (1979) 3–171.

Fitzgerald Allan D., ed. *Augustine through the Ages: An Encyclopedia*. Grand Rapids: Eerdmans, 1999.

Fitzmyer, Joseph. "The Matthean Divorce Texts and Some New Palestinian Evidence." *Theological Studies* 37 (1976) 197–226.

Ford, David C. *Women and Men in the Early Church: The Full Views of St John Chrystostom*. South Canaan, PA: St Tikon's, 1996.

Galen. *De usu partium corporis humani*. Claudio Galeni Opera. Vol. 4. Edited by Karl G. Kühn, 1–366. Leipzig: Cnobloch, 1822.

Gallagher, Clarence, SJ. "Marriage in Eastern and Western Canon Law." *Law and Justice: Christian Law Review* 7 (2006) 7–16.

———. *Church Law and Church Order in Rome and Byzantium*. Aldershot: Ashgate, 2002.

Garland, Lynda. *Byzantine Empresses*. London: Routledge, 1999.

Gasparro, G. S., et al. *The Human Couple in the Fathers*. Translated by Thomas Halton. Pauline Patristic Series 1. Staten Island, NY: Alba, 1999.

Gilbert, Peter, translator. *On God and Man, The Theological Poetry of St Gregory of Nazianzus*. Crestwood, NY: St Vladimir's Seminary Press, 2001.

Gilson, Étienne. *Introduction à l'étude de saint Augustin.* Paris, 1969. Originally published 1929.

Girard, René. *I See Satan Fall Like Lightning.* Translated with a foreword by James G. Williams. Maryknoll, NY: Orbis, 2001.

———. *Things Hidden Since the Foundation of the World.* Translated by Stephan Bann and Michael Metteer. London/New York: Bloomsbury Academic, 2016. Originally published in French, 1978, and in English: Stanford: Stanford University Press, 1987.

Goehring, James. *Ascetics, Society, and the Desert: Studies in Early Egyptian Monasticism.* Harrisburg, PA: Trinity, 1999.

Grubbs, Judith Evans. *Women and the Law in the Roman Empire: A Sourcebook on Marriage, Divorce and Widowhood translated from the Latin.* London: Routledge, 2002.

Gorman, Michael. *Abortion and the Early Church.* New York: Paulist, 1982.

Graf, Fritz. *Magic in the Ancient World.* Translated by F. Philip. Cambridge, MA: Harvard University Press, 1997.

The Greek Anthology. Translated by W. R. Paton. 5 vols. London: Heinemann, 1919.

Gregory of Nyssa, St. *On Virginity.* In *Ascetical Works,* translated by Virginia Woods Callahan, 3–75. Washington, DC: Catholic University of America Press, 1967.

———. *From Glory to Glory: Texts from Gregory of Nyssa's Mystical Writings.* Selected and with an introduction by Jean Daniélou, SJ. Translated and edited by Herbert Musurillo, SJ. London: John Murray, 1962.

Gregory the Theologian (Nazianzen). *Saint Grégoire de Nazianze: Correspondence.* Edited and Translated by Paul Gallay. Two vols. Paris: La Belle Lettres, 2003.

———. *Poem in Praise of Virginity.* PG 37, 521–78. Translated by Gilbert, *On God and Man* (Crestwood, NY: St Vladimir's Seminary Press, 2001), 88–118.

———. *Oration 37, On Matthew 19.1–12* (c. AD 380). PG 36 279–308. NPNF second ser. VII, 338–344.

———. *Oration 38, On the Theophany or the Nativity of the Savior* (c. AD 380). PG 36 311–334; NPNF second ser. VII, 345–351.

———. *Oration 38, On the Theophany or the Nativity of Christ* (c. AD 380). PG 36 309–334. NPNF second ser. VII, 345–351. (325B)

Grubbs, Judith Evans. *Women and the Law in the Roman Empire: A Sourcebook on Marriage, Divorce and Widowhood translated from the Latin.* London: Routledge, 2002.

Guernsey, Andrew. "Denzinger Timeline of the Controversy over Communion For the Divorced and Civilly 'Remarried' in Adultery in Church History and the Pontificate of Pope Francis." https://docs.google.com/document/d/1XKimKuzgH gbE9YsJXojwhiufsDosCURraly6mMXIxDE/edit#heading=h.3xw7qubn91ce.

Harkins, P. W. "John Chrysostom, St." In *Catholic Encyclopedia,* vol. 7, 1041–44. Washington, DC: Catholic University of America Press, 1967.

Harper, Kyle. *From Shame to Sin: The Christian Transformation of Sexual Morality in Late Antiquity.* Cambridge, MA: Harvard University Press, 2013.

Hart, David Bentley. *Atheist Delusions: The Christian Revolution and its Fashionable Enemies.* New Haven, CT: Yale University Press, 2009.

Hart, Mark D. "Reconciliation of Body and Soul: Gregory of Nyssa's Deeper Theology of Marriage." *Theological Studies* 51 (1990) 450–78.

Heaney-Hunter, Joann. "Gregory the Theologian: An Enlightened View of Marriage." *The Greek Orthodox Theological Review* 39 (1994) 227–41.

Hemelrijk, E. A. "Masculinity and Femininity in the *Laudatio Turiae*." *Classical Quarterly* 54 (2004) 185–97.

Hippocrates. *Hippocrates, with an English Translation*. Edited and translated by W. H. S. Jones. London: Heinemann, 1958.

Hofer, Andrew, OP. *Christ in the Life and Teaching of Gregory of Nazianus*. Oxford: Oxford University Press, 2013.

Hopwood, Bronwyn. "The Good Wife: Fate, Fortune, and Familia in Augustan Rome." In *The Alternative Augustan Age*, edited by Kit Morrell et al., 1–21. Oxford: Oxford University Press, 2018.

Hugo, John J. *St. Augustine on Nature, Sex and Marriage*. Chicago: Scepter, 1969.

Huizinga, Leroy. "Marriage and the Matthean Jesus: A First Response to John Martens." *Catholic World Report*, November 8, 2015. http://www.catholicworldreport.com/Item/4350/marriage_and_the_matthean_jesus_a_first_response_to_john_martens.aspx.

Hunter, David G. "Augustinian Pessimism? A New Look at Augustine's Teaching on Sex, Marriage and Celibacy." *Augustinian Studies* 25 (1994) 153–77.

———. *Marriage in the Early Church*. Minneapolis: Fortress, 1992.

Huntley, Thomas. "The Earliest Church Dedicated to Our Lady." *Annals Australasia* 122.1 (January–February 2011) 8–9.

Irenaeus of Lyons. *Adversus Haereses* (Against Heresies). PG VII, 433–1224.

Janzen, David. "The meaning of *porneia* in Matthew 5.32 and 19.9: an approach from the study of ancient Near Eastern culture." *Journal for the Study of the New Testament* 23 (2000) 66–80.

Jensen, Joseph. "Does Porneia mean Fornication? A Critique of Bruce Malina." In *Novum Testamentum* 20.3 (1978) 161–84.

John Paul II, Pope. *Patres Ecclesiae*. 1980.

———. *Familiaris consortio*. 1981.

———. *Mulieris dignitatem*. 1988.

———. *Guardian of the Redeemer/Redemptoris Custos*. 1989.

———. *Letter to Families*. 1994.

———. *Letter to Women*. 1995.

———. *Man and Woman He Created Them: A Theology of the Body*. Boston: Pauline, 2006.

Jurgens, William A., ed. *The Faith of the Early Fathers*. 3 vols. Collegeville, MN: Liturgical, 1970, 1979, 1979.

Kalavrezou, Ioli. "Irregular Marriages in the Eleventh Century and the Zoe and Constantine Mosaic in Hagia Sophia." In *Law and Society in Byzantium, Ninth-Twelfth Centuries*, edited by Angeliki E. Laiou and Dieter Simon, 241–59. Washington, DC: Dumbarton Oaks, 1994.

Kieckhefer, Richard. *Magic in the Middle Ages*. Cambridge: Cambridge University Press, 2000.

Laistner, M. L. W. *Christianity and Pagan Culture in the Later Roman Empire*. Ithaca, NY: Cornell University Press, 1951.

Lake, Kirsopp, trans. *The Apostolic Fathers*. 2 vols. London: Heineman, 1913.

Lienhard, Joseph T., SJ. *St Joseph in Early Christianity: Devotion and Theology*. Philadelphia: St Joseph's University Press, 1999.

Louth, Andrew. *The Origins of the Christian Mystical Tradition*. 2d ed. Oxford: Oxford University Press, 2006.
Mansi, J. D. *Sacrorum Conciliorum Nova et Amplissima Collectio*. 31 vols. Florence-Venice, 1757–98.
Martin, Francis. "Marriage in the New Testament Period." In Olsen, ed., *Christian Marriage* (New York: Crossroad, 2001), 50–100.
———. "Marriage in the Old Testament and Intertestamental Periods." In Olsen, ed., *Christian Marriage* (New York: Crossroad, 2001), 1–49.
Martyr, Justin. *First Apology*. PG VI, 327–440. English: ANF I, 159–187.
McGinn, Thomas A. J. *Prostitution, Sexuality and the Law in Ancient Rome*. New York: Oxford University Press, 2003.
McLaren, Angus. *History of Contraception from Antiquity to the Present Day*. Oxford: Basil Blackwell, 1990.
Meyendorff, John. *Byzantine Theology: Historical Trends and Doctrinal Themes*. New York: Fordham University Press, 1983.
Mishnayoth. Edited by Philip Blackman. 7 vols., 2d ed., rev., corrected. Gateshead: Judaica, 1983.
Morrell, Kit, et al., eds. *The Alternative Augustan Age*. Oxford: Oxford University Press, 2018.
Murray, A. T., trans. *Demosthenes, Private Orations*. Cambridge, MA: Harvard University Press, 1939.
Nicene and Post-Nicene Fathers, First Series. General editors Philip Schaff and Henry Wace, original edition, Christian Literature Publishing Co., 1886. Reprinted Peabody, MA: Hendrickson, 1995.
Nicene and Post-Nicene Fathers, Second Series. General editors Philip Schaff and Henry Wace, original edition, Christian Literature Publishing Co., 1895. Reprinted Peabody, MA: Hendrickson, 1995.
Nichols, Aidan, O.P. *Criticising the Critics*. Oxford: Family Publications, 2010.
Noonan, John T., Jr. *Contraception: A History of Its Treatment by the Catholic Theologians and Canonists*. Cambridge, MA: Harvard University Press, 1965.
Olsen, Glen W., ed. *Christian Marriage: A Historical Study*. New York: Crossroad, 2001.
Oulton, J. E. L., and Henry Chadwick. *Alexandrian Christianity*. London: SCM, 1954. Clement of Alexandria: "On Marriage" (*Stromateis* III) 40–92. "On Spiritual Perfection" (*Stromateis* VII) 93–170.
Pacwa Mitch, SJ. "Abortion, Contraception and the Church Fathers." http://www.ncregister.com/daily-news/abortion-contraception-and-the-church-fathers.
Paul VI, Pope. *Humanae Vitae*. 1968.
———. *Marialis Cultis*. 1974.
Pelikan, Jaroslav. *Confessor Between East and West: A Portrait of Ukrainian Cardinal Josyf Slipyj*. Grand Rapids: Eerdmans, 1990.
Pieper, Josef. *"Divine Madness": Plato's Case Against Secular Humanism*. San Francisco: Ignatius, 1995.
Pius XI, Pope. *Casti Connubii*. 1930.
Plato. *Plato: Euthyphro Apology Crito Phaedo Phaedrus*. Translated by Harold N. Fowler. London: Heinemann, 1913, 405–577.
———. *Plato: The Laws*. 2 vols. Edited and translated by R. G. Bury. London: Heinemann, 1926.

———. *Plato: Lysis Symposium Gorgias.* Translated by W. R. M. Lamb. London: Heinemann, 1925.

———. *The Republic.* 2 vols. Translated by C. Emlyn-Jones and W. Preddy. London: Heinemann, 1913.

Preisker, Herbert. *Christentum und Ehe in den ersten drei Jahrhunderten.* Berlin: Trowitzsch, 1927.

Quasten, Johannes. *Patrology.* 4 vols. First published Utrecht/Antwerp: Spectrum, and Westminster, MD: Newman, 1963. Reprinted Allen, TX: Christian Classics, 1996.

Ramsey, Boniface, OP. *Beginning to Read the Fathers.* London: Darton, Longman, and Todd, 1985.

Ratzinger, Joseph. "Concerning the Notion of Person in Theology." Translated by Michael Waldstein. *Communio* 17 (1990) 437–54.

———. *Faith and the Future.* San Francisco: Ignatius, 2009.

Riddle, John M. *Contraception and Abortion from the Ancient World to the Renaissance.* Cambridge, MA: Harvard University Press, 1992.

———. *Eve's Herbs: A History of Contraception and Abortion in the West.* Cambridge, MA: Harvard University Press, 1997.

Riddle, John M., and J. W. Estes. "Oral Contraceptives in Ancient and Medieval Times." *American Scientist* 80 (1992) 226–33.

Rist, John M. "'Amatorius': A Commentary on Plato's Theories of Love?" *The Classical Quarterly* 51.2 (2001) 557–75.

Rousseau, Olivier. "Divorce and Remarriage: East and West." In *Concilium* 4.3 (1967) 57–69.

Russell, Claire. *Glimpses of the Church Fathers.* London: Scepter, 1994.

Satinover, Jeffrey. *Homosexuality and the Politics of Truth.* Grand Rapids: Baker, 1996.

Saward, John. *Perfect Fools: Folly for Christ's Sake in Catholic and Orthodox Spirituality.* Oxford: Oxford University Press, 1980.

Schillebeeckx, Edward. *Marriage: Human Reality and Saving Mystery.* New York: Sheed and Ward, 1965.

Scola, Angelo. *The Nuptial Mystery.* Grand Rapids: Eerdmans, 2005.

Second Vatican Council. *Lumen Gentium: Dogmatic Constitution on the Church.*

———. *Dei Verbum: Dogmatic Constitution on Divine Revelation.*

———. *Gaudium et Spes: Pastoral Constitution on the Church in the Modern World.*

Severy, Beth. *Augustus and the Family at the Birth of the Roman Empire.* London: Routledge, 2003.

Sherrard, Philip. "*Humanae Vitae*: Notes on the Encyclical Letter of Pope Paul VI." *Sobornost* 5.8 (Winter-Spring 1969) 570–80.

Silvas, Anna M. *The Rule of St Basil in Latin and English.* Collegeville, MN: Liturgical, 2013.

———. *Macrina the Younger, Philosopher of God.* Turnhout: Brepols, 2008.

———. *Saint Gregory of Nyssa: The Letters.* Leiden: Brill, 2007.

———. *The Asketikon of St Basil the Great.* Oxford: Oxford University Press, 2005.

Sweeney, Conor, and Brian T. Trainor. *The Politics of Conjugal Love: A Baptismal and Trinitarian Approach to Headship and Submission.* Eugene, OR: Pickwick, 2019.

Tertullian. *Ad Uxorem (To his Wife).* CCSL Vol. 1. Edited by E. Dekkers et al. Turnhout: Brepols, 1954, 373–394.

———. *Apologeticum* or *Apologia.* CCSL Vol. 1. Edited by E. Dekkers et al. Turnhout: Brepols, 1954, 85–171. Cf. http://www.tertullian.org/works/apologeticum.htm.

———. *Liber de Praescriptionibus adversus haereticos* (Prescription against Heretics). PL 2, 9–74.
Theodore the Studite, St. *The Letters*. In PG 99, 903–1682. G. Fatouros, *Theodori Studitae Epistulae*, CFHB 31. 2 vols. Berlin: Walter de Gruyter, 1992.
———. *Eulogy of Platon*. In PG 99, 803–50.
Theodoret. *Historia Ecclesiastica (Ecclesiastical History)*. PG 82, 882–1280.
———. Letter 146. *Epistolae*, PG 83, 1173–1494.
Tosefta. Edited by Jacob Neusner. 6 vols. New York: Ktav, 1981.
Treggiari, Susan. *Roman Marriage: Iusti Coniuges from the Time of Cicero to the Time of Ulpian*. New York: Oxford University Press, 1991.
van Oort, J. "Augustine on Sexual Concupiscence and Original Sin." In *Studia Patristica* 22 (1989) 382–86.
Vasil, Cyril. "Separation, Divorce, Dissolution of the Bond, and Remarriage: Theological and Practical Approaches of the Orthodox Churches." In Dodaro, ed., *Remaining in the Truth of Christ* (San Francisco: Ignatius, 2014), 93–128.
Vawter, Bruce, "Divorce and the New Testament." *Catholic Biblical Quarterly* 39.4 (October 1977) 528–42.
———. "The Divorce clauses in Mt 5.32; 19.9." *Catholic Biblical Quarterly* 16 (1954) 155–67.
von Hildebrand, Dietrich. *Marriage: The Mystery of Conjugal Love*. Manchester, NH: Sophia Institute, 1991.
Wahba, Matthias F. *Honorable Marriage according to St Athanasius*. Minneapolis: Light & Life, 1996.
Walsh, Ephtalia Makris. "Saint Gregory the Theologian's Use of the Abraham and Sarah Tradition in Relation to Marriage." *The Greek Orthodox Theological Review* 39 (1994) 211–26.
Winger, Thomas M. *Ephesians*. St Louis: Concordia, 2015.
Ware, Timothy. *The Orthodox Church*. Harmondsworth: Penguin, 1963.
Wenham, Gordon, "Matthew and Divorce: An Old Crux Revisited." *Journal for the Study of the New Testament* 22 (1984) 95–107.
Zizioulas, John D. *Being as Communion: Studies in Personhood and the Church*. Crestwood NY: St Vladimir's Seminary Press, 1985.

SCRIPTURE INDEX

The author follows the Old Testament scriptural canon of the Catholic Church, largely based on the Septuagint as used in the early Church and the Fathers. Books not found in the later Rabbinic *Tanakh*, as coded in the Massoretic recension, are indicated with: (deuterocanonical). Psalms are listed according to their Septuagint numbering, followed immediately by the Massoretic numbering where applicable.

OLD TESTAMENT

Genesis

1:26–28	3–4
1:26	5n7, 6
1:27–28	7
1:27	4, 7, 50, 156
1:28	7, 40, 118, 119, 155
1:31	8
2:18	6
2:18–25	4
2:22	6
2:23	31, 80
2:24	6, 75, 115, 133, 156, 157
2:25	8
3:1–7	10
3:6	11
3:7	12, 145
3:15	12
3:16	12
4:1	29, 40, 46
4:5	15
4:8	13
4:10	13
4:16	13
4:17	13
4:25–26	15
5:1–2	4n3
5:24	16
12:3	19
13:8	21
14:14	19, 21
15:5–6	13
16:1–4	13
17:12–13	19
17:37	19
18:19	19
21:10–12	20
24:38	18, 19
24:40	18
25:28	19, 20
27	20
27:11–17	20
28:14	19
30:1	40
30:2	40
30:16	20
30:22	40

31:34	20
37:4	19
37:10	19
38:9–10	41
44:20	19
50:16	19

Exodus

2:7	21
2:9	21
12:26–27	19, 21
13:8	19
13:13	20
13:14–15	19
17:9–12	53n11
19:15	38
19:22	38
20:2	17
20:7	41
20:12	17
20:17	17
24:8	16, 79
33:18	33
34:12–16	25

Leviticus

15:16–18	18
15:19–30	18
17–26	18, 23
18:6–18	18
18:19	18
18:22	18
18:23	18
19:2	27
19:23	18
20:1–5	26
20:11–14	18
20:13	18
20:17	18
20:19–21	18
21:10	21
22:4	18
24:11–16	41
24:23	41

Numbers

25:1–3	25

Deuteronomy

1:31	20, 22
2:4	21
2:8	21
6:4–9	22
6:7	19
8:5	22
23:8	21
23:17	18
23:18	18
24:1	61, 64
24:1–3	18
24:1–4	28, 61
25:5–10	41
25:10	18
27:20	18
32:6	22

Judges

13:23	20
17:2–6	20

Ruth

4:13	40

1 Samuel

1:22–23	20
21:4	39
21:5	39

2 Samuel

11:9–11	39

1 Kings

2:19	20
11:1–8	25
14:21	20
15:13	20

2 Kings
8:1–6	20

2 Chronicles
15:16	20
36:14–21	26

Tobit (deuterocanonical)
4:3–4	22
8:4–8	35

Job
1:5	20

Psalms
6:6	87n15
15/16	32n8
21/22:27–28	43
25/26	32n8
35/36:9	7, 40, 41
41/42	32n8
41/42:8	2
43/44:21	50
45/46:5–6	42
47/48	42n6
62/63	32
83/84	32n8
83/84:2	40
86/87:5	42
88/89:26–27	50
90/91	32n8
101/102:10	14
102/103:13	19
105/106:39	25
112/113:9	41
121/122	42n6
124/125	42n6
126/127:1	18
126/127:3–5	18
127/128:3	18, 20
132/133:1	21
138/139	32n8
138/139:13–15	39–40

Proverbs
1:7	22
1:8	19, 20, 22
3:11–12	22
4:3	20
6:20	19
6:20–22	22
12:4	119
13:1	22
13:24	22
17:6	19, 119
17:17	21
19:18	22
19:26	22
20:20	23
22:15	22
23:13–14	22
23:25	19
29:17	22

Song of Songs
3:1–4	32
3:1–2	138
4:9	49
5:6–9	32
7:13	37

Wisdom (deuterocanonical)
2:21–24	9

Sirach/Ecclesiasticus (deuterocanonical)
1:23	37
3:1	22
3:2–3	23
3:12–14	23
7:23–28	22
47:19–20	25

Isaiah
2:2	43
2:9–10	26
6:3	26
7:14	43
23:22	42

24:1–13	109
43:5–7	43
49:15	20
49:18	29
49:23	29
54:1–10	29
54:2	53
54:5–6	30
54:6–7	35
55:3	29, 79
56:4–5	65
60:16	29
62:4–5	29
62:5	30
64:1	44
64:8	22
66:8–14	43
66:13	20
66:8	46

Jeremiah

2:1–12	29
3:1–14	29
3:1	28
3:2	26
3:1–4	23
3:20–25	29
4:11	42
8:13	42
16:1–2	38
17:9	71
19:4–5	26
31:1	24
31:9	24
31:31–34	29, 31
31:31	16, 79
31:32	79
35:6–10	19
47:3	19

Lamentations

1:15	42

Ezekiel

8:9–12	26
16	75
16:5–32	29
16:6–14	30
16:20–21	26
18:6	23
22:6–7	24
22:7	23
22:10–11	24
23:1–49	29
23:5–8	26

Hosea

1:2	28
3:3	34
2:14–20	29
5:4	28
8:7	11
11:1–3	20
11:1	22

Joel

2:21	42

Micah

4:5	24
7:6	23

Habbakuk

2:14	29

Zephaniah

3:14–17	43
3:14	42

Zechariah

2:10–13	43
9:9	42

Malachi

1:6	22
2:10	22
2:10–11	36
2:13–16	36

SCRIPTURE INDEX

2 Machabees

7	20

~

NEW TESTAMENT

Matthew

1:20	48
1:24	48, 139
2:14	139
3:11	63n3
5:3	63n3
5:13	69
5:28	60
5:31–32	60–64
5:32	61
6:2	115
6:4	70
6:5	115
6:10	63n3
6:13	63n3
6:16	115
10:10	120
10:34–38	67
11:6	32
12:29–30	22
12:39	70
12:46–50	53
13:3–24	118
13:12	63n3
14:12–23	73
15:1–9	67
16:16	63n3
17:2	87
18:20	116, 119, 122
19:1	60
19:1–12	132
19:3–9	60–64, 143
19:4–6	7
19:4	50
19:5	115, 156, 162
19:6	141
19:8	3, 157
19:9	62
19:10–12	65
19:10	63
21:2	63n3
22:2	72
22:4	72
25:1–12	72
25:31	115
28:8	33

Mark

1:8	63n3
2:19	74
4:25	63n3
5:25–34	51
5:40	67
7:20–23	72
7:21–23	162
8:29	63n3
8:38	70
9:44	162
10:1	60
10:2–9	36n1
10:2–12	60
10:6	50
10:11	60, 103, 106
10:12	64
10:14	67
10:23–28	66
10:38	73
14:3	51
16:9	51

Luke

1:8	39
1:17	24, 46, 72
1:35	54
1:42	46
1:48	20
1:49	46
2:1	82
2:48	51
2:49	51–52
2:51	51, 52, 53
2:54–55	47
3:16	63n3
3:38	78

6:20–21	63n3
7:38	51
8:18	63n3
9:20	63n3
10:23–24	44
10:38–42	51
10:51	52n11
11:2–4	63n3
11:49–52	15
12:32	58
12:51–53	67
13:33	73
13:34	71
14:26–27	67
16:18	106
18:29–30	66
20:34–36	68
20:38	107n19
22:15–16	80
22:29–30	80
22:20	16
22:61	51n9

John

1:1	45
1:1–2	3
1:11	71
1:12–13	45, 55
1:14	45, 53
1:26	63n3
2:1–11	73–75
2:11	2, 73
2:25	50
3:28–30	71
4	51
6:44	78
6:53	79
6:54–56	80
8:9–11	51
10:40	73
12:20–24	83
13:1	74
13:14	58
14:27	116
16:21	67
18:36–37	25
19:25–27	54

20:29	32
21:5	57

Acts of the Apostles

2:4	54
2:14	54
4:32–35	55
6:4	97
8:27–34	39
16:14–15	56
20:36–38	57
23:6	107n19

Romans

1:3	132
1:24–32	83
5:12	147
5:14–15	78
6:11	107n19
7:2	163
7:2–3	63
7:12	121
8:5	102
16:1	57
16:3–4	56
16:13	57

1 Corinthians

2:9	3
4:9–13	58
6:9	162
6:12–17	7
7	67, 143
7:1–6	149, 154
7:2	155
7:3–6	149
7:4	144
7:5–6	130
7:5	113, 149, 154, 157, 158
7:6	149
7:10–11	63, 144
7:15	141
7:20	174
7:29–31	68
7:35	69

SCRIPTURE INDEX   191

7:39	99, 106, 129, 141
11:25	79
15:45	78

2 Corinthians

4:4	5
4:6	87
11:2	157

Galatians

1:8	171
3:13	47
3:26	54
3:27	129
3:28	114
4:47	54
5:19–21	86n12, 101
5:23	110
6:7	11

Ephesians

1:3–10	2
2:19	55
3:14	67
3:15	19
5:19	115
5:21–33	74–75
5:25	99
5:30	157
5:31	115, 132
5:32	132, 145
6:1–4	160

Philippians

2:13	72
3:13	137
3:20	102, 128

Colossians

1:15	5
1:26–27	76
1:26	53
2:8	92n14
3:16	115
4:9	57

1 Thessalonians

1:9	7
2:11	57
5:17	158

2 Thessalonians

2:7	14

1 Timothy

3:14	47
3:15	55
5:14	144
5:2	56

2 Timothy

2:17	92n14

Titus

3:9	92n14

Hebrews

1:6	53
10:1–3	2
10:22	121
12:23	55
12:24	15
13:4	113, 114
13:14	68

1 Peter

1:10–12	2
1:14	58
1:22	58
4:17	47

2 Peter

1:4	80

1 John

2:1	57
3:1	55
4:8, 16	6, 78, 138

Apocalypse/Revelation

2:7	80
9:21	101
13:18	80
19:6–7	81
19:9	81
21:2	81
21:5	47, 74, 80
21:8	101
21:9	81
22:17	81
22:20	81

GENERAL INDEX

Abel, children of, 15
Abortion, 84–87, 101, 105n16, 108, 116, 118–19, 131, 148
Adultery, 17, 26, 35, 60–64, 70–71, 100, 103–4, 131, 169–70
    Jewish tradition, 90
    Roman society, 90, 132, 169–70
Akiva, Rabbi, 31n6, 61
Ambrose, 50n7, 51n9, 77n3, 139–41
Angels, 9
Arianism, 78, 94, 135, 137
Aristotle, 84, 92
Athenagoras of Athens, 105–7
Athenagoras, Patriarch, 175
Augustine, 5n7, 50n7, 127n6, 142–51, 152, 158
    Three goods of marriage, 143–45
    Concupiscence, 146–50

Barnabas, Letter to, 102
Basil the Great, Saint, 124–25, 128
    On marriage, 130–32
    Canons, 168–70
Benedict XVI, Pope, 4n5, 5n7, 58n14, 78n5, 135n18
Bernadine, Saint, 49n6

Cain, children of, 13–14
Canon Law, in East and West, 164–66
Clement of Alexandria, 116–22
Creation mandate, see fruitfulness
Catechism of the Catholic Church, 6, 66, 140, 154

Chrysostom, John, Saint, 126, 153–63
    On divorce and remarriage, 161–63
    On family as domestic church, 160–61
    On the purpose of marriage, 154–56
Comiskey, Andrew, 27
Concupiscence, 131, 145–51
    And shame, 12
Continence / Sexual abstinence, see Virginity, 18, 65
Contraception, see Fruitfulness, 8, 40, 85–87, 101, 108, 118, 142, 174
    And *pharmakeia* / drugs, 86, 95, 101, 148
Coptic Church, 173–74
Covenant, 13, 16, 79
    With Noah, 16–17, 95–96
    Of Sinai, 17–18, 21–22, 23–24, 44, 45, 65, 72, 79
    Marital, 28–32, 34, 36, 40, 69, 79, 81, 137, 139
    New, 30–31, 38, 45, 47, 79–80
Coptic Church, 173–74

Damascene, John, 114
Didache, 100–101
Digamy, 104n15, 106, 107n19, 109, 133, 169, 173
Diognetus, Letter to, 102, 108
Dionysius Exiguus, 164–66
Dionysius, Pseudo-, 57n12

GENERAL INDEX

Divorce, 18, 35–36, 60–64, 106n17, 109, 132–33
Domestic church, 122, 55, 66, 116, 122–23, 160–61

Elliott, Peter, 6n7, 127
Elohim, 6
Emmelia, Saint, 123–28, 134
Encratism, 48, 110–14, 120, 122, 143
Eros, 32, 93, 136, 138
Essenes, 36, 38–39, 71
Eucharist, 55–56, 79–81, 129n7, 131, 156–57
Evagrius of Pontus, 98
Evdokimov, Paul, 175

Family / household, see Domestic Church, 18–19, 21–22
　Decay of, 23–24
　Holy Family, 47–51
　Household of the Church, 47, 53–58
　Greek, Roman, 91
　Recovery of, in Israel, 24
Fallashas, of Ethiopia, 39
Father / fatherhood, 19–20, 50
　God as Father, 6, 17, 22, 24, 36, 49, 51–52, 53
　Apostles as fathers, 56–57
　Fathers of the Church, 97–98
Feminine persona of Zion, 42–44, 45–46
Fitzmyer, Joseph, 83n3
Fruitfulness, 4, 7, 9, 40–41, 46, 77n3, 118–19, 155

Gallagher, Clarence, 164, 167, 172
Gaudium et Spes, 4n4
Girard, René, 2n1, 10n10, 87n16
Gregory of Nyssa, 106n19, 124, 135–38
Gregory the Theologian, 5n7, 114, 124, 126, 132–35

Headship, male, 77–79
Hermeneutic approach to the Scriptures, 2–3

Hermas, 102–4, 105, 108, 133
Hippocratic medicine, 86, 96
Human sacrifice, 26–27, 87–88
Humanae Vitae, 85, 107, 148, 175

Idolatry and sexual depravity, 25–27, 70
Ignatius of Antioch, 99–100
Image of God, 3–5, 8, 9, 17, 176
Irenaeus, 5n7, 111, 117
Isaac of Stella, 77n3

John the Baptist, 38, 48n4, 60–61, 71–73
John-Paul II, Pope, 4n6, 31n5, 50n7, 53n11, 57, 66, 98, 117, 124, 136n21, 137, 140, 153, 161
Jesus
　The Bridegroom, 30, 69, 71–75, 77, 79, 81, 138, 154
　On divorce and remarriage, 60–64
　Incarnate as male, 78
　His stricter standard, 60
　At twelve years, 51–52
　And women, 50–51
Joseph, Saint, 46–53, 73, 139–40
Justin Martyr, 101–2, 104n14, 105, 107, 108
Justinian, 166–67

Macrina the Elder, Saint, 123, 125, 126–27
Macrina the Younger, Saint, 106–7n19, 123, 127–128, 169n13
Manichaeism, see Encratism, 48, 110–11, 143n10
Marriage, see Nuptial Mystery
　In Roman law, 88–90, 133
　A holy way of life, 120–21, 124, 161
　As liturgy, 136–37
　Remediation of, in Israel, 34–36
　"Triangular" relationship of, 5, 11, 35, 40, 104, 176
Mary, 20, 39, 46–54, 73–74, 77n3, 139–40, 147, 157n10

Mother / motherhood, 20, 40-41,
    42-43, 77n3n4, 79, 88, 91,
    121, 125, 128, 153, 156, 159
Mulieris Dignitatem, 6n7, 12n11, 77
Mysterion, 75-77, 79

Nakedness
    Without shame, 8
    With shame, 12, 30
    To God, 12, 51
Natural law, 94, 117-18
Nuptial Mystery / nuptial, 1, 6, 7,
    8, 9
    Imagery applied to God and
        Israel, 27-29, 31-33, 34, 71
    Imagery applied to Christ and
        Church, 30, 79

Oikonomia, Eastern Orthodox, 132,
    168, 171-72
Oral Law, 36, 39, 61

Paul VI, 107, 148, 161, 174
Philo, 5n7, 38
Pius XI, 88n18, 144n10, n11
Plato, 84, 85, 87n16, 93-94, 118

Quasten, Johannes, 97n2, 117
Qumran / Qumranis, see Essenes

Roman law on marriage, 80, 88-91,
    95-96
    v. Christian law, 105-6, 133-34,
        161-63, 166-67

Ratzinger, Joseph, see Benedict XIV

Satan / Devil / Serpent / Enemy,
    9-11, 82, 87n16, 130, 132,
    149
Satinover, Jeffrey, 27, 28
Scola, Angelo, 6n7, 7n9, 40n4
Spousal imagery, see Nuptial
    Imagery
Sterilizing the marital act, see
    Contraception
Stoics, Stoicism, 86, 94-95, 110,
    117, 131
Sweeney, Connor, xi, 12, 79n7

Tertullian, 88n17, 92n24, 114-16,
    141, 161
Theodore the Studite, Saint, 170-71,
    173
Therapeutae, 38
Troitsky, Hilarion (?), 172-73

Virginity, see also continence, 37-
    39, 49, 65-69, 100, 110-14,
    122, 127-29, 134, 139-40,
    143, 154
    And eunuchs for the Kingdom,
        65-66
    And marriage, 69, 111-12

Zizioulas, 78n5

www.ingramcontent.com/pod-product-compliance
Lightning Source LLC
Chambersburg PA
CBHW020340240426
43662CB00048B/805